Enterprise Security Risk Management (ESRM) in the Real World

This book bridges the critical gap between Enterprise Security Risk Management (ESRM) theory and practical implementation.

While ESRM principles have gained widespread acceptance, particularly following ASIS International's endorsement of the approach, security professionals in real-world implementations consistently struggle with translating concepts into actionable strategies. This practical guide introduces a simple, operational framework centered around three core questions that help security leaders map ESRM directly to business outcomes and strategic decision-making. This book addresses the persistent "how-to" questions that practitioners face when attempting to implement ESRM in complex organizations. This book includes actionable field lessons, case examples, and practical tools that transform theory into measurable security impact. It addresses many of today's most urgent security challenges: organizational resilience amid a fast-changing global risk landscape, accelerating technology adoption (including AI), and an increasingly complex business and operational environment. As security programs face mounting pressure to demonstrate value, integrate with enterprise risk management, and build trust with non-security stakeholders, this accessible guide equips professionals to move beyond theoretical understanding and confidently lead ESRM implementation.

This book serves as an essential resource for security leaders ready to translate ESRM principles into measurable outcomes that align the security strategy with broader business objectives.

Enterprise Security Risk Management (ESRM) in the Real World

A Field Guide for Security Leaders Who Get Things Done

Rachelle Loyear

CRC Press
Taylor & Francis Group
Boca Raton London New York

CRC Press is an imprint of the
Taylor & Francis Group, an **informa** business

Designed cover image: Shutterstock

First edition published 2026
by CRC Press
2385 NW Executive Center Drive, Suite 320, Boca Raton FL 33431

and by CRC Press
4 Park Square, Milton Park, Abingdon, Oxon, OX14 4RN

CRC Press is an imprint of Taylor & Francis Group, LLC

Library of Congress Cataloging-in-Publication Data
Names: Loyear, Rachelle author
Title: Enterprise security risk management (ESRM) in the real world : a field guide for security leaders who get things done / Rachelle Loyear.
Description: First edition. | Boca Raton, FL : CRC Press, 2026. |
Includes bibliographical references and index. |
Identifiers: LCCN 2025045970 (print) | LCCN 2025045971 (ebook) |
ISBN 9781041193616 hardback | ISBN 9781041193593 paperback | ISBN 9781003711346 ebook
Subjects: LCSH: Risk management | Financial risk management
Classification: LCC HD61 .L69 2026 (print) | LCC HD61 (ebook)
LC record available at https://lccn.loc.gov/2025045970
LC ebook record available at https://lccn.loc.gov/2025045971

ISBN: 9781041193616 (hbk)
ISBN: 9781041193593 (pbk)
ISBN: 9781003711346 (ebk)

DOI: 10.4324/9781003711346

Typeset in Caslon
by codeMantra

To all the participants in the ESRM trainings I have been privileged to lead and join, who asked powerful and often challenging questions. You helped sharpen the ESRM conversation and expand my thinking. Your curiosity and persistence made the ideas stronger and the lessons more real.

And to the many security professionals whose insights, critiques, and collaboration have shaped my perspective over the years— JP, BA, McCreight, Paul, Amy, Jeff. This work is as much a reflection of your shared wisdom as it is my own experience.

Contents

About the Author

Rachelle Loyear is a seasoned security executive with 15 years of experience in corporate security and risk management. As Vice President of Integrated Security Solutions at one of the largest security services providers in the world, she works with clients across the globe in Enterprise Security Risk Management (ESRM) programs, focusing on aligning security strategies with organizational objectives. Her expertise encompasses both physical and cyber risk domains, ensuring comprehensive enterprise resilience.

Preface

A Note from the Author—Lessons Learned from a Decade of ESRM

When I first began speaking and writing about Enterprise Security Risk Management (ESRM) as a concept, the message was primarily rooted in a theoretical foundation. A significant amount of research, discussion, and analysis by an extensive group of people went into developing a solid model that aligned security activities with business strategy. Over the past decade of ESRM in practice, however, I've learned a lot about what works in the concept (and, just as importantly, what doesn't) when it comes to bringing ESRM into real-world security programs.

What became clear to me is that while ESRM absolutely makes security programs more effective, it can also feel overwhelming to those who are first introduced to it. For many security professionals and business leaders, the original presentation of ESRM seemed complex, even intimidating. Security teams often worried that shifting to a risk-based approach would require more bureaucracy, more processes, and more difficulty in securing executive buy-in.

But the reality is that ESRM does not have to be complicated. In fact, it is meant to simplify security decision-making, ensuring that organizations focus on the most important risks instead of being caught up in reactive measures, "best practices," or compliance checklists.

So, I felt that it was time to update the ESRM message. Through my work teaching ESRM with multiple co-teachers over the years and helping different organizations implement ESRM, I've learned a few key lessons that shape the approach of this book:

Lesson 1: We Have to Speak the Language of Business

If security professionals can't communicate why security matters in business terms, we will struggle to gain influence. Business leaders don't think in terms of security gaps and vulnerabilities; they think in terms of reputation, revenue, operational resilience, and competitive advantage. We must build relationships in the business by becoming an integral part of the business and being known to our stakeholders as supporters, not blockers, of their critical processes. ESRM helps security leaders position the security function as a strategic enabler, not just a defensive measure.

Lesson 2: We Can't Make Risk-Based Security More Difficult than the Old Way

If shifting to ESRM makes security harder to implement, more resource-intensive, or overly bureaucratic, organizations will resist it. ESRM has to be practical, actionable, and designed to integrate seamlessly into existing business operations.

Lesson 3: We Have to Accept That Businesses Inherently Take Risks, and That's OK

One of the hardest parts of adopting ESRM seems to be the acknowledgement that the business is allowed to take risks—acceptance is a core tenet of most risk management standards. Some business leaders are far more comfortable with that idea than the average security professional. Understanding that we are there to help our partners accomplish their goals helps us give them the options they need to either implement security to mitigate risk or to understand exactly what risk they are accepting if they decide differently.

I wrote this book to reflect how I think about ESRM a decade after writing *Enterprise Security Risk Management: Concepts and Applications.* A simpler approach to security will help us connect better with our business partners and ultimately be more impactful in our security programs.

Case Examples and Anonymity

The field lessons, examples, scenarios, and case studies described in this book are drawn from a combination of the author's professional experience, publicly available information, and anonymized composites. No real organizations or individuals are referenced. Any resemblance to unacknowledged persons, living or dead, or to unreferenced entities is coincidental. These examples are presented for educational purposes only and do not constitute legal or professional advice.

Author Note on Use of Generative AI and Copyright

As I wrote this book, I used ChatGPT, a generative AI tool developed by OpenAI, to brainstorm and develop phrasing and sharpen clarity. All concepts, frameworks, and conclusions are my own; no AI-generated text was accepted without my review and revision, and no third-party copyrighted material was inserted by the tool.

This work cites and lightly quotes the published research of others. All such references are identified in the text and listed in the bibliography. All quotations fall within customary fair-use limits; no additional permission was required. Responsibility for the accuracy of citations and permissions rests solely with the author.

Introduction
Simplifying Security in a Complex World

Introduction: Simplifying Security in a Complex World

Every security professional has been in a meeting where leadership dismisses concerns with statements like:

> "We've never had a problem with security before—why change anything?"

And

> "That scenario is too unlikely to happen; we don't need to waste resources on it."

These statements expose two of the biggest psychological barriers to effective security risk management:

- People believe bad things won't happen to them.
- People assume risk management is too complicated.

These beliefs persist not because business leaders don't care about security, but because they align with deep human tendencies. Psychologists call the first one *optimism bias*: the tendency to assume that negative events are more likely to happen to others than to oneself.[1] Leaders are no different. A CEO who has never faced a major incident can easily fall into the trap of thinking, "our company is different," or "those headlines don't apply here." That bias provides short-term comfort, but it also leads to underestimating genuine vulnerabilities.

The second barrier reflects what behavioral economists call *complexity aversion*. When confronted with processes that look technical

DOI: 10.4324/9781003711346-1

or abstract, people gravitate toward simpler explanations[2]—even if they are wrong. Security risk management can sound intimidating, filled with scoring models, probability scales, and matrices. Leaders may tune out, defaulting instead to gut instinct or reactive fixes. "Just put more guards on the gate" feels actionable in a way that structured analysis does not, even if it's far less effective.

I've personally seen these dynamics play out across industries. After years of smooth sailing, one company in a flood-prone region built offices without proper disaster contingencies and with an inadequate backup plan. It only took one severe storm to wipe out both a facility and an entire operational van fleet. In healthcare, executives a decade ago often resisted investing in cybersecurity controls, convinced that hackers were more interested in banks and retailers than hospitals, until ransomware attacks brought emergency rooms to a standstill. A clear pattern emerges: optimism bias and complexity aversion give the illusion of safety, but that illusion crumbles quickly under pressure.

These misconceptions lead directly to poor security planning, lack of preparedness, and ultimately, greater vulnerability. Taking a *risk-based* approach to your security program offers a path out of that cycle.

This is where Enterprise Security Risk Management (ESRM) comes in. By simplifying the process, grounding it in business priorities, and making risk conversations accessible without oversimplifying the reality of threats, ESRM provides a practical way to counter both of these myths and engage leaders in meaningful dialogue.

The First Myth: "That Won't Happen Here"

Human beings like to believe that if something hasn't happened before, it won't happen in the future. Psychologists describe this as the "illusion of safety": the assumption that the absence of past incidents guarantees future security. For leaders, this bias can be especially powerful. If the business has operated for years without disruption, it is tempting to conclude that its safeguards are sufficient and that rare, high-impact events are someone else's problem.

History proves otherwise. This mindset has contributed to some of the most costly security failures on record:

- Before September 11, 2001, U.S. national security agencies had contingency plans for hijackings, but they all assumed a familiar pattern. A hijacker would demand money, safe passage, or the release of prisoners, and the objective of authorities was to negotiate and preserve life until the standoff ended. The idea that terrorists might weaponize passenger planes themselves was so far outside the conventional model that, although fragments of intelligence hinted at the possibility, the threat was never prioritized.[3] The failure to challenge the "that won't happen here" assumption meant that on the morning of the attacks, security processes, training, and infrastructure were not designed to prevent the catastrophic use of commercial airliners as missiles. The consequences reshaped global aviation security and national defense policy overnight.

- Apollo 1 Disaster: In the mid-1960s, NASA engineers and astronauts were pushing toward the moon with an ambitious pace. Concerns about fire hazards inside the oxygen-rich Apollo command module were raised, but they were brushed aside with the assumption that ignition was "impossible unless astronauts brought cigarettes aboard." This misplaced confidence meant that emergency escape procedures were not fully developed, and the hatch design required more than 90 seconds to open under pressure. On January 27, 1967, during what was supposed to be a routine ground test, an electrical fault triggered a cabin fire. With no viable escape path, astronauts Gus Grissom, Ed White, and Roger Chaffee perished in less than a minute. The tragedy forced NASA into an 18-month stand-down and a complete redesign of the spacecraft, delaying the moon program and permanently altering the agency's approach to safety.[4]

The lesson for business leaders is that a risk that has never happened before is not the same as a risk that cannot happen. For security professionals, ignoring low-probability but high-impact threats can be disastrous. History shows that it is often the unconsidered event, the one dismissed as too unlikely to bother with, that causes the greatest disruption when it finally arrives. The point is not that every risk can be foreseen, but that dismissing new or unusual warnings creates blind spots with devastating consequences.

This is where ESRM changes the conversation. Instead of relying on assumptions or past experience, ESRM encourages practitioners to ask what the real consequences would be if the "unlikely" were to occur. That shift, from focusing only on probability to

Pro Tip: Don't just ask leaders whether a scenario is likely—ask them what the cost would be if it happened. Shifting the focus from probability to impact reframes the discussion and helps executives see why preparing for "unlikely" risks is still smart business.

weighing impact, allows leaders to see that resilience is not about predicting the future with perfect accuracy. It is about preparing the organization so that even if the unexpected happens, operations continue, people remain safe, and the business mission endures.

In this way, ESRM offers a disciplined response to the illusion of safety. It replaces comfort with clarity, equipping security leaders to counter the easy narrative of "that won't happen here" with structured analysis and business-aligned planning. And while this addresses one major barrier to effective risk management, it leads us directly into another: the perception that the process itself is overly complex and difficult to implement.

The Second Myth: It's Too Complicated

If the first myth is rooted in optimism, the second stems from avoidance. Many organizations fail to implement strategic security risk management because they believe it is too difficult, too expensive, or too disruptive to existing operations. Leaders may hear terms like "probability matrices" or "threat modeling" and assume that only specialists can understand them. Faced with this perceived complexity, it feels easier to default to instinct, copy what peers are doing, or purchase the latest technology as a quick fix.

But the irony is that structure actually makes things simpler. A disciplined risk process does not overcomplicate decision-making; it *clarifies* it. When risks are defined, ranked, and tied to business priorities, executives can see which issues truly require investment and which do not. Instead of leaving decisions to gut instinct, what other people are doing, or personality, the ESRM process gives more people the ability to weigh in and increases the likelihood of reaching a sound, defensible outcome.

We've seen the cost of ignoring this. In one large healthcare system incident, cybersecurity was treated as a separate technical problem, left solely to the IT team. Physical security, fraud prevention, and clinical risk management each operated in their own silos, with little communication across departments. When ransomware attacks began targeting hospitals, the gaps became painfully obvious. The IT team had robust firewalls, but medical devices were still running outdated software; physical security had contingency plans for power outages but not for locked computer systems; fraud teams monitored billing irregularities but never considered what would happen if data became inaccessible. When an attack finally struck, emergency rooms were forced to divert patients, elective surgeries were canceled, and the organization lost millions in revenue over just a few days.

The damage was magnified by three interconnected failures:

- A lack of cross-functional communication, leaving each team blind to the others' vulnerabilities.
- Overconfidence in partial protections, such as strong firewalls but weak device security.
- No enterprise-wide plan to sustain operations if critical systems went down.

Tactically focused security programs tend to repeat this pattern. They overreact to isolated incidents, such as installing expensive new controls after a single event. They fail to focus resources on critical risks, spending budgets on low-priority issues instead of real threats. And they fragment security into disconnected units, where physical, cyber, and fraud teams all work hard but rarely together.

ESRM is designed to solve these problems. It reframes risk management as a methodology, not intended to be a complicated academic exercise, but a practical, business-oriented process that any organization can adopt. By ensuring that strategies are aligned with business priorities, ESRM directs attention to the risks that

Pro Tip: If leaders push back that risk analysis is "too complex," frame it as a set of clear choices. Show two or three options with costs, benefits, and risks side by side—decision-makers engage faster when the trade-offs are obvious.

matter most. By promoting resource efficiency, it avoids wasteful spending on ineffective controls. And by integrating security functions across the enterprise, it creates a unified approach that supports business operations instead of disrupting them.

Both of these myths, complacency and complexity, undermine security at its core. ESRM addresses them directly with a process that leaders can understand and practitioners can apply.

Bringing ESRM Into the Real World

By the mid-2010s, security leaders faced a growing dilemma related to the preceding myths and many other historical factors. Physical and cyber programs often operated in isolation, executives viewed security largely as a cost center, and most strategies were reactive, driven by incidents rather than by business priorities.

Security teams wanted a framework that could unify these functions and put them on equal footing with other enterprise disciplines. Out of that need, ESRM began to gain traction across the profession.

Written in 2017, the book *Enterprise Security Risk Management: Concepts and Applications*, by Brian J. Allen and this author, defined ESRM as:

> Enterprise security risk management is the application of fundamental risk principles to manage all security risks - whether information, cyber, physical security, asset management, or business continuity - in a comprehensive, holistic, all-encompassing approach.[5]

It was described as a formal cycle that requires

1. Identifying and Prioritizing Assets
2. Identifying and Prioritizing Risks
3. Mitigating Prioritized Risks
4. Improving and Advancing the Program Over Time

These four steps gave the profession a common language. They emphasized that security is not a one-time project, it is a cycle: start with what matters most, understand the risks, implement proportional safeguards, and continually improve. At the same time, the definition reinforced a vital point: ESRM is not a theory that sits in a binder on a shelf. It is enacted by security professionals in partnership with their organizations, tailored to unique industries, cultures, and operating environments.

It also clarified what ESRM is *not*. It is not an attempt to predict and mitigate every possible threat. No program in a world of fiscal constraints can do that. Instead, ESRM is about making security a business function and acting like a business function, ensuring that we:

- Identify our organization's most critical assets. These are the crown jewels; the systems, people, and capabilities that drive the success of the mission. Protecting everything equally dilutes resources, but protecting the essentials ensures resilience.
- Assess real risks, not just perceived ones. ESRM pushes us beyond chasing the last incident or the loudest concern and toward evaluating actual threats, vulnerabilities, and impacts.
- Allocate resources effectively and efficiently. Budgets are finite. ESRM helps leaders become good stewards of the security investment, ensuring that dollars, time, and effort deliver measurable value.
- Enable continuous adaptation. Risks evolve constantly—new technologies, new regulations, and new adversaries. ESRM embeds improvement into the cycle so the program never stagnates.

Those early definitions gave the security profession a much-needed foundation. In the years that followed, I had the opportunity to speak, teach, and consult with organizations around the world, helping practitioners understand and apply ESRM.

What I quickly discovered was that the framework worked. But the way it was communicated often determined whether it gained traction. Security professionals appreciated the clarity of the four-step cycle, yet when presenting to executives, I often saw eyes glaze over as soon as the conversation turned technical.

Leaders wanted the benefits of ESRM, but they needed the language to be accessible, the process to feel manageable, and the outcomes to be clearly tied to business goals.

Further refinements to my thinking on ESRM came during my time with dozens of different security clients at G4S and later with Allied Universal. In practice, I found that executives rarely engaged with formal definitions or long process cycles. What resonated were three simple, operational questions:

- What am I trying to protect?
- What does it truly need to be protected from?
- How can we most effectively and efficiently protect it?

This approach was clear, memorable, and actionable, and became the foundation for how I've helped organizations move ESRM from theory to practice in the past few years.

These three questions now guide the structure of this book. And although I have reworded them slightly since my initial adoption, they remain, to this day, the clearest path I know to building a security program that is both strategic and business-aligned.

At the end of the day, well-implemented security cannot be about fear or compliance alone. Fear sells short-term fixes, but it does not build long-term trust. Compliance satisfies regulators, but it does not guarantee resilience. ESRM provides the middle ground: a disciplined, risk-based process that earns security leaders a seat at the table by enabling the business to operate confidently in a world of constant risk. That is what ESRM is all about.

What to Expect in This Book

This book is designed to get beyond theory and be a practical field guide for security leaders who want to get things done. You will find real-world examples, lessons learned from failure as well as success, and practical frameworks you can adapt to your own environment. Each chapter is written to bridge strategy and operations, showing how to take big ideas like ESRM and translate them into daily decisions and conversations that make security a trusted partner in business success.

The book is organized into three sections that build on one another.

Section 1: Changing the Way We Think About Security

- **Chapter 1: The ESRM Difference** explores how Enterprise Security Risk Management shifts security from a reactive, tactical function to a proactive, business-aligned discipline.
- **Chapter 2: Thinking Like a Risk Manager** examines the fundamentals of risk thinking—how to understand, frame, and communicate risk in ways that support smarter decision-making and align with business goals.

Section 2: Turning Strategy into Action—The Three Essential Questions

- **Chapter 3: What Am I Trying to Protect? – Understanding Critical Assets and Their Impact** walks through identifying both tangible and intangible assets and determining which ones are truly critical to the business.

- **Chapter 4: What Does It Truly Need to Be Protected From? – Understanding Threats to Evaluate Risk** focuses on how to assess threats, vulnerabilities, and likelihood to determine actual—not assumed—risk, using practical frameworks to rate and prioritize risk.
- **Chapter 5: How Can We Most Effectively and Efficiently Protect It? – Choosing the Best Mitigations for Your Risk Profile** introduces the concept of Effects-Based Security to help security professionals select the right mix of measures that deliver the greatest impact with the most efficient use of resources.

Section 3: Sustaining ESRM Success

- **Chapter 6: Continual Improvement Strategies**
  Shows how to monitor controls, measure effectiveness, and adapt programs through structured feedback loops, ensuring resilience in a changing environment.
- **Chapter 7: Required for Success—Making the Shift to a Security-Driven Culture**
  Explains how employee mindsets, incentives, and leadership modeling transform ESRM from a strategy on paper into a daily practice that drives resilience.

Section 4: What's Next for ESRM?

- **Chapter 8: The Future of ESRM—Adapting to an Accelerating World**

This capstone chapter looks forward, exploring how ESRM positions security leaders to navigate accelerating change, AI integration, and the evolving risk landscape with clarity and confidence.

Taken together, these chapters show not only what ESRM is, but also how it works in practice. The goal is to equip you with tools and insights you can use immediately, regardless of your industry or organizational size.

Security leaders who embrace ESRM will not only improve today's resilience but also prepare their organizations for tomorrow's uncertainty. Whether facing new technologies, shifting regulatory demands, or emerging global risks, the ESRM approach ensures that security is never just reacting to the world; it is helping to shape a confident, resilient future.

Let's dive in.

–Rachelle

Notes

1 Kendra Cherry, "What Is the Optimism Bias?" *Verywell Mind*, updated June 7, 2023, https://www.verywellmind.com/what-is-the-optimism-bias-2795031.

2 Geoffroy de Clippel, Paola Moscariello, Pietro Ortoleva, and Kareen Rozen, "Caution in the Face of Complexity," Working Paper, March 2025, https://pietroortoleva.com/papers/CautionComplexity.pdf.

3 National Commission on Terrorist Attacks upon the United States, *The 9/11 Commission Report: Final Report of the National Commission on Terrorist Attacks upon the United States* (Washington, DC, U.S. Government Printing Office (GPO), 2004).

4 NASA, *Report of Apollo 204 Review Board to the Administrator, National Aeronautics and Space Administration* (Washington, DC: NASA Headquarters, 1967).

5 Brian Allen and Rachelle Loyear, *Enterprise Security Risk Management: Concepts and Applications* (Brookfiled, CT, Rothstein Associates, 2017).

Section 1

CHANGING THE WAY WE THINK ABOUT SECURITY

Before a security program can become truly risk-based, the people leading it must shift how they think. Section 1 lays the foundation for Enterprise Security Risk Management (ESRM) by challenging the traditional, tactical mindset of security as a reactionary function and introducing a new vision of security as a proactive business partner.

These opening chapters explore how ESRM redefines our role as security professionals, transforms decision-making, and positions security as a strategic enabler rather than just a compliance-driven cost center.

Here's what this section sets out:

- **Chapter 1: The ESRM Difference** explores how ESRM shifts security from a reactive, tactical function to a proactive, business-aligned discipline.
- **Chapter 2: Thinking Like a Risk Manager** examines the fundamentals of risk thinking—how to understand, frame, and communicate risk in ways that support smarter decision-making and align with business goals.

DOI: 10.4324/9781003711346-2

Chapter 1

The ESRM Difference

Why ESRM, and Why Now

Enterprise Security Risk Management (ESRM) is not a brand-new idea. This model of risk-led security has been developing for more than a decade, steadily gaining traction in professional associations, academic programs, and conference discussions. Security leaders have been learning the theory, debating the principles, and experimenting with pilot projects for years. In this sense, ESRM has progressed well beyond the "emerging concept" stage.

Over the past decade, ESRM has also gained institutional recognition. Professional associations, such as ASIS International, have formally endorsed ESRM as a core practice. Universities have begun teaching the approach in risk and security curricula, while many corporate organizations are adopting a risk-led approach in their security vendor requirements.

This growing body of adopters signals a turning point: ESRM is no longer just a niche theory. It is steadily becoming the accepted language of modern security leadership, giving practitioners confidence that they are aligning with global best practice.

At the same time, the broader security landscape has undergone rapid evolution. Global risks are more interconnected, business operations are more digitized, and the speed of change is outpacing traditional playbooks. Boards and executives now expect security leaders to be fluent in business practices, resilience, continuity, and risk, in addition to having robust tactical incident response capabilities. In this environment, the limitations of old, activity-driven models are impossible to ignore.

We are at an inflection point. ESRM is no longer just something to learn *about*; it is something to put into practice. In the

DOI: 10.4324/9781003711346-3

security industry, we have reached a moment where theory must translate into execution. Security teams that move now, adjusting from siloed and tactical approaches to applying ESRM in the real world, have the opportunity to position security as a value-driving partner rather than a cost center. Those who do not act risk being left behind, stuck in reactive cycles, while their peers integrate security into their business strategy and become part of overall organizational leadership.

This book is written for that moment. ESRM has matured, the profession has prepared, and now is the time to act.

The Problem with Tactical Security

For decades, many enterprises have approached security as a checklist of tasks rather than as a function of business risk. On the surface, this style of "tactical security" seems practical: it creates visible actions for security teams and offers stakeholders quick reassurance that something is being done. But tactical security is built on activity, not outcomes. That distinction makes all the difference in the perception of what security is for.

The familiar cycle looks like this:

1. Recognize a need—The organization decides it "has security risks" or "needs security."
2. React to incidents or fears—An actual theft, vandalism, or trespassing event sparks a response, or leaders grow anxious about potential or perceived threats, like active assailants or civil unrest, that may never materialize. New controls are added in reaction.
3. Measure activity—Success is reported in terms of patrols completed, alarms installed, or doors locked, without connecting these activities to actual business performance.

At first glance, this cycle looks entirely reasonable. It creates clear tasks and visible outputs. But in practice, it leaves organizations vulnerable. By treating all concerns as equal and by focusing on activity counts rather than risk impact, tactical security often diverts resources to the wrong problems. The security team ends up protecting what is loudest, or "scariest," not what is most operationally critical.

Tactical security persists in our organizations today because it's a comfortable and familiar business interaction for both security leaders and our business partners in the organization. Visible security measures, such as guards at a lobby or cameras on a warehouse wall, provide reassurance to executives and employees alike that they are in a "safe" environment. Compliance auditors reward precise adherence to regulations with a passing grade for the team. Security teams have also historically been praised for reacting quickly to ensure a problem is resolved immediately. These incentives create a cycle where activity is equated with impact, even if the actual risks remain unaddressed. ESRM challenges this pattern by redefining success. What matters is not how many controls are deployed or the hours worked, but whether the business remains resilient against the threats most likely to disrupt it.

A Tactical Failure in Action

Consider this case of an automotive parts distributor facing unexplained product loss at one of its regional warehouses. To senior leadership, the explanation seemed obvious: employees or contractors must be stealing. Their directive was equally straightforward: "Get more cameras."

The organization invested heavily in video surveillance, installing cameras across the facility and contracting for 24/7 monitoring with analytics software. On paper, this looked like a decisive response. Executives could point to the visible action of implementing more technology and increased monitoring. At the same time, the security team could report increased activity in the form of patrols, footage reviews, and incident checks. In short, it looked like progress.

Yet the losses continued. After months of frustration, further investigation revealed the actual problem: an inventory control failure. The warehouse was overstocked with aging parts that weren't selling, and managers, fearful of being penalized for inefficiency, under-reported availability. The "losses" existed only in the data, not in physical theft.

This was a costly lesson. The organization spent significant capital and staff effort on controls that did nothing to reduce the underlying business risk. Security may have been visible, but it was not effective.

How ESRM Would Change the Outcome

Now imagine the same scenario approached through an ESRM lens. Instead of rushing to deploy cameras, the security team would start by asking a different set of questions, questions designed to align with business priorities rather than assumptions about theft.

They might ask:

- *What assets are most critical to the business?*
  Rather than treating all inventory as equal, the security team collaborates with operations to identify which parts drive revenue, which are most vulnerable to disruption, and which directly affect production schedules.
- *What is the real risk to those assets?*
  ESRM broadens the scope beyond theft as a threat to assets to include supply chain breakdowns, counterfeit components entering the system, process issues, or cyber vulnerabilities in the warehouse management platform.
- *What security investment will have the most significant business impact?*
  The focus shifts from visible activity to solutions that close the most critical vulnerabilities. Solutions are chosen that could disrupt operations, erode customer trust, or have the most significant impact on revenue.

From this starting point, even without having discovered the procedural issues, the ESRM-driven strategy might lead to a very different set of recommendations:

- Strategic Camera Placement—Rather than blanketing the warehouse, cameras could be deployed in places where they could have the most impact to protect high-value inventory, at loading bays, and at choke points where unauthorized access could be concealed.
- RFID-Based Inventory Tracking—Implementing RFID tagging ensures real-time visibility of stock movement, allowing anomalies to be flagged and corrected before they cascade into costly "losses."
- Vendor and Contractor Controls—Procurement and supply chain teams partner with security to vet vendors, check for counterfeit risks, and tighten oversight of third-party logistics partners.
- Insider Threat Prevention—HR and security co-develop stronger screening, targeted access policies, and awareness programs that treat employees as partners in protection rather than suspects.

- Shared Training and Response—Warehouse staff receive incident-prevention and reporting training, so the responsibility for security is distributed across the business, not siloed in the security function.

The impact could have been profound. Instead of chasing the wrong problem, the company would have addressed the real vulnerabilities that were undermining its performance. The investigation into potential threats could have uncovered the real issue before any mitigation decisions were made. Security could have gone from being a reactive cost to an active enabler of operational continuity, supply chain resilience, and cost control.

Even if not every recommendation is adopted, the very act of approaching the problem through ESRM changes the conversation. Security is no longer positioned as the department that reacts to incidents, but as a partner embedded in the daily decisions that shape resilience.

With this model, security can be seen as:

- A proactive enabler of business continuity—Helping the organization prevent costly disruptions before they occur.
- A trusted partner to operational teams—Collaborating across supply chain, HR, IT, and procurement to close gaps that no single department could address alone.
- A risk-management leader that safeguards critical assets—Ensuring the company's most valuable resources, whether physical, digital, or reputational, remain protected.
- A driver of cost savings and revenue protection—Shifting investments away from reactive spending and toward controls that deliver measurable returns.

This warehouse example highlights a common theme: tactical responses often create the appearance of security without addressing the risks that truly matter. To move beyond that cycle, security decisions must be rooted in risk analysis and business impact, not simply in compliance requirements or the urge to "do something."

This is the true power of ESRM. Security becomes a strategic function that allows the business to operate safely, efficiently, and with confidence. More importantly, this approach scales. Whether the challenge is inventory loss in a warehouse, cyber threats in the data center, or workforce safety across multiple sites, ESRM ensures decisions are guided by risk, aligned with strategy, and defensible to leadership. In doing so, security transitions from being an overhead to an essential and integrated contributor to overall business success.

Pro Tip: Anchor every recommendation to a business consequence. Instead of "we need more cameras," frame it as "improved monitoring could reduce $X in inventory write-offs."

Why Compliance Alone Falls Short

It is tempting for organizations to equate "compliance" with regulation and "industry practice" with "security." Regulatory checklists provide clear rules to follow, auditors reinforce them annually, and executives can point to a binder of policies as evidence that the company is "secure." For leaders under pressure, compliance feels like a simple solution: meet the requirement, pass the audit, and move on.

The problem is that compliance with checklists is not equivalent to risk reduction. A control that satisfies a regulation may or may not address the actual threats facing the business. In many cases, compliance-driven decisions give a false sense of security. Action is taken, money is spent, metrics are collected, reports are written, boxes are checked... but vulnerabilities remain.

Take video surveillance as an example. A compliance mandate may require cameras in a sensitive area, and they can easily be ordered and hung. However, a risk-based approach poses a deeper question: *what do we need to observe, and why?* The answer drives the specification. Cameras covering five doors, added solely to satisfy a checkbox, may capture hours of footage that no one ever sees or needs. In contrast, a camera placed strategically in response to risk can monitor choke points where a single failure would halt operations. The intent behind the placement makes all the difference.

The same is true for perimeters. Compliance may require a boundary line, such as a fence around the property. But what is that perimeter meant to achieve? Is it to mark territory for insurance purposes? To guide pedestrian flow? Or to stop a speeding vehicle from breaching the facility? Each of those purposes requires a radically different design, from signage to bollards to reinforced barriers. Without asking the risk question, the design team risks building controls that look secure but fail under real pressure.

ESRM shifts the conversation from "Are we compliant?" to "Are we effectively mitigating the risks that matter most?" The difference is not just about how we are saying things. Changing the approach can determine whether resources are spent on protections that can really make a difference, or on one-off measures that do little to reduce real exposure.

Taken together, these examples reveal the central challenge facing security leaders today. Tactical reactions create activity without impact, while compliance-driven approaches produce controls that look solid on paper but may not protect against real threats. Both approaches consume resources, generate reports, and satisfy stakeholders in the short term, but neither consistently safeguards the business in the long run. To break out of this cycle, security requires a different model that starts with business risk and builds outward from there. That model is ESRM.

Making the Shift to ESRM—What Security Leaders Need to Do

The transition to ESRM does not mean discarding everything security teams have done before. It means elevating security to a strategic function that actively supports business objectives. Traditional security measures, such as guards, cameras, access control, and alarm systems, still have their place. However, under ESRM, these tactics are no longer the starting point. We ask, "Why do we need these systems and guards?" Then we select and prioritize our controls based on real business risk rather than instinct, routine, or regulatory mandates.

The fundamental shift from tactical security to risk-based security requires a new mindset, one that positions security professionals as business partners rather than isolated security specialists. It means stepping beyond day-to-day incident response and becoming an essential part of the organization's risk management framework.

This shift is not always easy. Tactical approaches can feel comfortable because they are visible, familiar, and easy to measure. Installing cameras or hiring more officers provides a quick answer when executives demand action. By contrast, ESRM requires asking more complex questions, engaging multiple business units, and sometimes challenging assumptions about what "good security" looks like. It asks security leaders to slow down in order to speed up, to pause before spending, so that investments truly protect what matters most.

💡 **Pro Tip**: Build credibility by showing where not to spend. Saying "this control is unnecessary" demonstrates stewardship of resources and earns leadership trust.

Importantly, making the shift does not mean abandoning tactical measures. People, process, and technology solutions remain critical tools to our security programs. What changes is the sequence: they are no longer deployed simply because "that's what we've always done," but because they are the right solutions to defined risks. In other words, tactics are reframed as outcomes of strategy, not substitutes for it.

Implementing ESRM in a real-world organization requires security leaders to fundamentally rethink our role within the business. For many of us, the most significant shift is not in the technical tools we use, but in how we define our value. We must become translators of risk into business language, facilitators of cross-functional solutions, and partners in achieving the enterprise's mission. We can accomplish this by following the steps outlined in this chapter and the rest of the book.

Understand the Business You Protect

The first and most critical step is to understand the business itself. Security cannot align with a strategy it does not understand. This means more than the typical advice we hear about scanning the annual report. As an integral part of the business, it involves examining the organization's day-to-day operations in depth.

Security leaders need to understand the big picture,[1] including:

- Revenue Streams—How does the company actually make money? A manufacturing firm has significantly different exposures compared to a professional services company or a hospital. If you do not understand the flow of revenue, you cannot anticipate the risks most likely to disrupt it.
- Operational Priorities—Which business processes are most critical to success? For some organizations, uptime in a data

center may be the lifeblood; for others, it is uninterrupted access to a warehouse or the ability to open a retail store safely every morning.

- Growth Objectives—Where is the company headed? Expansion into new regions, services, or product lines introduces fresh risks. If security does not understand the growth strategy, it cannot prepare for the exposures that will accompany it.
- Business-specific Strategies—Every organization has unique approaches. They might be just-in-time supply chains, franchise models, or intellectual property development. Each comes with distinct vulnerabilities. Security leaders must understand these nuances to design relevant protections.
- The Language of Business—Perhaps most importantly, security leaders must translate their recommendations into terms the business cares about. Executives think in categories such as cost control, revenue protection, liability avoidance, and brand reputation. A risk framed in those terms will resonate far more than one described only in terms of guards, gates, or gadgets.

Leaders who neglect this understanding inevitably run into conflict. A security posture designed in isolation will eventually conflict with operational or financial priorities. And when that clash happens, it is rarely security that wins. Even if a security position does prevail, it often comes at the expense of valuable political capital, ultimately weakening the program in the long run. Far better to understand the landscape of the business, anticipate where friction points will emerge, and frame security as the enabler of safe, efficient operations rather than the department of "no."

Pro Tip: Learn the language of finance. Translating risk into terms like "avoided losses" or "protected revenue" makes security recommendations resonate with executives.

Build Authentic Relationships across the Business

Learning how the business operates is only the first step. Security leaders also need genuine relationships with the people who own those functions. Without trusted connections, insights about revenue streams, growth plans, or operational challenges may never surface in time to influence risk decisions. Too often, security discovers important business changes after they are already underway, when controls are more complex and more expensive to implement.

Relationships grow from consistency and credibility. A single presentation to executives does not build lasting trust. Influence comes from regular conversations, curiosity about colleagues' challenges, and a willingness to connect security to their goals. When operations leaders see security asking how a plant expansion might affect production, or when finance hears security explain risks in terms of cost avoidance, trust builds. Over time, security shifts from being the group that reacts to incidents to the partner invited to planning sessions.

A practical way to begin building these inter-personal bridges is by scheduling recurring stakeholder conversations. These meetings do not need to start as formal risk assessments. They can be informal discussions. Try taking a colleague out for coffee. Have a conversation about them that might uncover business priorities and eventually lead to opportunities where security can provide value.

Stakeholder Conversation Guide

Sometimes it isn't easy to know how to begin building relationships across the business. A simple set of questions can help start the conversation and uncover what matters most to each team.

Getting to Know Their Function

- What does success look like for your team in the short and long term?
- Which processes or resources are most essential to your daily operations?
- Where do you feel pressure points—budget, staffing, regulations, or customer expectations—that influence how you work?
- What keeps your team from moving faster or more efficiently?
- What are the top goals or challenges for your team this quarter or year?
- Are there upcoming changes, such as new projects, market entries, or technology rollouts, that may shift your priorities?

Exploring Risks

- If your goals were disrupted, what would be the biggest impact on finances, operations, or reputation?
- Where do you see potential vulnerabilities or friction points that could slow you down?

Connecting to Security

- How does your team currently think about risk in your area?
- Where could security support your objectives beyond compliance or incident response?

Closing

- What is the best way for us to stay connected as things change?
- Are there forums or meetings I should join to understand your priorities better?

Building relationships in this way ensures that security is part of the conversation before decisions are made, rather than trying to influence them afterward. Once security leaders understand both the business landscape and the people who drive it, the next step is recognizing that security itself is one function among many that must integrate into the larger enterprise you've been exploring.

Recognize Security as One Business Function among Many

Security must recognize that it is one function among many that make up the enterprise. When security operates in a silo, it is almost inevitably seen as a cost center, or worse, the department that hinders innovation and impedes progress. This perception damages security's credibility. It also undermines the organization's ability to make truly risk-informed decisions. To shift this perception, security must deliberately embed itself into the broader business framework.

That means being:

- Integrated into overall strategy, risk management, and resilience planning -

  Security cannot be an afterthought. When strategic plans are being developed, whether for entering a new market, launching a new product, or reorganizing operations, security input must be part of the discussion. This ensures that potential risks are addressed at the planning stage, rather than being added later at a greater cost.

- Involved in the early stages of new projects, mergers, and expansion plans -

  Too often, security is brought in only after a deal is signed or a facility is already under construction. By joining at the front end, security professionals can highlight exposures early, reduce costly redesigns, and build controls that support both safety and efficiency.
- A partner in decision-making rather than just a policy enforcer -

  Policies are essential, but they are not enough. Security earns influence when it can sit at the table with finance, operations, and legal leaders to weigh trade-offs and shape solutions that protect the business while still enabling growth. There's little influence if people are scared or annoyed when they see you.

What does this look like in practice? It means security is part of strategic planning sessions, not just incident debriefs. It means that risk assessments are completed before major decisions, such as international expansion, adopting a new technology platform, or reshaping supply chains, are made, rather than as an afterthought once threats have already materialized. Further, it requires that security leaders collaborate directly with business executives to identify which assets are truly critical, prioritize protection strategies accordingly, and ensure that controls do not simply "check the box" but actively contribute to business resilience.

When security is viewed as part of the broader picture, and we can help ensure that the organization can achieve its mission without unnecessary disruption, we are far more likely to be embraced as a valuable partner. At that point, security is no longer the department of "no." Instead, it becomes the department of "how," helping the organization pursue opportunities while managing risk deliberately and strategically.

Move from Reactive Tactics to Proactive Strategy

Tactical security teams often find themselves reacting to problems only after they occur. Whether it is a data breach, a physical intrusion, or an incident of workplace violence, they are called only once the issue is already causing an impact. This reactionary stance reinforces the perception that security is simply a cost of doing business rather than a proactive partner[2] in protecting operations. It also places the organization at a disadvantage, because responding after the fact is almost always more expensive[3] and more disruptive than preventing the incident in the first place.

The ESRM approach turns this cycle on its head. Instead of waiting for problems to surface, ESRM positions security to anticipate risks, identify vulnerabilities, and design protections before a disruption occurs. This mindset elevates security from a crisis-response function to an active contributor to operational continuity and business resilience.

Consider the case of a retail company preparing to expand into international markets. A tactical security approach might involve selecting storefronts first and then adding alarms, cameras, and personnel after leases are signed. While this provides visible security, it does little to address broader risks that could threaten the venture's success.

A proactive ESRM approach would bring security into the expansion process from the start. The security team would collaborate with executives to evaluate:

- The political and economic stability of candidate markets, and how instability could affect customer and employee safety.
- Supply chain vulnerabilities that might disrupt product delivery or create opportunities for counterfeit goods.
- Fraud and theft risks associated with unfamiliar vendors and partners in new regions.
- Cybersecurity and privacy obligations under local laws that could expose the company to fines or reputational damage if overlooked.

By engaging at the planning stage, security leaders help the business avoid costly missteps, such as choosing a market where instability leads to prolonged store closures or where compliance failures expose the company to penalties. Instead of being perceived as an obstacle that slows down expansion, security is reframed as a guide that helps leadership choose the safest and most profitable path forward.

This distinction between reactive and proactive security is summarized in Table 1.1. The left-hand column reflects the hallmarks

TABLE 1.1 Tactical vs. Strategic Security

Tactical Security	Strategic, Risk-Based Security (ESRM)
Focuses on known security threats (for example, workplace violence, fraud, and cyberattacks) and deploys security measures accordingly.	Focuses on mission-critical assets first, determining how security supports the overall operation.
Reacts to incidents and compliance requirements.	Aligns security efforts with risk intelligence and business objectives.
Measures success based on activity (for example, patrols completed, doors locked).	Measures success based on incident reduction trends and business continuity.
Security often operates in a silo, separate from business operations.	Security is an integrated business function that enables business growth and resilience.
Driven by fear, recent incidents, or external pressure.	Driven by structured risk assessments and data-informed decision-making.
Perceived as a cost center or barrier.	Perceived as a partner that enables safe and profitable operations.

of tactical security: a narrow focus on individual threats, activity-based metrics, and siloed operations. It is often driven by fear of the latest incident or external pressure to "do something," which reinforces the perception of security as a costly but necessary burden. The right-hand column illustrates the ESRM mindset, where security aligns with mission-critical assets, integrates with business decisions, and measures success in terms of resilience and continuity. Instead of reacting to headlines, ESRM utilizes structured risk assessment and business data to inform its decisions, positioning security as a trusted partner and enabler of safe and profitable operations.

INSIGHT: TABLE 1.1—TACTICAL VS. STRATEGIC SECURITY

This table highlights the mindset shift at the core of ESRM. Tactical security feels productive because it produces visible activity like guards on post, cameras installed, or patrols logged. But activity is not the same as impact. Without alignment to business priorities, these measures often become costly signals of safety rather than actual safeguards. Strategic, risk-based security reframes the conversation by asking what assets matter most, what risks truly threaten them, and how controls can be prioritized for resilience. This shift is more than operational. It reshapes how organizations protect reputation, manage finances, and build culture. Staying tactical locks security into chasing yesterday's problems, while ESRM positions it as a partner in tomorrow's growth.

Use Business Impact and Data to Drive Security Decisions

Security recommendations carry the most weight when they are anchored in business impact and supported by current data. Rather than defaulting to what has always been done or reacting to the last incident, ESRM insists that leaders ask: *How will this risk, if realized, affect production, services, revenue, or reputation?* When security is framed in these terms, executives can clearly see how decisions translate into real business consequences.

One of the core weaknesses of tactical models is their reliance on two unreliable guides: worst-case scenarios and headline-driven incidents. Planning only for the most extreme case often results in controls that are too expensive to maintain and that still fail to address the issues most likely to occur. Likewise, reacting to the latest high-profile event elsewhere can drain resources away from the risks that are actually material to the organization. Neither approach delivers lasting value.

Pro Tip: Use scenario-based conversations with executives. Phrasing risk as "If X happens, then Y impact follows" keeps discussions practical and avoids abstract security jargon.

ESRM advocates for using traditional risk-led approaches and international standards such as ISO 31000, which call for a disciplined process of data-driven analysis that takes into account both the probability and the business impact of potential events.[4] By grounding decisions in evidence, security leaders avoid the trap of chasing every possible threat and instead build programs that are proportionate, sustainable, and credible to the business.

ESRM replaces fear-based responses with researched, risk-informed decision-making. The goal is not to ignore catastrophic threats, but to allocate resources in a way that balances preparedness for extreme events with practical protection against everyday risks. This shift ensures that scarce security budgets are invested where they deliver the highest business return.

For example:

- Instead of installing miles of perimeter fencing because of vague concerns about criminal trespassing, an ESRM analysis might reveal that insider fraud is the greater exposure, leading to investments in stronger employee screening, access management, and audit controls.
- Instead of deploying armed guards at every facility to counter the specter of an active shooter, ESRM may direct resources toward workplace violence prevention training, behavioral threat assessment teams, and employee assistance programs that reduce risk at its root.
- Instead of applying cybersecurity tools uniformly across the network, an ESRM approach prioritizes business-critical systems first, ensuring that essential operations and sensitive data are protected before expanding outward.

Each of these examples underscores the same principle: We can both improve protection and demonstrate measurable value to organizational leadership by linking security decisions to business impact that is supported by real data.

Move Beyond Compliance to Build Real Security

Regulations and industry standards are essential, but they are only a starting point. Too often, organizations treat compliance as the finish line, assuming that once the required boxes are marked, the enterprise is secure. In reality, compliance frameworks are designed to establish minimum expectations, rather than to guarantee protection. Adversaries do not measure their attacks against regulations, and incidents rarely unfold neatly along audit lines.

The ESRM perspective is different. It treats compliance as a baseline that must be met, but not as the goal. Real security comes from asking whether mandated controls actually address the risks that matter most to the organization, and whether those controls are implemented in a way that protects critical assets and keeps the business running.

Take the healthcare sector, for example. Compliance with HIPAA requires technical measures such as encryption, user access controls, and regular audits.[5] These steps are essential, but they do not in themselves prevent a malicious insider from exfiltrating sensitive patient records, nor do they guarantee resilience if ransomware locks down an entire hospital network. ESRM adds another layer of scrutiny by asking:

- Who poses the greatest threat to patient data, outside hackers, dishonest employees, or untrained staff making accidental errors?
- What is the real business impact of a breach? Look beyond the regulatory fines; also consider the damage to reputation, patient trust, and continuity of care.
- Where are the organization's most exploitable vulnerabilities? Are technical safeguards enough, or are cultural and procedural gaps more dangerous?
- How will the hospital continue to operate if an incident occurs? What recovery plans are in place to ensure patient safety and clinical services are not disrupted?

The same challenge is evident in other highly regulated sectors. Aviation, for instance, operates under strict mandates[6] from the TSA, ICAO, and national regulators. Meeting these requirements ensures a baseline of safety, but it does not guarantee resilience against today's evolving risks. For example, an airline may comply with passenger screening standards, baggage checks, and cockpit access rules, yet still face exposure to cyberattacks targeting reservation systems, insider collusion among ground staff, or disruptions in the global parts supply chain.

An ESRM perspective reframes this challenge. Instead of stopping at "we are compliant with regulations," security leaders ask:

- Who are the actual adversaries? Are threats more likely from external hackers probing flight systems, insiders with access to secure areas, or criminal groups seeking to exploit cargo shipments?
- What are the business impacts of an incident? Beyond passenger safety, how would prolonged delays, reputational damage, or financial penalties from regulators affect operations?

- Where are the most significant vulnerabilities? Is the weak point perimeter fencing, insider access, or reliance on a single IT vendor?
- How will continuity be maintained if disruptions occur? What plans are in place to restore flight schedules and passenger confidence quickly?

By layering these questions over compliance obligations, ESRM ensures that aviation security addresses both regulatory audits and the real threats that could ground planes, erode customer trust, and weaken business resilience.

Taken together, the healthcare and aviation examples illustrate the same truth across industries: compliance defines a minimum standard, but only a risk-based ESRM approach ensures that protections are tailored to real threats, aligned with business priorities, and capable of sustaining long-term resilience. This shift ensures that compliance obligations are met while also strengthening security where it truly matters. In practice, ESRM makes regulatory adherence more meaningful because it embeds required controls into a broader strategy that considers actual risk, operational impact, and business resilience.

Key Takeaways from Chapter 1

- Tactics aren't strategy: Activity-based security looks busy but often misses the risks that matter most.
- Compliance isn't security: Meeting regulations sets a floor, not a ceiling.
- Risk is the real driver: ESRM aligns controls with business impact, not with fear, headlines, or things done in the past.
- Security is a business function: When integrated into strategy and operations, it enables continuity and growth.
- The shift starts with mindset: ESRM reframes security from reacting to incidents to shaping resilience and outcomes.

Security Leader Toolkit: Chapter 1

ESRM Implementation Checklist

- Have I reviewed my current security program and identified which measures are activity-driven (e.g., patrols, cameras,

locks, audits) versus risk-driven (aligned with asset criticality and business goals)?
- Do I understand the organization's top revenue streams, operational priorities, and growth plans?
- Have I reframed at least one recent security recommendation in terms of its business impact (e.g., avoiding losses, maintaining operational continuity, or protecting the brand)?
- Have I built or begun building authentic relationships with at least three key non-security business stakeholders?
- Do I have a plan to explain security decisions in business terms rather than security jargon?

Tactical vs. Strategic Diagnostic Worksheet

Use this template to map where your current activities fall—are they tactical "activity-based" measures or strategic "risk-based" measures?

Security Activity/ Technology	How Often Is It Done?	Current Reason It's Done	Primarily Tactical or Strategic?
Example: Nightly perimeter patrols	Daily	Prevent intrusion	Tactical (activity-driven)
Example: Badge-based server room access	Continuous	Protect IT infrastructure from insider threat	Strategic (risk-driven)
Example: Annual audit of contractor badges	Annual	Audit requirement	Strategic (risk-driven)

How to Use It

- List 10–15 of your current controls.
- Fill in the reason your team performs each one.
- Decide if it's primarily tactical (done for activity, visibility, or compliance) or strategic (directly tied to business risk to critical assets).
- Highlight which "tactical" items might be re-evaluated through the ESRM lens.

Notes

1 ASIS International, *Senior Security Executive Standard* (Alexandria, VA: ASIS International, 2022).
2 Tim Malcom Vetter, "Proactive Security 101: Discover, Prioritize, Remediate," *NetSPI Blog*, May 22, 2024, https://www.netspi.com/blog/executive-blog/proactive-security/proactive-security-101-discover-prioritize-remediate/.
3 IBM Security, *Cost of a Data Breach Report 2024*, Conducted by Ponemon Institute (Armonk, NY: IBM, 2024), https://www.ibm.com/reports/data-breach.
4 International Organization for Standardization, *ISO 31000:2018: Risk Management—Guidelines* (Geneva: ISO, 2018).
5 U.S. Department of Health and Human Services, *Health Insurance Portability and Accountability Act of 1996 (HIPAA)*, Pub. L. No. 104–191, 110 Stat. 1936 (1996).
6 U.S. Department of Homeland Security, Transportation Security Administration. *49 CFR Part 1542: Airport Security* (Washington, DC: U.S. Government Publishing Office, current through August 2025), https://www.ecfr.gov/current/title-49/subtitle-B/chapter-XII/subchapter-C/part-1542.

Chapter 2

Thinking Like a Risk Manager

Many security professionals start our careers by responding to threats. A breach occurs, an incident disrupts operations, or a high-profile crime makes headlines. In response, leadership demands an immediate solution: often a visible, tactical fix that creates the perception of safety. More guards, more cameras, more access restrictions. These measures may address immediate concerns, but they rarely take a long-term, strategic approach to risk reduction. They are often left in place regardless of their efficacy, simply because "it's what we've been doing."

This cycle of incident, reaction, and short-term solution is the hallmark of fear-based security. It relies on responding to events rather than preventing them. It prioritizes high-profile threats over the most pressing business risks. And, ultimately, it limits the ability of our security teams to contribute meaningfully to business resilience.

Consider the case of a manufacturing company that suffered a significant theft of copper wiring from its storage yard. Executives, alarmed by the financial loss and attention from the local paper, immediately ordered the facility manager to add perimeter patrols and additional guard hours.

While the extra presence provided reassurance, it also came at a recurring cost that eventually exceeded the value of the stolen material. Worse, the actual vulnerability, which was a lack of secure storage and poor inventory controls, remained unaddressed.

The company was spending more to *feel* safer, but not to *be* safer.

But reacting to incidents, even with preventive measures, is not the same as managing risk. Security Risk Management professionals need to go further, anticipating risks, assessing their impact, and directing resources where they will have the most significant effect.

DOI: 10.4324/9781003711346-4

Pro Tip: When executives demand an immediate fix, consider asking whether the solution is meant to address the *actual* risk or provide visible reassurance. It's a bold question, but it can help them see that comfort measures may calm fears, but only risk strategies reduce exposure.

Moving from "What If" to "What Matters"

Reactive security conversations are easy to spot. When they begin, they often start with fear-driven hypotheticals. Leaders and employees alike frame the discussion around "what if" scenarios. What if there's an active shooter? What if someone tricks our staff with a phishing email? What if protesters show up at the front gate? Each of these scenarios highlights a genuine concern, and each generates a fairly obvious and quickly implementable tactical response: developing a workplace violence program, providing cybersecurity training, or tightening access control.

These measures are not wrong, but they do reflect a limited mindset. "What if" thinking focuses on individual threats in isolation. It drives tactical programs that address visible risks, yet it rarely connects those risks back to the broader mission of the business. When resources are limited, as is always the case, responding to every possible "what if" leaves organizations spread thin, chasing every scenario without asking whether those scenarios are the ones that truly matter. This is a challenging position to be in when the security function is a secondary responsibility of a team such as Facilities, Real Estate, or Administration, which may not have previously considered real security risk.

Enterprise Security Risk Management (ESRM) reframes the conversation. Instead of asking only what could happen, it asks what matters most. What assets are essential to the business? What damage would have the largest effect on operations, reputation, or revenue? How can security protect those assets while still enabling the organization to function smoothly? These questions shift the focus from fear to value, from theoretical threats to real business priorities. Table 2.1 presents several examples of how this shift might be framed in various security environments.

TABLE 2.1 Examples of "What If" vs. "What Matters" across Industries

Industry	"What If" Question	"What Matters" Question	Example Security Focus
Healthcare	What if a patient gets aggressive in the ER?	How can we ensure that emergency care continues uninterrupted?	Staff safety protocols that also protect patient throughput
Retail	What if shoplifters target our flagship store?	How do we minimize revenue loss across the chain?	Data-driven deployment to the highest-loss locations
Manufacturing	What if an intruder jumps the fence?	How do we prevent downtime that halts production lines?	Asset-focused access controls and backup suppliers
Finance	What if hackers attack our website?	How do we maintain customer trust and compliance?	Layered defenses are prioritized around critical systems.
Hospitality	What if protesters gather outside the hotel?	How can we ensure guest safety and maintain our brand reputation?	Crowd management plans tied to customer experience.

INSIGHT: TABLE 2.1—EXAMPLES OF "WHAT IF" VS. "WHAT MATTERS" ACROSS INDUSTRIES

Executives raise "what if" questions because they want assurance that visible threats are covered. Dismissing those concerns outright risks losing credibility. The ESRM approach is to acknowledge the scenario, then redirect toward the larger issue: what the organization values most and what risks truly threaten those priorities. This reframing keeps leaders engaged while elevating the discussion from tactical fixes to strategic risk management.

What Risk Really Means: Intelligent Trade-Offs

When most people hear the phrase "security risk," they picture the threat itself: hackers, intruders, and insiders. Fear focuses attention on what might happen, but that view is incomplete. Security risk is not solely about the presence of a threat. It is about the *business impact* if that threat materializes into an incident, and whether the cost of prevention is justified.

This is where intelligent trade-offs come in. No organization can block every risk, and trying to do so wastes resources while creating unnecessary friction. A risk-led approach asks three practical questions:

- What is the actual impact of this potential incident on the business?
- What level of mitigation is appropriate, given our risk tolerance?
- What security solutions provide the best return on investment?

Consider an insurance company facing an uptick in stolen laptops. Leadership's instinct before understanding the cost is to issue every employee a hardened, encrypted device to protect data. But this is a fix that could cost millions. A proportional response might be simpler: mandate encryption on existing devices, update secure storage policies, and provide lockboxes for field vehicles. These steps reduce exposure at a fraction of the cost, aligning protection with the true scale of business impact.

Risk management is not about eliminating every danger; it's about mitigating risks, making informed investments, and reducing the risks that matter most, while avoiding overspending on controls that appear reassuring but deliver little real value.

Pro Tip: When someone says, "Do whatever it takes to stop this from happening again," ask what level of financial loss is acceptable to prevent it. That question reframes the discussion and opens the door to a real ESRM conversation.

A strategic risk-based approach begins with this reminder:

- *Not every threat demands the same level of mitigation.*

The ISO 31000 standard on risk makes this explicit, noting that the role of risk professionals is to help leaders make informed choices, rather than eliminating every possible danger.[1] Just because an incident occurs somewhere does not mean the proper response is, "do whatever it takes to stop this from happening here."

Let's look at a real-world example to see how that might play out in practice.

The Cost of Overreaction vs. Strategic Risk Management

Consider a regional retail chain operating 300 stores with $600 million in annual revenue. Like many retailers, it suffers from shrinkage, losses from shoplifting, employee theft, and errors. On average, shrinkage in the retail sector runs 1–2% of sales.[2] In this case, the chain is reporting losses closer to 2.5%, or about $15 million annually. Executives are understandably alarmed.

Frustrated, the CEO calls for a zero-tolerance policy: every store entrance staffed with a uniformed officer. Without thinking it through, the idea carries a certain appeal. A guard at every door signals control, reassures customers, and sends a message that theft will no longer be tolerated. Yet beneath the optics, the numbers tell a different story. At roughly $100,000 per officer per year, once salary, benefits, training, scheduling coverage, and overhead are included, the program would cost $30 million annually. That is double the actual shrink losses, and a level of spending that would eat directly into profits without addressing the root causes of the problem. Needless to say, it quickly becomes "not an option."

What appears to be a bold and decisive request in the boardroom is, in practice, a fear-based overreaction. It provides visibility, but not necessarily value. Security that relies on visibility alone tends to become financially unsustainable, delivering diminishing returns as costs escalate while theft adapts to the new environment. Worse, such measures are often misaligned with the actual drivers of loss, creating a false sense of security without delivering the operational resilience the business truly needs. But just because the initial demand is not feasible, that doesn't mean doing nothing (Figure 2.1).

An ESRM perspective reframes the discussion. Instead of asking, *How do we stop every theft?* The better question is, how do we reduce shrinkage *to an acceptable level while supporting the business?* That shift changes the conversation from one of absolutes to one of balance. No retailer can realistically reduce theft to zero, but every retailer can determine what level of loss is tolerable and how to address it without undermining profitability or customer experience.

The security leader in this case would start with the data: analyzing which stores contribute most to the shrinkage problem, mapping loss patterns against local crime rates, and projecting where theft is most likely to escalate. With that insight, the company can focus resources where they will make the most difference, rather than spreading them thin across all 300 locations.

From there, the organization can build a layered mitigation program. Targeted training equips staff to recognize and respond

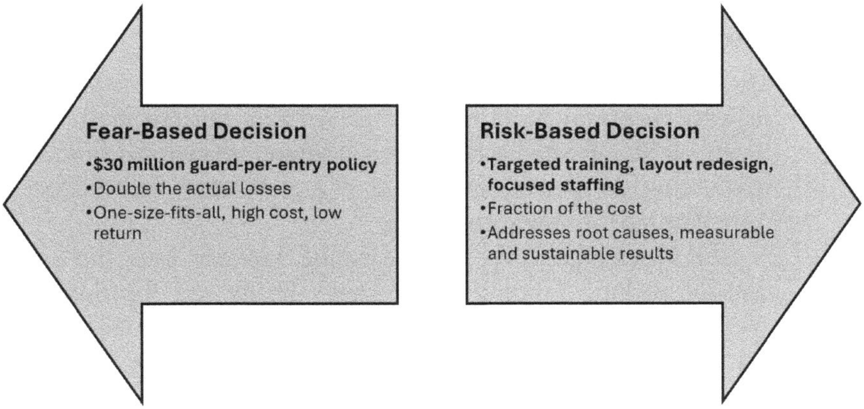

FIGURE 2.1 Fear-Based vs. Risk-Based Response

to theft attempts. Focused deployment of security officers in the handful of high-loss stores provides visible deterrence without chain-wide expense. Redesigning layouts to reduce blind spots, securing the most vulnerable merchandise, and using signage to discourage casual theft all reinforce the effect. In some cases, even modest technology investments, such as smarter video analytics or improved inventory tracking, can further amplify these efforts.

Together, these measures cost a fraction of the $30 million guard blanket while producing a sharper, more sustainable reduction in losses. More importantly, they demonstrate that security decisions, when guided by risk management principles, create value by aligning solutions directly to business priorities.

This example illustrates the key distinction. A fear-based approach might spend heavily to project control, often without changing outcomes. A risk-based approach aligns investments with business priorities, thereby reducing losses in a proportionate, data-driven, and financially sound manner.

INSIGHT: REAL-WORLD RISK IMPLICATIONS FOR SECURITY LEADERS

- Not every threat requires the same response; context determines the right level of action.
- Eliminating all risk is impossible; proportionality is the goal.
- Security recommendations must be framed around business impact, not fear or visibility.

The "Bottom Line": Security Risk Is Business Risk

One of the most essential lessons for security professionals is that security risk must be framed as *business risk*. For too long, organizations have treated security as a separate, specialized function, reinforcing the perception that it is a cost center rather than a contributor to strategic outcomes.

ESRM changes this by integrating security into the same decision-making processes executives already use for financial, operational, and reputational risks. Instead of standing apart, security enters the boardroom conversation on equal footing, guided by the same cost-benefit logic and trade-off thinking that leadership applies elsewhere.

1. **What is the business impact of this risk?**

   Not all threats have the same consequences. A minor data breach involving non-sensitive information is inconvenient but not catastrophic. A cyberattack or sabotage that shuts down production lines for a week could have severe and lasting consequences. Understanding the difference and quantifying the impact of a security risk on revenue, operations, or reputation helps leaders make informed trade-offs.

   Example: A pharmaceutical company losing access to its research data for even a few days could delay clinical trials and result in millions of dollars in lost market opportunity. By contrast, the theft of a few outdated laptops may create minimal business disruption.
2. **What is the likelihood of this threat materializing?**

   Business leaders do not allocate millions of dollars to ensure against highly unlikely, low-impact operational or financial risks. The same logic applies to security. Some risks, while catastrophic in theory, may be statistically improbable. ESRM ensures that decisions are data-driven rather than fear-driven, so resources are directed where they make a measurable difference.

   Example: A regional utility might face the theoretical risk of a nation-state cyberattack, but the far more likely risk is copper theft at substations. Focusing first on the high-probability, high-impact theft problem prevents outages and protects revenue.

3. **What is the most cost-effective mitigation strategy?**
   No business would spend $10 million to mitigate a $500,000 risk. Security investments must follow the same principle: proportional spending tied to realistic exposure. The goal is not to implement the most expensive or most visible solution, but the one that delivers the best balance of protection, efficiency, and value.
   Example: A financial services firm facing insider fraud might be tempted to deploy a costly AI monitoring platform across all employees. A more balanced solution would target monitoring to high-risk functions, such as trading desks, paired with robust ethics training, thereby cutting costs while maintaining focus where the risk is highest.
4. **How does this mitigation support the company's overall mission?**
   Security should never become a barrier to business success. Well-designed strategies enhance operations rather than obstruct them. The role of the security leader is to align controls with organizational priorities, ensuring that risk mitigation enables efficiency and growth, rather than creating unnecessary friction.
   Example: A logistics company can mandate multi-factor authentication for drivers accessing route systems without slowing down daily dispatch. Controls that protect information while keeping trucks on schedule directly support the company's mission of reliable delivery.

A risk-based security mindset ensures that organizations stay focused on what matters most, not just on what feels most urgent in the moment. By evaluating and discussing threats in the same way executives evaluate financial or operational risks, security leaders reposition their function as an integrated partner in business resilience.

The Risk Triangle: A Practical Framework for Educating Decision-Makers in ESRM

Most security professionals are already familiar with the concept of the risk triangle, even if they don't use the term explicitly. It is the foundation of nearly every risk discussion, and one of the

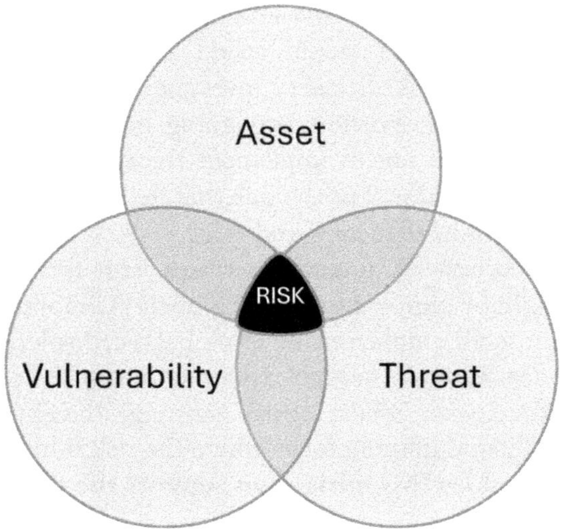

FIGURE 2.2 The Risk Triangle

clearest ways to help internal business partners understand how security decisions should be made. Unlike complex matrices or lengthy reports, the triangle is easy to visualize: three points that show the relationship between assets, threats, and vulnerabilities (Figure 2.2).

At its core, the risk triangle consists of three components:

Assets—The things that need to be protected because they are critical to the business.

> *Example:* At a university, students' academic records are a core asset. They exist in both digital form, stored in information systems, and physical form, such as transcripts and paper files in registrar offices. Both versions are essential for ensuring compliance, maintaining a positive reputation, and enhancing the student experience.

Threats—The external or internal forces that could cause harm to those assets.

> *Example:* A cybercriminal attempting to breach the student information system is one threat. Another could be a dishonest employee altering grades, or even a break-in where physical files are stolen or tampered with. Each threat type can damage trust and trigger regulatory or legal action.

Vulnerabilities—The weaknesses that could allow a threat to exploit an asset.

Example: If the university relies on outdated software or leaves accounts active for former students and staff, those vulnerabilities increase the likelihood of a successful cyberattack. Physical exposures matter too: unsecured data entry stations in registrar offices, or server rooms without strong access controls, create openings for unauthorized access.

Pro Tip: Define Your Terms. Before a risk discussion, state clearly what you mean by "security risk." It avoids executives mapping the word onto finance, legal, or other definitions.

The Risk Formula: A Simple Math Problem

Risk is not an abstract concept. It is a calculation of three factors: assets, threats, and vulnerabilities. The intersection of these three points gives us the actual level of risk to an organization from any particular category of threat.

At its core, risk is a function of these factors:

1. Assets have value.
2. Threats are what could reduce that value.
3. Vulnerabilities are what allow threats to impact assets.

Applying the thinking from multiple risk standards,[3] we can (in a highly simplified way) conclude that:

Risk = Asset Value × Threat × Vulnerability

This is not the exact math used to calculate risk; we will look at that in more detail in Chapter 4, but it reveals a fundamental truth. If any of these factors is zero, the risk itself is zero. If an asset has no value, there is no business reason to protect it. If the threat level is nonexistent, it does not require mitigation. If vulnerabilities are eliminated, threats cannot cause harm.

In the real world, of course, risk is never truly zero. However, risk can be effectively managed by adjusting these variables, which is precisely where ESRM shifts the conversation from reacting to threats toward managing them strategically.

By breaking risk into assets, threats, and vulnerabilities, the triangle strips away jargon and makes risk easy to explain. Its real value is in communication: business leaders can quickly see what drives exposure and where trade-offs matter most, without getting lost in technical detail. At the same time, its simplicity has boundaries, and security leaders must understand where the model falls short in order to use it responsibly.

INSIGHT—THE LIMITS OF THE TRIANGLE

The Asset × Threat × Vulnerability model is a practical teaching tool, not a statistical formula. It simplifies complex dynamics into a shape executives can quickly understand, but security leaders should recognize its boundaries:

- Threat likelihood is rarely linear -
  In many models, the probability curve accelerates: the jump from "4" to "5" may signal a steep rise in frequency, far more than a small step up. Treating scores as evenly spaced can distort the actual severity of the risk.
- Vulnerability is never truly zero -
  Even when controls appear strong, residual weaknesses remain: systems can fail, users make errors, and new attack methods emerge. Zero-vulnerability exists only in theory.
- Multiplying qualitative scores gives directional results, not absolutes -
  The purpose is to compare across assets and scenarios, not to make predictions. What matters most is consistency in scoring and clarity in how results are used.

Simplified models are well-suited for many organizations, particularly when the goal is to achieve a shared understanding. But industries such as aviation, healthcare, or energy often require more advanced quantitative models to meet regulatory or operational demands. In Real-world ESRM, the triangle should be treated as a decision-support framework, a means to guide discussion, rather than generate statistically precise answers.

Translating the Risk Triangle

Security professionals sometimes overcomplicate risk discussions with technical jargon that loses the attention of business leaders. Instead of discussing "threat vectors," "attack surfaces," or "risk matrices," ESRM practitioners need to translate these three elements into plain language, framing them in ways that business partners can understand and act on.

Part of the challenge is that the very word *risk* means different things to different people. For a finance executive, risk may be synonymous with market volatility. For a general counsel, it may mean liability or regulatory exposure. For operations leaders, risk often translates into downtime. In my own conversations with executives, I've frequently found that what I meant by "security risk" wasn't the picture they had in mind at all. They were attempting to process a highly technical definition through their own business lens, resulting in disconnects and frustration on both sides.

That is why reframing risk into simpler, universal questions is so effective. A practical way to translate both the ESRM cycle and the risk triangle is by putting them into plain language:

1. **What am I trying to protect?** (The Asset)—Identifying what is most valuable to the business.
2. **What does it truly need to be protected from?** (The Threats that have associated Vulnerabilities)—Understanding both the external threats and the internal weaknesses that create risk.
3. **How can I most effectively and efficiently protect it?** (The Mitigation Strategy—Removing the Vulnerabilities)—Allocating resources to manage risk in a way that aligns with business priorities.

By structuring conversations around these three questions, we avoid abstract jargon and keep discussions relevant, clear, and actionable for leadership. Later in this book, we will explore each question in detail, with tools and tactics for applying them in practice.

Risk Tolerance and Trade-offs

Not all risks bring the same level of concern, and not all require the same level of response. Consider two very different situations: a manufacturer deciding whether to keep a factory running during hurricane season, or a fast-moving tech startup willing to launch a new product with minimal testing to beat competitors to market. Both decisions involve risk, but the level of tolerance is very different. That tolerance, or the amount of risk an organization is willing to take on, is the real driver of the actions leadership will take.

Defining Risk Tolerance

Formally, risk tolerance refers to *the amount of risk an organization is willing to accept in pursuit of its business goals before intervention is required.*[4]

It represents the variation from expected levels of loss or harm that the company can absorb without severe operational or financial consequences. In practice, it shows up every day in boardrooms and project meetings. When executives weigh a merger, choose between suppliers, or debate how much insurance coverage to buy, they are signaling their tolerance for uncertainty. Security leaders must connect their own recommendations to those same conversations. Table 2.2 illustrates what this might look like in practice within low- and high-tolerance organizations.

This contrast shows how two organizations can face the same threat yet respond in opposite ways, depending on their tolerance for uncertainty. Take "control philosophy," for example: a nuclear power plant will naturally emphasize strict, layered defenses, while a fintech startup may prefer an agile, minimum-viable-control approach. Both are rational choices within their respective tolerance levels.

Pro Tip: Listen for language. Leaders often reveal their risk tolerance in how they talk. Phrases like "near zero tolerance" or "we can live with it" are signals to frame your recommendations accordingly.

It is also important to remember that tolerance is not a static concept. It varies depending on the industry, market conditions, and business cycles. A company in rapid expansion mode may accept higher risk, while the same company facing regulatory audits or shareholder pressure may suddenly demand strict controls. After a major incident, tolerance often narrows temporarily, then rebalances over time. For security leaders, the task is to recognize these shifts and recalibrate recommendations so they remain aligned with the organization's current priorities.

TABLE 2.2 Levels of Risk Tolerance

Aspects of Tolerance	Low-Tolerance Organization	High-Tolerance Organization
Strategic posture	"Protect at all costs" mindset; prioritizing the elimination or transfer of risk.	"Pursue opportunity" mindset; accepts more uncertainty to seize market/innovation gains.
Investment pattern	Larger, up-front spend on preventive controls (e.g., redundancy, premium insurance).	Leaner baseline controls; funds flow to growth projects first, then to risk mitigation as needed.
Decision trigger	Any risk rated moderate or above prompts executive review and a mitigation plan.	Only risks rated high and above trigger board attention; moderate risks are often accepted.
Control philosophy	Defense-in-depth and strict change-control processes; preference for proven solutions.	Agile, minimum-viable-control approach; willingness to pilot emerging solutions with limited safeguards.
Residual risk threshold	Targets "as low as reasonably achievable" (ALARA[5]); near-zero tolerance for surprise.	Willing to carry visible residual risk if the ROI justifies it; focuses on rapid response capability.
Metrics focus	Lagging indicators (incident count, loss events) and leading indicators (test coverage, control uptime) to stay ahead of risk.	Primarily, lagging indicators are used to assess the cost of accepted risk; leading metrics are added only after issues have emerged.
Cultural signal	"Safety blanket" culture. Employees escalate early and seek explicit permission.	"Calculated bet" culture—teams empowered to act quickly within broad risk guardrails.

INSIGHT—RISK TOLERANCE IN DIFFERENT INDUSTRIES

Risk tolerance varies significantly across different industries. That's because the impact of loss differs dramatically from one to another. A threat that is existential in one sector may be a manageable nuisance in another. Understanding this context is essential for security leaders.

- Financial Services—A bank typically has an extremely low tolerance for cybersecurity risk. A single breach can trigger regulatory fines, legal liability, reputational collapse, and even systemic financial disruption. As a result, banks invest heavily in multi-factor authentication, continuous monitoring, layered encryption, and strict access controls. For them, the cost of robust prevention is small compared to the potential impact of a breach.
- Food Service—A regional restaurant chain, by contrast, may view cyber risk very differently. While no company wants to be hacked, the direct impact of a breach in this environment is far less severe. Leadership may decide that enterprise-grade monitoring and top-tier authentication controls are simply too expensive relative to the value of their data. Instead, they accept a higher level of residual risk, focusing on affordable measures like employee awareness training, sound password practices, and clear response policies. The goal is not to eliminate the risk but to keep it within acceptable bounds.
- Manufacturing—A global manufacturer faces a third kind of challenge. While cyber compromise of financial data may not be as catastrophic as in banking, downtime on the production floor can cost millions per day. Their risk tolerance prompts them to make substantial investments in industrial control system security, supply chain visibility, and physical safeguards for critical machinery, even if other risks are partially accepted.

These examples highlight a central truth: risk tolerance is not about right or wrong; it is about alignment. Each organization chooses which risks it is willing to carry and which it must mitigate aggressively, based on what would most disrupt its mission. ESRM equips security leaders to navigate these choices with clarity and confidence.

Aligning with Business Risk Appetite

Even when security teams adopt a risk-based mindset, friction can still emerge if security strategies do not align with leadership's overall risk appetite. This tension often shows up in two predictable ways:

1. Security as a barrier. If the business is willing to accept higher levels of risk in pursuit of growth, but security insists on stringent controls that slow down operations, leadership may view security as a drag on innovation.

2. Security as a gap. If security ignores or underestimates leadership's risk tolerance, it may provide too little protection. In that case, executives inherit unmitigated risks that could ultimately lead to financial, operational, or reputational crises.

Both extremes—overcontrol and undercontrol—erode trust. The risk-based approach aims to strike a balance by ensuring that risk management practices align with the organization's stated appetite for risk.

Imagine a global corporation planning to expand operations into a country with high levels of organized crime, kidnappings, fraud, and corruption.

- A risk-averse approach might advise against entering the market at all, pointing to the potential for theft, bribery, reputational damage, or even harm to personnel. From a purely protective standpoint, "no" feels like the safest answer.
- A risk-based ESRM approach begins with the recognition that leadership has already signaled a willingness to accept the risk of operating there, because the potential business reward outweighs the dangers. The role of security is not to veto the decision but to shape it by presenting options to mitigate those risks to a level the business finds tolerable.

The first step is to clarify what assets will actually be at risk in this market. Will the company be moving high-value physical shipments across unsecured routes? Will expatriate executives or traveling staff be present and therefore exposed to kidnapping risk? Will the assets at stake primarily consist of financial transactions and intellectual property, making fraud and cybercrime the most significant concerns? Security leaders cannot propose adequate controls until they understand what the organization is implementing.

Once the asset picture is clear, the security team can design and suggest mitigations that align with business priorities:

- Rigorous background checks for all local hires, with escalation procedures for red flags.
- Secure logistics planning to protect shipments from theft or tampering.
- Enhanced fraud detection systems in financial operations.

- Stronger partnerships with local law enforcement or vetted private security providers.
- Protective travel protocols for executives and staff, ranging from itinerary control and safe-route planning to, if justified, specialized kidnap-prevention training or response support.

In this way, ESRM keeps the business opportunity on the table, while ensuring that the organization fully understands its exposures and applies practical safeguards where they matter most.

Why Risk Tolerance Alignment Matters

Risk appetite is ultimately a board-level directive. When security recommendations align with that appetite, leaders view security as a partner in achieving strategic goals rather than a barrier to progress. By contrast, when security is perceived as ignoring or overriding leadership's stated tolerance, credibility erodes quickly, and security becomes sidelined from key decisions.

For ESRM practitioners, the goal should be to meet the business where it is, then try to guide leaders toward smarter, better-informed choices within that business framework. Part of that guidance includes documenting those choices. A signed record of what risks leadership has chosen to accept protects both the organization and the security leader by ensuring transparency and accountability.

Pro Tip: Request Sign-Off. If leadership accepts a level of risk that concerns you, request formal sign-off. This fosters accountability and ensures shared clarity on risk tolerance.

Trade-Offs in Risk Management

Every risk decision comes with trade-offs. Absolute security does not exist, and every additional control has a cost, whether financial, operational, or cultural. No business decision is entirely risk-free, and every security measure must be evaluated against the balance of its benefits and drawbacks.

- Too little security—leaves the organization exposed. Unmitigated risks can cascade into financial loss, operational disruption, regulatory penalties, or reputational harm. In some industries, a single lapse can be existential.

- Too much security—creates its own problems. Excessive controls can slow down business processes, frustrate employees, drive up costs, and ultimately hinder growth. In many cases, leaders will bypass or circumvent such controls, thereby defeating their intended purpose.

A practical example is access control. A facility may require multi-factor authentication, armed guards, and escort policies for all visitors. That would maximize security, but it could also cripple productivity and alienate partners. On the other end of the spectrum, a building with unlocked doors and no monitoring minimizes friction but leaves the company exposed. The correct answer lies between these extremes, tailored to the organization's risk tolerance and business needs.

The key for ESRM practitioners is to frame recommendations in terms of business impact rather than security concerns alone. When we clearly articulate why specific controls are necessary, or why others may be excessive, security gains credibility as a trusted partner rather than a roadblock.

Security as a Business Enabler: Thinking Like a Business Leader

In many boardrooms, security is still introduced as a budget line item rather than a business driver. The conversation begins with cost: the annual spend on guards, cameras, access cards, or alarms. Executives nod, approve what seems "reasonable," and move on. Rarely do they hear security framed as something that can protect revenue streams, accelerate expansion, or safeguard reputation. This dynamic reinforces the perception of security as overhead—necessary, but not value-generating.

Too often, security teams unintentionally reinforce that view. They report on inputs (hours worked, patrols logged, cameras maintained) instead of outcomes (losses reduced, disruptions prevented, markets safely entered). These metrics demonstrate activity, but not impact. And in an era when executives expect every function to prove return on investment, activity alone does not earn a seat at the strategy table.

The Business Mindset Shift

Thinking like a Risk Manager with ESRM reframes the conversation. Rather than asking, "What are we spending on security?" leaders begin to ask, "What value is security delivering to the business?" Security becomes a business enabler when it demonstrates how it prevents revenue loss, maintains operational uptime, supports market entry, and strengthens customer trust.

Consider a few examples:

- A pharmaceutical company's distribution depends on the integrity of its cold chain. Security measures that protect shipments from diversion or sabotage directly ensure the company can deliver life-saving drugs on time, preserving both revenue and brand credibility.
- A tech startup's most valuable asset may be its intellectual property. By investing in insider threat monitoring and secure data handling, the company prevents data loss while also reassuring investors and partners.
- For a transit authority, disruption is catastrophic. Security programs that protect control centers, safeguard passenger areas, and ensure continuity of operations are fundamental to both regulatory compliance and public trust.

These examples illustrate the key fact that when security aligns itself with outcomes that executives already value (such as revenue, reputation, and resilience), it shifts from a cost center to a growth partner.

Speaking the Language of Business

To make this shift, security leaders need to adopt a mindset to match their business leaders. Instead of counting the number of incidents that occurred, we ask: *What financial loss did we prevent? How many hours of downtime did we avoid? How did we preserve our license to operate in this market?* This reframing helps executives view security as the business performance driver it is, instead of looking at it through a "cost center" lens.

Just as importantly, security teams must avoid becoming barriers to progress. If security policies continually create obstacles that slow operations or frustrate employees, they will be ignored and bypassed. An effective ESRM approach allows you to integrate seamlessly into operations, reducing risk without adding unnecessary drag.

The path to making this change is outlined in Table 2.3. The left-hand column brings integration and collaboration. The right-hand column leads to isolation and friction.

TABLE 2.3 Do's and Don'ts to Shift Mindset

Do	Don't
Frame security initiatives in financial terms: showing cost savings, loss prevention, and return on investment.	Focus solely on security-specific metrics, such as the number of threats detected or patrols conducted.
Align security efforts with business continuity and operational resilience to ensure seamless operations.	Treat security as a separate function, distinct from business priorities and objectives.
Explain how security enhances customer trust, promotes regulatory compliance, and fosters a strong brand reputation.	Overload executives with technical jargon that doesn't translate to business outcomes.
Demonstrate how security mitigates real business risks, including fraud, supply chain disruptions, and regulatory penalties.	Assume that security concerns alone will drive executive decision-making.
Integrate security seamlessly into business operations, making it an enabler rather than an obstacle.	Implement security measures that hinder efficiency or create unnecessary friction.
Develop partnerships across departments, collaborating with finance, HR, IT, and operations.	Operate security in a silo without engaging other business units.
Utilize data, trends, and risk analysis to anticipate issues before they escalate into crises.	Wait for incidents to occur and then layer on reactive controls.
Design security processes that enable employees and customers to operate efficiently and securely.	Create rigid policies that frustrate users and drive workarounds.

INSIGHT: TABLE 2.3—DO'S AND DON'TS TO SHIFT MINDSET

This table highlights the mindset shift at the core of ESRM. Tactical security feels productive because it produces visible activity: guards on post, cameras installed, patrols logged. But activity is not the same as impact. Without alignment to business priorities, these measures often become costly "security theatre" rather than real safeguards.

Strategic, risk-based security reframes the conversation by asking what assets matter most, what risks truly threaten them, and how controls can be prioritized for resilience. Organizations stuck in tactical mode will continue to chase yesterday's problems, while those that adopt ESRM position security as a partner in tomorrow's growth.

Ultimately, though, ESRM is about far more than changing an approach. It is about changing how the business perceives security itself. A well-run risk-based security program enables innovation, supports market growth, protects reputation, and reduces volatility. That is the definition of a business enabler. Making this change helps security leaders and their teams move into that coveted "seat at the table" and gets us recognized as an essential investment in the organization's future.

Key Takeaways from Chapter 2

- Fear-driven security wastes resources: Tactical overreactions rarely match the real business risk.
- Risk decisions are trade-offs: ESRM focuses effort where it delivers the most value.
- Speak in business terms: Framing around outcomes makes security relevant to leadership.
- The ESRM model clarifies risk: Asking "What Am I Trying to Protect?, What Does It Truly Need to Be Protected From? And, How Can We Most Effectively and Efficiently Protect It?" makes the process actionable.
- Risk tolerance belongs to leadership: Security guides the discussion, but executives set the threshold.

Security Leader Toolkit: Chapter 2

ESRM Implementation Checklist

- Have I clearly defined "risk" in terms of asset × threat × vulnerability for my organization?
- Have I introduced the Risk Triangle (Asset–Threat–Vulnerability) to at least one stakeholder group?
- Have I documented my organization's agreed-upon risk tolerance or appetite (low, medium, high)?
- Do I have a simple method to explain trade-offs when leaders ask for costly or fear-based fixes?
- Have I established a living Risk Register to track and prioritize risks consistently?

Risk Trade-Off Worksheet (Template)

Use this template to practice turning fear-driven "what if" scenarios into business-aligned trade-off decisions.

Fear-Based "What If?"	Underlying Asset	Real Business Impact if Incident Occurs	Likelihood (Low/Med/High)	Proportional Response Options	Risk Tolerance Check	Preferred Action
"What if protesters gather outside the hotel?"	Guest safety & brand reputation	Injury, negative media, cancellations	Medium	Visible security at entrances, liaison with local police, communication plan	Medium	Preparedness plan, not blanket guard deployment
"What if hackers attack our website?"	Customer trust & compliance	Loss of customer data, fines, reputational harm	High	MFA, monitoring, incident response	Low	Invest in layered defenses

How to Use It

1. Write down the fear-based question or demand you've heard.
2. Identify the **asset** that's truly at stake.
3. Translate it into the **business impact** if disrupted.
4. Estimate **likelihood** (qualitative at this stage).
5. Outline **response options**—both visible and proportional.
6. Compare to the organization's **risk tolerance**.
7. Decide on the **preferred action** that is proportionate, risk-driven, and defensible.

Notes

1 International Organization for Standardization, *ISO 31000:2018 – Risk Management – Guidelines* (Geneva: ISO, 2018), Section 6.5.

2 National Retail Federation, *2023 National Retail Security Survey* (Washington, DC: National Retail Federation, 2023), https://nrf.com/research/national-retail-security-survey-2023

3 ASIS International, *General Security Risk Assessment (GSRA) Guideline* (Alexandria, VA: ASIS International, 2019); National Institute of Standards and Technology, *Guide for Conducting Risk Assessments*, NIST Special Publication 800–30 Revision 1 (Gaithersburg, MD: NIST, 2012); International Organization for Standardization, *ISO 31010:2019 – Risk Management – Risk Assessment Techniques* (Geneva: ISO, 2019).

4 Stephen Quinn et al., *Enterprise Impact of Information and Communications Technology Risk: Governing and Managing ICT Risk Programs Within an Enterprise Risk Portfolio*, NIST Special Publication 800–221 (Gaithersburg, MD: National Institute of Standards and Technology, November 2023), https://doi.org/10.6028/NIST.SP.800-221

5 U.S. Nuclear Regulatory Commission, "ALARA – As Low As Reasonably Achievable," NRC Glossary, Last reviewed/updated March 9, 2020, https://www.nrc.gov/reading-rm/basic-ref/glossary/alara.html

SECTION 1

CLOSE AND TRANSITION

In Section 1, we establish the foundations of ESRM.

Chapter 1 introduced the ESRM approach as a practical, business-focused alternative to tactical, fear-based security, showing how alignment with organizational priorities produces stronger outcomes.

Chapter 2 explained how security leaders must balance likelihood, impact, and vulnerability to assess real risks, confronting the trade-offs that shape every decision.

Together, these chapters demonstrate that effective security begins not with activity, but with clarity on what matters most.

Section 2 builds directly on this foundation, moving deeper into how organizations define and assess risk. We look at what assets truly matter, what threats endanger them, and how security leaders can use that knowledge to shape more sustainable strategies.

Field Lesson: When Opportunity Overshadows Risk

The Situation

At a global consulting firm's corporate headquarters, a contract cleaner was discovered wandering into a restricted IT server room after hours. The individual had trailed an employee through an elevator bank and gained access with a generic janitorial badge—one that was never intended to function beyond 6 p.m.

DOI: 10.4324/9781003711346-5

No data was compromised, but the incident rattled senior leadership. The CEO pictured potential investors asking why critical systems weren't better controlled. The COO imagined the reputational fallout of headlines about unsecured infrastructure. Within hours, a leadership meeting was convened.

In that meeting, the CSO was asked the golden question: "What do you need to secure us?"

Not wanting to squander the moment, the CSO offered a long-standing list of projects he'd requested over the last two years:

- New card readers on every restricted floor
- Biometric locks on all server rooms
- Expanded evening security staff coverage

The proposal carried a mid-six-figure price tag, and to the executives, who were still shaken by the incident, it sounded like a decisive plan to fix the problem. They approved the budget, and within a few months, the upgrades were in place.

The Missed Risk

The problem was that the investment targeted *symptoms, not causes.*

Several months later, during an audit, the analyst team uncovered the actual vulnerability: an outdated contractor access policy. For ease of use, facilities had been reusing janitorial badges across multiple contractors without thorough review, and no one had looked at the ruleset for off-hours access in more than three years. The badges worked because no one had ever declared them expired, disabled them, or changed them out.

Security's "fix" was visible, reassuring, and expensive. However, the underlying issue, a neglected policy and unmonitored badge provision process, remained unresolved until after the money had been spent.

This kind of overreaction is common in solution-based security. Leaders equate large, visible investments with safety. Security teams, eager for executive buy-in, sometimes seize the moment to fund long-desired projects. The result may be new hardware, more people, or stronger locks, but not necessarily an absolute reduction in risk.

What ESRM Would Have Changed

An ESRM approach would have reframed the discussion entirely:

1. **What am I trying to protect?**
   The business mission depends on the continuity and security of its IT infrastructure, not on the presence of guards or security technology.
2. **What does it truly need protection from?**
   The incident (eventually) revealed risks not of deliberate intrusion, but of unmanaged vendor processes, outdated access rules, and a lack of accountability.
3. **How can we most effectively and efficiently protect it?**
   By updating contractor access policies, conducting a credential audit, assigning ownership for oversight, and reinforcing with modest technology adjustments, at a fraction of the six-figure spend.

A targeted ESRM response would have provided both better security and better alignment with business priorities. The resources freed from unnecessary upgrades could have been reinvested in higher-value initiatives, such as enhanced monitoring of critical business systems or insider threat prevention.

The Lesson: Don't Let the Opportunity Define the Defense

When executives finally engage, security leaders may feel pressure to deliver sweeping fixes. But seizing that moment without applying ESRM discipline often results in money spent on visibility rather than impact. The firm ended up with stronger doors, but the same open back gate.

The real lesson for Section 1 is this: fear-based or solutions-driven decisions produce fast activity, but risk-based management produces lasting value. ESRM ensures that when opportunity knocks, security leaders use it to align protection with business priorities, not just to buy more locks.

SECTION 2

TURNING STRATEGY INTO ACTION—THE THREE ESSENTIAL QUESTIONS

With the risk-based mindset shift in place, it's time to put Enterprise Security Risk Management (ESRM) to work.

Section 2 introduces the heart of the ESRM methodology through three deceptively simple, yet highly impactful, questions: *What am I trying to protect? What does it truly need protection from? How can we most effectively and efficiently protect it?* These questions offer a structured and repeatable approach to aligning security decisions with business value.

In Chapters 3 through 5, we break down how to identify critical assets, assess real-world threats and vulnerabilities, and apply the right mix of people, processes, and technology to mitigate risk. The goal is not just to protect our organizations, but to do so with purpose, precision, and partnership.

Here's how the next three chapters bring the ESRM model to life:

- **Chapter 3: What Am I Trying to Protect?—Understanding Critical Assets and Their Impact**

  Helps identify and prioritize both tangible and intangible assets based on their importance to business continuity, revenue, compliance, and reputation.

DOI: 10.4324/9781003711346-6

- **Chapter 4: What Does It Truly Need to Be Protected From?—Understanding Threat to Evaluate Risk**
  Equips security leaders to evaluate a wide range of threat types, analyze likelihood versus perception, and assess vulnerability using real-world data and organizational context.
- **Chapter 5: How Can We Most Effectively and Efficiently Protect It?—Choosing the Best Mitigations for Your Risk Profile**
  Introduces the Effects-Based Security model, which aligns security controls with threat behavior, enabling layered, efficient, and outcome-focused mitigation strategies.

CHAPTER 3

What Am I Trying to Protect?—Understanding Critical Assets and Their Impact

Modern security is about more than just keeping bad things from happening to the enterprise. Security today is fundamentally about protecting what truly matters to the organization, the things the organization needs to fulfill its mission. In the real world, when managing the risk tradeoffs of cost vs. impact we discussed in Chapter 2, every security decision, whether it is where to post an officer, how much video coverage to place, how to design access control, or how much to invest in a new technology, must begin with a clear understanding of the assets that are most critical to the business. Without that foundation, even the best-intentioned efforts can end up misaligned and inefficient, or at worst, completely ineffective.

This first question is deceptively simple. It is easy to point to a building, a fleet of trucks, or a server room and declare them "assets." Some assets are visible and tangible, including facilities, equipment, personnel, and technology. Others are less obvious but equally vital: brand reputation, intellectual property, customer trust, and compliance standing. Still others sit in the middle ground, where tangible and intangible intersect. For example, data centers that house both physical infrastructure and the sensitive information that flows through them. But the real question is not about what property an organization owns; it is about what the organization *cannot afford to lose.*

DOI: 10.4324/9781003711346-7

A risk-based approach, such as Enterprise Security Risk Management (ESRM), emphasizes this question: *What am I trying to protect?* Because it is the starting point for everything else. If the wrong assets are prioritized, then the subsequent steps of identifying threats to them, assessing vulnerabilities, and designing mitigation measures will all be skewed. Conversely, when an organization has a clear picture of its undisputedly critical assets, security decisions can be aligned with business priorities, resources can be directed toward the most critical problems, and leaders can have confidence that security is enabling resilience rather than reacting to the latest incident.

In this chapter, we will explore how to identify, classify, and prioritize critical assets in practice. We will look at the distinction between tangible and intangible assets, explore how different industries define their "crown jewels," and introduce frameworks that help assess which assets truly drive business value. We will also discuss common mistakes organizations make in asset identification, highlight dependencies and ecosystem risks that are often overlooked, and provide practical tools to facilitate conversations with stakeholders.

Identifying Assets: Tangible and Intangible

When most people think about "assets," they picture physical things. The property that can be touched, seen, weighed, and measured. In fact, much of the history of corporate security has been rooted in this perspective. Early security programs were designed to safeguard factories from theft, protect office buildings from vandalism, and secure warehouses full of goods awaiting distribution. These were the assets that executives could walk through and accountants could assign a dollar value to, so they naturally became the focal point of protection efforts.

This emphasis on the tangible made sense in an era when a company's value was closely tied to its physical footprint. The risk of a factory fire, a stolen shipment, or a break-in at headquarters represented direct, visible losses. Security measures like locks, guards, fences, and cameras provided equally visible reassurance that those risks were under control. Tangible assets were easier to inventory, easier to quantify in financial statements, and easier to justify protecting in a budget discussion.

Yet the modern business environment tells a different story. Today, the majority of a company's market value is not stored in its warehouses or office towers. More value now lies in intangible assets, including the trust of its customers, the strength of its brand, the proprietary knowledge of its employees, and the intellectual property that fuels innovation. Data from the S&P 500 shows that in 1975, physical assets accounted for more than 80% of corporate value; by 2020, intangible assets made up nearly 90%.[1] This shift has profound implications for security.

A cyberattack that leaks customer data, a scandal that erodes public trust, or the sudden loss of a key research team can be more devastating to an organization's survival than the theft of physical goods. Consider the difference between losing a truckload of merchandise and suffering a reputational collapse after a massive data breach. The truck can be replaced, insurance can cover the loss, and operations can move forward. Reputation, trust, and intellectual property, once compromised, may take years to rebuild, if they can be rebuilt at all.

The challenge for security professionals is that intangible assets are trickier to define, measure, and visibly protect. They don't sit behind a locked door or show up in a warehouse log. Their value is realized in customer loyalty, regulatory compliance, operational continuity, and investor confidence. This makes them easy to overlook when organizations compile their "critical assets" list, but the cost of that oversight can be staggering.

That is why when we take the first step in a risk-based security program, it is not to "make a list of stuff to protect," but to take a holistic view of the enterprise. The data center is essential, but so is the data inside it. The headquarters building matters, but so does the corporate reputation that it represents to the outside world. The fleet of delivery trucks enables revenue, but so does the trust that customers place in the company to deliver their products safely and on time. In reality, tangible and intangible assets are tightly linked. Harm to one often causes or amplifies harm to the other. Protecting them in isolation leaves gaps that adversaries can exploit.

By helping business leaders expand their view of the assets the security function protects beyond the purely physical, security professionals can shift the conversation from guarding property to safeguarding value. This mindset shift opens the door to a more mature discussion of risk and a different perspective on the security leader.

Tangible Assets: The Physical and Technological Backbone of the Business

Tangible assets form the visible foundation of an organization's operations. They are the physical components, whether owned, leased, or shared across business locations, that enable day-to-day activities and the organization's critical mission. Because they can be counted and depreciated on a balance sheet, these assets are often the first to come to mind when executives think about security's role in protection. They are also the most straightforward to inventory, assess for vulnerabilities, and protect through traditional physical security measures. Yet their true value is often tied to less obvious factors, such as the people who use them or the data they contain.

People

While some hesitate to call people "assets," employees, executives, contractors, and even customers are often the foundation on which every part of the operation depends. Their safety and well-being underpin continuity, morale, and trust. A workplace violence incident, industrial accident, or failure to protect executives during travel can halt production and damage reputation far faster than the loss of a piece of equipment. Beyond safety, people also carry institutional knowledge and judgment that cannot be replaced overnight. For example, a manufacturing plant may have redundant machines, but the specialized operators who run them are not easily substituted. Protecting people requires ensuring physical security, addressing insider threats, handling executive protection, developing evacuation plans, and maintaining health and safety compliance.

Buildings and Infrastructure

Facilities such as office towers, manufacturing plants, warehouses, and retail stores are where the core business activities take place. They house other tangible assets like staff, critical equipment, and inventory, making them central to both productivity and identity. A well-secured headquarters can reassure investors and customers, while a poorly protected facility invites theft, vandalism, and disruption. Facilities are also symbolic assets. Headquarters often represent the brand itself, meaning damage or an incident there can carry both reputational weight and operational impact.

IT Servers, Data Centers, and Networks

Although digital in function, servers and data centers are still tangible infrastructure, occupying physical space and requiring physical protection. These systems form the backbone of modern business by storing and transmitting proprietary information, financial records, and customer data. They are vulnerable not only to cyberattacks but also to physical risks such as fire, flood, or power failure. A single server room outage can paralyze operations for days, or a data center breach may result in fines, lawsuits, and other consequences. For this reason, organizations are increasingly combining physical and cyber measures, such as access control, CCTV, redundant power supplies, and strict visitor policies, alongside firewalls and encryption.

Vehicles, Delivery Fleets, and Supply Chain Hubs

For organizations that rely on the movement of goods or people, vehicles and logistics facilities are lifelines. Delivery trucks, cargo fleets, and warehouse distribution centers ensure that products reach customers on time, allowing revenue to continue flowing. Yet these assets are highly exposed: fleets can be hijacked, stolen, or disrupted by accidents; warehouses can become targets for theft or sabotage. Real-world examples include theft of pharmaceuticals from distribution trucks or organized crime rings targeting high-value cargo at port facilities. The security of these assets, therefore, extends beyond theft prevention to continuity planning, which involves ensuring alternate routes, redundant suppliers, and contingency storage.

Manufacturing Equipment and Proprietary Machinery

Specialized production tools and machinery represent both enormous capital investment and a source of competitive advantage. A single piece of custom-built equipment may enable production that no competitor can replicate. As a result, sabotage, theft, or even extended maintenance downtime can lead to millions of dollars in lost revenue. For example, an automobile manufacturer whose robotic welding systems fail will see its production line grind to a halt, delaying product launches and jeopardizing contracts. Protecting such assets requires a blend of physical access controls, insider risk monitoring, and rigorous maintenance protocols.

Raw Materials and Finished Goods

The physical inventory of a business, what it makes, stores, and distributes, is often the most visible target for crime. Raw materials may be stolen or diverted for black-market resale, while finished goods face risks of theft, counterfeiting, spoilage, or damage in transit. Retailers and consumer goods companies are well aware of these risks: shrinkage from theft erodes margins, and counterfeit products undermine brand integrity. For industries such as pharmaceuticals or food, contamination or spoilage adds another layer of risk, with regulatory and reputational consequences that far exceed financial loss.

These categories are summarized in Table 3.1, which provides examples of tangible assets and highlights why they matter most to organizational security.

Pro Tip: Ask your leadership what event, loss, or outage would cause them to call an emergency meeting. The answers usually reveal your most critical assets.

TABLE 3.1 Categories of Tangible Assets

Category	Examples	Why It Matters
People	Employees, executives, contractors, customers	Safety and well-being are essential for all operations; loss of talent or injury disrupts continuity.
Buildings	Offices, warehouses, plants, retail stores	Central hubs for operations are vulnerable to crime, disasters, and reputational damage.
IT Infrastructure	Servers, data centers, networks	Backbone of modern operations; vulnerable to both physical and cyber risks.
Logistics	Delivery fleets, distribution hubs	Enable revenue flow; vulnerable to theft, hijacking, and supply chain disruption.
Machinery	Proprietary equipment, production tools	High capital value; downtime directly halts production and revenue.
Inventory	Raw materials, finished goods	Direct revenue value; exposed to theft, counterfeiting, spoilage, or damage.

Tangible assets are usually the easiest to conceptualize and, as a result, often dominate security discussions. But additional significance lies in how they connect and interact with intangible assets. A server's value lies not in the hardware but in the intellectual property and customer trust embedded in its data. A facility is more than walls—it is the workplace that sustains people and processes. By framing tangible assets in this broader context, security professionals can better demonstrate why physical protections must be integrated with strategies for safeguarding data, brand, and continuity, and paired with the intangible assets that are tied to them.

Intangible Assets: The Hidden Value Driving the Business

Intangible assets may not have a physical form, but they are just as necessary for a company's success. These assets carry value because they are unique to the business, generate trust with stakeholders, or ensure compliance with legal obligations. The challenge is that a single scandal, breach, or disruption can erase years of careful investment in these areas.[2]

Unlike property or machinery, intangible assets are challenging to inventory and protect, yet their loss often has a greater impact than the destruction of any building or fleet. Modern organizations are frequently worth more for what they know, represent, and the trust they hold than for what they physically own. A single breach, scandal, or vendor failure can erode reputation or intellectual property in ways that no rebuild can recover. Protecting intangible value requires not only security controls but also effective governance, a strong culture, and foresight.

Intellectual Property (Patents, Trade Secrets, Proprietary Research)

Innovation is at the heart of competitive advantage, and intellectual property is what keeps that advantage secure. Whether it is a key business strategy, a patented medical formula, a software algorithm, or a trade secret process, IP underpins future revenue streams. If compromised through espionage, insider theft, or careless handling, it can weaken a market position overnight and force costly legal battles to regain control.

Customer Trust and Brand Reputation

A company's reputation takes years to build but can collapse in an instant. When customer data is leaked, products fail, or an organization is caught engaging in unethical practices, the resulting loss of confidence can be devastating. For many businesses, reputation is more valuable than any single asset, because it directly influences consumer loyalty, investor confidence, and long-term market share.[3]

Regulatory Compliance and Legal Standing

Every industry operates under a framework of regulations that dictate how sensitive data is managed, how products are made, and how services are delivered. Assets tied to compliance, such as protected health information under HIPAA (Health Insurance Portability and Accountability Act) or financial records under SOX (Sarbanes-Oxley Act), carry both business value and legal risk. Losing control of these assets can result in penalties, lawsuits, and loss of the license to operate.

Business Relationships and Vendor Agreements

Partnerships, contracts, and supplier arrangements may not appear on a balance sheet as assets, but they define an organization's ability to function smoothly. If a key vendor fails due to a security breach, financial collapse, or political disruption, the ripple effects can disrupt production lines, delay deliveries, and harm customer relationships.

Corporate Data and Business Intelligence

Proprietary insights, from customer analytics to pricing models, form the backbone of strategic planning. When these assets are leaked or stolen, competitors can gain an unfair advantage, sometimes years ahead of schedule. Protecting this category requires not only cybersecurity controls but also strict governance around who can access, share, or copy sensitive internal information.

Workforce Knowledge and Expertise

Beyond the workforce as individuals, organizations depend on the skills, judgment, and institutional memory that employees possess. This knowledge can't be easily codified or replaced. When experienced staff depart suddenly or when insider threats exploit privileged access, the loss can leave organizations exposed in ways that no insurance policy can cover.

These categories are summarized in Table 3.2, which illustrates examples of intangible assets and why they represent some of the most difficult yet critical elements to protect.

TABLE 3.2 Categories of Intangible Assets

Category	Examples	Why It Matters
Intellectual property	Patents, trade secrets, proprietary research	Foundation of innovation and competitive advantage; loss undermines market position.
Customer trust & brand reputation	Loyalty, public perception, investor confidence	Built over years, but can collapse overnight; loss directly impacts revenue and growth.
Regulatory compliance & legal standing	GDPR (General Data Protection Regulation), HIPAA, SOX, licensing, industry standards	Ensures a license to operate; violations result in fines, lawsuits, and reputational harm.
Business relationships & vendor agreements	Supplier contracts, strategic alliances	Enable continuity of supply chains and services; disruption cascades through operations.
Corporate data & business intelligence	Market research, pricing strategies, product roadmaps	Informs decision-making and strategy; leaks give competitors an edge.
Workforce knowledge & expertise	Institutional memory, specialized skills, workflows	Difficult or impossible to replace quickly; the departure of key staff can halt operations.

INSIGHT: THE INTERSECTION OF TANGIBLE AND INTANGIBLE ASSETS

Tangible and intangible assets rarely exist in isolation from one another. One reinforces the other, and leaving either underprotected creates vulnerabilities that can undermine the whole enterprise. Let's look at an example:

A pharmaceutical company may spend millions securing its research facilities with cameras, guards, and access controls. Yet the real value driver often lies in the intangible: the proprietary drug formulas and clinical trial data inside. If competitors or criminals gain access, years of research and billions in potential revenue could be lost. In this case, physical security of the lab is important. Still, without equally strong protections for data and intellectual property, such as insider threat monitoring, cybersecurity controls, and restricted access, the investment falls short of its potential.

This example shows that protecting facilities without equal attention to intellectual property and data leaves the enterprise exposed.

Assets across Industries

Every organization depends on a mix of tangible and intangible assets. The balance shifts by sector, but even so, both categories matter and need to be documented as part of the ESRM process. Table 3.3 provides examples of various critical assets across different industries.

Executives often view their organizations as unique, but examining industries across the board reveals that critical assets follow similar patterns. Hospitals, retailers, manufacturers, and utilities may operate differently, yet all rely on a combination of physical infrastructure and intangible assets, including trust, reputation, and intellectual property. By framing discussions

TABLE 3.3 Examples of Tangible and Intangible Assets Across Industries

Industry	Tangible Assets	Intangible Assets & Why They Matter
Healthcare	Facilities, medical devices, patient records	Patient trust and regulatory compliance: ransomware can halt care and erode confidence.
Utilities	Distribution networks, plants, control centers	Reliability and public trust: outages damage confidence in essential services.
Retail	Stores, warehouses, POS systems, delivery fleets	Brand reputation and customer data: breaches cost more in loyalty than theft.
Finance	Data centers, trading floors, ATMs	Compliance and credibility: reputational missteps cascade into systemic risks.
Manufacturing	Plants, proprietary machinery, supply hubs	Intellectual property: stolen designs can erase years of R&D overnight.
Higher education	Campuses, labs, housing facilities	Research integrity and student trust: scandals undermine enrollment and funding.
Houses of worship	Worship spaces, congregational facilities, artifacts	Community trust and freedom of practice: incidents resonate far beyond the walls.
Cultural properties	Museums, archives, historic landmarks	Heritage value and identity: theft or damage erodes national and community identity.
Hospitality	Hotels, event venues, guest facilities	Guest trust and comfort: incidents ripple across bookings worldwide.

through cross-industry comparisons, security leaders can swing conversations from generic best practices toward tailored priorities. This approach builds credibility and also highlights overlooked vulnerabilities, particularly intangible ones that leadership may undervalue.

Determining Asset Criticality

As we discussed in Chapter 2, not all assets carry the same weight in supporting the business, and not all require the same degree of protection. The goal of taking a risk-based approach to security is not to protect everything equally but to protect what matters most, in proportion to its criticality and vulnerability.[4] That requires moving from an inventory of "what we have" to a sharper lens on "what we can't fulfill our mission without."

Understanding criticality is not only about ranking assets, but also about aligning protection with consequences. A piece of equipment may be expensive, but if its loss causes only a minor delay, it is less critical than a modest database that underpins compliance with government regulations.

For example, a CEO's lost laptop may generate urgency because of its visibility. Still, payroll servers that fail just before annual bonus time could trigger far greater consequences: missed paychecks, loss of employee trust, or potential lawsuits. Criticality comes from impact, not perception.

Assessing Asset Criticality

A practical approach to prioritizing assets starts with a few key factors that help ensure security resources are directed where they will have the most significant impact. When meeting with asset owners, frame the discussion around these questions so they can evaluate criticality in business terms rather than abstract technical language.

1. **Business Impact**

   How essential is this asset to the organization's revenue, operations, or strategic objectives? If compromised, would it disrupt business continuity, result in financial losses, or impact customer service?

   - *High criticality example*: An e-commerce company's payment processing system is mission-critical because its failure immediately halts transactions and revenue.

- *Low criticality example*: A break room coffee machine is stolen. Annoying, but no disruption to core business operations.

Within this category, consider both operational value (would work activity cease without it?) and regulatory value (would its loss result in compliance violations?). For instance, losing a patient records system in a hospital disrupts care and creates HIPAA exposure, making it doubly critical.

2. **Monetary Value**

   Can the asset be assigned a clear dollar value? Some assets, such as financial reserves or high-value goods, have an obvious monetary worth. Others, like intellectual property, may have an indirect but outsized financial impact.

   - *High criticality example*: A biotech firm's proprietary drug formula, potentially worth billions in future revenue, is one of the company's most valuable assets.
   - *Low criticality example*: Art used to provide a pleasant office atmosphere, while technically an asset, has a negligible financial impact on the organization.

3. **Replacement Difficulty**

   If the asset is lost or compromised, how hard is it to restore? What time and resources are needed to recover function in part or in full?

   - *High criticality example*: A sole-source supplier for a patented manufacturing component. If disrupted, operations could halt for months, no matter if it is an expensive item or not.
   - *Lower criticality example*: Commodity items like printer paper, which can be replaced with minimal delay or cost.

   A structured framework is helpful, but sometimes stakeholders respond best when the conversation feels concrete and guided. To move from theory into practice, you can use a simple checklist that translates the criticality factors into direct questions. Table 3.4 shows a framework that keeps discussions focused on what matters most and helps stakeholders articulate risks in their own business language.

The checklist provides stakeholders with a structured way to surface what truly matters. Turning those questions into conversations can uncover hidden dependencies and business priorities. By walking through scenarios and pressing for specifics, security

TABLE 3.4 The Critical Asset Checklist

Dimension	Questions to Ask Stakeholders
Operational dependence	What assets must function every day for your team to meet its goals? Which processes stop immediately if this asset is unavailable?
Regulatory & legal requirements	Are there assets tied to compliance obligations or legal exposure? Would regulators, auditors, or courts take issue if this asset were compromised?
Financial impact	What is the dollar value of this asset, or of the revenue it enables? How long can we operate without it before losses become significant?
Reputation & trust	Which assets, if harmed, would cause customers, investors, or the public to lose confidence? What incident would make headlines that would damage our brand?
Recovery & replacement	How difficult or time-consuming would it be to restore or replace this asset? Do we have backups, substitutes, or contingency plans in place?

leaders can translate abstract risks into concrete impacts that resonate with executives. The following example illustrates how this dialogue unfolds in practice.

Example: Turning the Checklist into Dialogue

Security Leader: Let's talk about what would cause the most disruption if it failed. What's the one thing your team absolutely cannot function without?

Business Executive: Our customer ordering portal. If that goes down, orders stop immediately.

Security Leader: Understood. Beyond revenue, what else would be affected if it were unavailable?

Business Executive: Customer trust. Our competitors would capitalize on the downtime, and regulators might question whether we have proper continuity plans.

Security Leader: So, we're not just protecting a website… we're protecting customer trust and regulatory standing. That tells me it belongs on the critical asset list.

By structuring conversations this way, security leaders move beyond abstract debates about "what's important" and instead guide stakeholders through practical lenses: operations, compliance, finances, trust, and recovery. The result is a clearer, business-aligned inventory of critical assets. It sets the stage to prioritize and assign levels of criticality to the assets identified.

Prioritizing Asset Criticality

Assigning criticality is not something the security team can do alone. The people who own and operate assets every day must be part of the discussion, since they best understand how failure would affect the business. The security leader's role is to bring structure to the conversation, translating business impact into clear levels of priority that guide protection strategies.

A practical way to do this is through a three-step process:

1. Present the criteria—Share the factors of business impact, monetary value, and replacement difficulty so stakeholders know how the scoring works.
2. Facilitate dialogue—Walk through each asset with its owner, pressing for concrete impacts ("If this system went offline, what would happen in the first hour? The first day?").
3. Agree on a level—Document whether the asset is High, Medium, or Low criticality, with the owner's input, so prioritization becomes a joint decision rather than a security decree. Examples of criticality level descriptions are seen in Table 3.5.

TABLE 3.5 Example Assets and Criticality Levels

Criticality Level	Description	Example Assets
High	Essential to continuity, revenue, compliance, or trust; loss causes severe disruption or damage.	Payment processing system, patient records database, and executive leadership safety.
Medium	Significant to operations, but loss does not cause immediate collapse; moderate disruption.	Regional office building, secondary supplier contracts, departmental file shares
Low	Valuable but minimal direct impact; loss is inconvenient but not catastrophic.	Break room equipment, surplus inventory, general office supplies

Pro Tip: Ask stakeholders to identify their top three "can't-lose" assets. Ranking forces trade-off decisions and creates a shared understanding of what truly matters most.

Case Study: Misjudging the Most Critical Asset

A national retail company took pride in the security of its distribution network. Warehouses and shipping hubs were surrounded by fencing, armed guards, access controls, and extensive camera coverage. Security budgets flowed to these sites because leadership saw them as the direct link between shelves and customers, the revenue engine of the business.

By contrast, the company's administrative headquarters, a modest multi-story office building downtown, received minimal investment. Visitors could walk into the lobby with little screening; there were no off-hours security officers on site, and sensitive records were stored in office areas with no specialized, role-based access control. The rationale was simple: if operations were running smoothly, the business was secure. Headquarters, in their view, was "just office space."

That assumption collapsed when a disgruntled employee entered the building after business hours undetected and set fire to the records storage area. While no one was injured, the damage was severe: payroll records, vendor contracts, and regulatory compliance files were destroyed. The result was weeks of chaos, delayed vendor payments, missed reporting deadlines, strained supplier relationships, and a regulatory investigation that led to substantial fines.

Despite significant budget spent on securing warehouses, additional critical assets (financial operations, compliance documentation, and institutional knowledge) had been left vulnerable. Protecting the visible supply chain while neglecting the administrative heart of the business brought the company to the brink of collapse.

Lessons Learned

- Criticality is contextual. Warehouses were vital, but the office housed equally irreplaceable processes and data.

- Symbolism can skew priorities. Leadership assumed that the most "important-looking" assets were the most valuable.
- People and processes matter. HR, finance, and compliance may not generate revenue directly, but their loss can grind operations to a halt.
- Balanced investment is essential. Security strategies must look beyond the obvious to safeguard less visible, but equally mission-critical, assets.

This case study also applies in reverse. In some organizations, leadership allocates significant budgets to securing headquarters facilities with guards, visitor management, and layered access controls, while often treating regional or field offices as afterthoughts, sometimes providing little more than a key in the door and a camera at reception. Yet those locations may house customer data, operational processes, or regional leadership teams that are every bit as critical to continuity. Whether the imbalance skews toward field sites or headquarters, the risk remains the same: misalignment between perceived importance and actual business impact leaves essential assets exposed.

Dependencies and Ecosystem Assets

No asset exists in isolation. Even the most carefully protected manufacturing line, warehouse, data center, or executive office depends on a web of supporting systems and external partners. These dependencies often remain invisible until they fail, yet they can be the weak points that bring down critical operations. Recognizing that assets are embedded in ecosystems is essential for accurate security planning.

Consider the example of a small manufacturer. Its plant may be well-secured with access controls, cameras, and perimeter fencing; yet, a significant exposure lies in its reliance on a single overseas supplier for key components. A labor strike, port closure, or cyberattack on that vendor could halt production more effectively than any intruder breaching the factory fence.

Dependencies also extend beyond suppliers and technology. Logistics partners, such as trucking fleets or port operators, can become chokepoints when fuel shortages or natural disasters strike. Critical infrastructure, such as power, telecom, and water, can fail without warning, instantly taking facilities and networks

INSIGHT: HIDDEN DEPENDENCIES ARE OFTEN THE MOST DANGEROUS

The most critical exposures often lie in what is invisible—the dependencies of operational activities, such as outsourced IT providers, small vendors, or global logistics networks. Mapping these dependencies with business stakeholders helps reveal where resilience investments are genuinely needed.

offline. Even internal processes like payroll, compliance reporting, or vendor management can create vulnerabilities if they are poorly designed, under-resourced, or reliant on a single key individual.

Dependencies remind us that assets rarely fail in isolation. A factory floor, a payroll system, or a corporate reputation can all be compromised by a host of direct threats, as well as by failures in the broader ecosystem that supports them. Recognizing these interconnections is critical. However, equally important is recognizing where organizations routinely misjudge what truly matters. Too often, security efforts are skewed by assumptions, visibility, or convenience, leaving critical blind spots.

Common Mistakes in Identifying Critical Assets

Even experienced organizations can stumble when it comes to defining what truly matters. The problem doesn't typically occur due to a lack of effort. However, when discussing the things we see around us day in and day out, assumptions and habits can skew our priorities. Sometimes security plans are developed in isolation, without the ability to get meaningful input from executives or operations leaders, leaving blind spots in what the business actually relies on. In other cases, security teams focus too narrowly on physical assets, such as buildings and equipment, overlooking digital, reputational, or compliance assets that carry equal or greater risk.

A different mistake comes from trying to treat everything the same, applying uniform controls across the board. This wastes resources on low-value items while leaving critical assets underprotected. Finally, many organizations neglect dependencies. A factory or data center may appear secure. However, the real exposure may lie with a single fragile vendor, a cloud provider, or even an internal process that everything else depends on.

Key Takeaways from Chapter 3

- Not all assets are physical: Tangible assets like buildings and fleets are visible, but intangible ones—reputation, intellectual property, customer trust—often hold greater long-term value.
- Asset value is contextual: Criticality comes from role, impact, and recovery difficulty, not just price tags. A modest system can sometimes be more vital than a high-cost piece of equipment.
- Tangible and intangible assets are interdependent: Losing one often amplifies risk to the other. Protecting only the physical "container" without safeguarding the value inside leaves dangerous gaps.
- Criticality is a business decision: Security leaders provide frameworks and context, but executives and asset owners ultimately define what the enterprise cannot afford to lose.
- Prioritization drives proportional investment: Over-securing minor assets drains credibility and resources, while under-securing core ones creates existential risk. Security must scale with business impact.

Security Leader Toolkit: Chapter 3

ESRM Implementation Checklist

- Have I defined what my organization considers an **asset** (both tangible and intangible)?
- Have I started a list of assets beyond just physical property (e.g., intellectual property, customer trust, compliance)?
- Have I discussed asset criticality with business stakeholders, not just security staff?
- Have I considered how assets interconnect (e.g., a server room that supports both IT and customer data)?
- Have I identified the top five to ten critical assets my program must protect?

Critical Asset Inventory Worksheet (Template)

Use this template to document and prioritize your organization's most important assets.

Asset Name	Tangible or Intangible	Business Value (High/Med/ Low or $ Estimate)	Replacement Difficulty (Easy/ Moderate/ Hard)	Interdepen- dencies (What Relies on It?)	Owner/ Custodian
Data Center	Tangible	High—supports operations across regions	Hard—months to rebuild	Customer data, operations, compliance reporting	CIO (Chief Information Officer)
Brand Reputation	Intangible	High—drives customer loyalty & investor confidence	Hard—years to rebuild	Marketing, sales, customer trust	CMO (Chief Marketing Officer)
Delivery Fleet	Tangible	Medium—revenue continuity	Moderate—can lease but with delays	Warehouses, customer service	COO (Chief Operating Officer)

How to Use It

1. List assets across both tangible (facilities, IT, fleets) and intangible (IP, trust, relationships).
2. Rate value based on contribution to revenue, compliance, continuity, or reputation.
3. Estimate replacement difficulty—can you replace it in days, months, or not at all?
4. Identify interdependencies—which other assets/functions rely on it?
5. Assign ownership—who in the business is accountable for its protection?

Notes

1 Shufang Pan, "Effects of the Growth of Intangible Capital Value on Firms," *American Journal of Industrial and Business Management* 12 (2022): 1552–1563, https://doi.org/10.4236/ajibm.2022.1210085

2 Larry Ponemon, et al. *2025 Cost of Insider Risks Global Report*. Ponemon Institute, February 2025. https://ponemon.dtexsystems.com/.

3 Edelman, *2025 Edelman Trust Barometer Special Report: Brand Trust, From We to Me*, June 2025. https://www.edelman.com/sites/g/files/aatuss191/files/2025–06/2025%20Edelman%20Trust%20Barometer%20Special%20Report%20Brand%20Trust%2C%20From%20We%20to%20Me%20%281%29.pdf
4 International Organization for Standardization, *ISO 31010:2019 – Risk Management – Risk Assessment Techniques* (Geneva: ISO, 2019).

Chapter 4

What Does It Truly Need to Be Protected From?—Understanding Threats to Evaluate Risk

Once we have identified and documented our critical assets to answer the first question, "What am I trying to protect?," the next step in both the formal risk triangle and our simplified three-question model is answering:

"What does it truly need to be protected from?"

The security environment is full of potential dangers, but organizations cannot spread resources across every imaginable possibility. The focus needs to be on those threats that could realistically lead to material harm to critical assets. By focusing on these areas, security leaders ensure that investments are tied to critical asset protection, business continuity, regulatory obligations, and the long-term resilience of the enterprise.

To move this conversation from theory to real-world practice, security professionals need to equip stakeholders with a clear framework for understanding the definition of threat.

This includes:

- The major categories of security threats to consider
- How threats map to assets in the risk picture
- How the intent and capability of a human actor, or the power of a natural hazard, define threat level
- How historical data and forward-looking intelligence combine to create a reliable view of the threat landscape

DOI: 10.4324/9781003711346-8

This chapter examines each of these elements and provides practical tools to help security leaders communicate the nature of threats in terms that resonate with executives and asset owners.

Categories of Security Threats

At the most basic level, a threat or hazard is any potential danger that could harm an asset. Threats may be external, such as crime, competition, or cyberattacks, or internal, such as insider fraud, process failures, or workplace violence. In most cases, they stem from a human "threat actor." Hazards are slightly different: they are systemic or natural events, such as weather disasters, pandemics, or economic upheavals, that can still disrupt critical operations and damage assets.

For the sake of ease and clarity in this book, we will use the term "threat" broadly to encompass both human-driven threats and environmental hazards. While security and risk standards[1] often define these categories differently, business leaders benefit most from a simplified model that captures the full spectrum without unnecessary complexity.

In practice, we can group threats into four broad categories that reflect both their source and their impact on organizational assets:

- Intentional Threats (Human-Caused, Malicious)
- Unintentional Threats (Human-Caused, Accidental)
- Environmental and Infrastructure Hazards (Natural or Systemic)
- Emerging and Future Threats

This simplified framework helps security leaders explain where risks come from, how they may evolve, and what steps the organization can take to prepare. It also sets the stage for mapping each threat category to specific assets, which brings the discussion directly into the context of business continuity, compliance, and resilience.

Intentional Threats (Human-Caused, Malicious)

Intentional threats come from individuals or groups who deliberately seek to cause harm. Their actions may be motivated by financial gain, ideology, personal grievances, or a desire for competitive advantage. Because their objectives are purposeful, these adversaries are often adaptive. Once a protective control is in place, it's not unlikely that determined actors will adjust their tactics, probing for gaps or shifting to softer targets.

Understanding intentional threats requires more than simply listing possible attack types. It means recognizing that behind every incident is a decision-maker weighing costs and benefits. A disgruntled insider, an organized crime ring, and an extremist group may approach targets in very different ways. Each, however, can inflict severe damage when its actions intersect with organizational vulnerabilities. I have seen cases where a single insider with modest access caused more disruption than an external group with far greater resources, simply because the opportunity was there.

Examples of Intentional Threats

- Violence Against People—Workplace violence, assault, robbery, kidnapping, or targeted threats against executives. In healthcare, for example, staff have faced increasing workplace assaults from frustrated patients and visitors, leading to both safety concerns and regulatory scrutiny.
- Theft of Property or Information—Physical theft of goods, diversion of shipments, or digital theft of sensitive data. Retailers might experience organized theft rings that strip shelves, while financial institutions confront account takeovers and credential theft.
- Property Violations—Vandalism, sabotage, or unauthorized facility access. A manufacturer may face sabotage from competitors or disgruntled employees seeking to halt production.
- Cyberattacks—Phishing, ransomware, malware, insider cyber threats, or attacks on physical infrastructure through connected control systems. Recent ransomware campaigns have shown how cyber incidents can paralyze hospitals, logistics companies, or entire municipal governments.[2]
- Disinformation Attacks—Fake news campaigns, misinformation-driven stock manipulation, or fraud through social engineering. A global consumer brand, for instance, could see its reputation damaged within hours if activists spread false claims about product safety.
- Terrorism and Extremism—Attacks by domestic or international extremist groups targeting critical infrastructure, executives, or public-facing facilities. Energy and transportation sectors remain high-profile targets.
- Fraud and Financial Crimes—Identity theft, insider trading, payment fraud, or money laundering schemes. Fraud

can erode public trust and invite regulatory action that far outweighs the immediate financial loss.

- Corporate Espionage—Theft of intellectual property, unauthorized surveillance, or competitor-driven intrusions. Technology firms and pharmaceutical companies often face these threats due to the immense value of their proprietary designs and formulas.

Intentional threats remain some of the most visible and concerning risks for organizations, but they are also the most dynamic. Recognizing the human drivers behind them helps security leaders anticipate how adversaries may shift and ensures that protective measures evolve in step with those changes.

Pro Tip: When explaining intentional threats, focus on the *actor*, not just the *method*. Executives connect more with the motives and goals of adversaries than with a technical list of tactics.

Unintentional Threats (Human-Caused, Accidental)

Not all security failures stem from malice. In many cases, incidents arise from human error, negligence, or systemic breakdowns. A careless employee with no intent to cause harm can expose sensitive data just as easily as a malicious hacker, and a single overlooked safeguard in an industrial process can lead to injuries, lawsuits, or costly downtime.

Unintentional threats are often underestimated because they lack a visible adversary. Yet across industries, they have proven just as damaging as deliberate attacks, such as in the story of a global firm that left misconfigured cloud storage environments open to all employees, exposing executive payroll data for days before anyone noticed or another case of a technician's failure to follow a safety step which triggered a chemical spill that shut down production and led to a regulatory investigation. These incidents were not acts of hostility, but their impact on business continuity and reputation was significant.

Most unintentional threats fall into three recurring patterns:

- Simple Human Errors—Mistakes are a leading cause of security incidents. Employees may send sensitive information to the wrong recipient, mishandle access credentials, or click on a phishing link. In the financial services industry, even a single misdirected email containing confidential data can prompt a regulatory investigation or reputational fallout.

- Systemic Process Failures—Weak enforcement of protocols, inadequate oversight, or reliance on unapproved tools often create hidden vulnerabilities. Employees uploading company materials to free cloud tools or downloading productivity apps without IT's knowledge may inadvertently create a backdoor for attackers. Shadow IT like this often bypasses formal controls and increases exposure.
- Miscommunication and Misunderstanding—Security procedures only work if employees are aware of and follow them. A misunderstanding of emergency protocols could lead to an evacuation when sheltering in place is safer, and failure to understand the criticality of anti-tailgating processes might open private areas to intruders. Training gaps, unclear policies, and ineffective communication all increase the likelihood of these failures.

Accidental damage also extends to physical infrastructure. In utilities, contractors have cut buried fiber lines, halting power delivery for days, while in transportation, equipment maintenance lapses have led to operational shutdowns and safety investigations.

These incidents remind us that the absence of intent does not reduce the severity of impact. Errors, oversights, and miscommunication can be just as costly as deliberate attacks, and they must be addressed with the same rigor in a risk assessment.

Environmental and Infrastructure Hazards (Natural or Systemically Caused)

Unlike intentional or unintentional threats caused by people, environmental and infrastructure hazards arise from forces largely outside the organization's control. These risks are often unpredictable and typically impossible to prevent. Severe weather, infrastructure failures, or geopolitical shifts can disrupt business operations, compromise supply chains, and pose risks to employees. While organizations cannot stop a hurricane or prevent a regional power outage, they can prepare for these hazards through resilience planning, redundancy, and infrastructure hardening.

Across the security industry, we see how these hazards can often be overlooked until they strike. A logistics company lost its central distribution hub to floodwaters because drainage upgrades had been deferred year after year; recovery took months and cost millions. A small rural health facility had invested well in cyber defenses but discovered during a regional blackout that its backup generators were insufficient for long-term operation, forcing patient transfers. In another case, a manufacturer faced repeated shipment delays due to political protests that shut down a critical port, highlighting the company's dependency on a single supply chain route. These scenarios were not the result of adversaries with intent, but the effect was just as disruptive as a deliberate attack.

Examples of Environmental and Infrastructure Threats

- Natural Disasters—Earthquakes, hurricanes, floods, wildfires, and tornadoes. In the retail sector, hurricanes have shuttered entire regional markets for weeks at a time.
- Hazardous Material Accidents—Chemical spills, gas leaks, or nuclear accidents affecting production facilities or surrounding communities. Industrial operators face both direct disruption and long-term regulatory consequences when these occur.
- Infrastructure Failures—Power grid outages, telecommunications breakdowns, or transportation network disruptions. For banks, even short network failures can halt transactions and undermine customer trust.
- Pandemics and Public Health Crises—Illness outbreaks that reduce workforce availability and interrupt business operations. COVID-19 highlighted how fast these disruptions cascade across industries, but even smaller outbreaks in food processing or healthcare can have severe localized impacts.
- Geopolitical Instability—Trade restrictions, mass migration, wars, sanctions, or sudden government changes that ripple across supply chains and business operations. Manufacturers dependent on cross-border suppliers often feel these shocks first.[3]

Environmental and infrastructure hazards remind us that not every threat is the result of malicious intent. Security and risk professionals add value when they help the business prepare for these broader disruptions, ensuring that critical assets can withstand forces far outside the organization's direct control.

Emerging & Future Threats

Some threats have not yet occurred, or have not occurred at scale, but they are on the horizon. These emerging risks require leaders to "think the unthinkable" and prepare for disruptions that may not yet be part of day-to-day operations. While not every forecasted hazard will materialize, ignoring the signals of change leaves organizations vulnerable to crises that can outpace their ability to respond.

The risks of tomorrow will likely emerge from three drivers of change: advances in technology, shifts in the natural environment, and instability in global systems.

- Technological Drivers

  Advances in quantum computing could eventually render traditional encryption methods obsolete, thereby compromising the confidentiality of financial transactions, government records, and intellectual property.[4] Autonomous drones and robotics, once limited to defense contractors, are becoming accessible to private actors who may deploy them maliciously. Cyber-physical attacks that once seemed theoretical are now disrupting utilities, logistics, and manufacturing by targeting industrial control systems.
- Environmental and Biological Drivers

  Synthetic biology, still largely an experimental field, carries both promise and risk. Unregulated use could lead to new forms of bioterrorism or contamination with wide-scale consequences. Climate change is also creating new patterns of disruption, from increasingly destructive storms to mass population displacement, which puts pressure on agriculture, manufacturing, and commercial real estate.
- Geopolitical and Economic Drivers

  Space-based infrastructure, such as satellites and GPS, is now essential to commerce, transportation, and defense—interference, whether accidental or intentional, could disrupt operations across multiple industries. Economic instability, including hyperinflation or sharp currency collapses, has historically been linked to spikes in fraud, theft, and social unrest, all of which impact business continuity and safety.

What matters for executives is not whether each of these threats will materialize, but that they represent the kinds of shocks the enterprise may face in the years ahead. The role of security leaders is to monitor signals, model plausible scenarios, and ensure programs are adaptable. The forward-facing approach of Enterprise Security Risk Management (ESRM) equips organizations to look beyond today's crises and invest in resilience for whatever comes next.

The Relationship between Threat Categories and Assets

While the list of potential threats like workplace violence, fraud, theft, or hacking may be universal across industries, the threats that will matter most to an organization depend on the type of assets it relies on the most. Different assets carry distinct vulnerabilities, and recognizing these distinctions enables security leaders to design targeted, business-relevant mitigation strategies.

Pro Tip: When threats feel overwhelming, tie them back to assets. Always ask, "Which critical asset would this actually impact—and how badly?" It keeps risk conversations grounded and actionable.

Mapping Threats to Assets

Not every asset is susceptible to every threat. A natural disaster could devastate infrastructure, but may have no direct effect on intellectual property. A disinformation campaign could damage a company's reputation and customer trust while leaving its physical facilities untouched.

This nuance is important because it enables security teams to prioritize where protections will have the greatest impact. By analyzing which threats are most relevant to each critical asset, security leaders can align controls with business risk and avoid wasted effort on low-impact scenarios.

Table 4.1 shows how different asset categories align with the threat types most likely to impact them:

TABLE 4.1 Mapping Assets to Threats

Asset Type	Most Impactful Threats
People	• Assault • Robbery • Workplace violence • Sexual assault • Stalking • Harassment • Targeted threats against executives • Kidnapping • Active shooter incidents • Insider threats • Public health crises (pandemics, bioterrorism)
Information	• Data breaches • Insider threats • Cyber espionage • Hacking • Malware • Intellectual property theft • Social engineering • Accidental data exposure • Unauthorized access • Third-party vendor data leaks • Regulatory non-compliance (GDPR, HIPAA, etc.)
Infrastructure	• Natural disasters (earthquakes, floods, hurricanes, wildfires) • Sabotage • Terrorism • Cyber-physical attacks on industrial control systems • Power outages • Telecommunications failures • Water supply contamination • Transportation network disruptions • Supply chain failures
Reputation & brand	• Disinformation campaigns • Regulatory violations • Major fraud incidents • Social media attacks • Activist targeting • Exposure of unethical business practices • Product recalls • Customer data mismanagement • Corporate scandal leaks • Media manipulation

INSIGHT: TABLE 4.1—MAPPING ASSETS TO THREATS

This table indicates that the same list of potential threats does not apply equally to all asset types. By making the connection explicit—people-to-workplace violence, infrastructure-to-natural hazards, brand-to-disinformation—leaders can see why security cannot treat all threats as interchangeable. It shifts conversations from "what threats worry us most" to "which threats could disrupt the assets our business depends on." That change in framing helps keep the discussion grounded in continuity, compliance, and resilience, rather than fear or headlines.

Threats across Industries

While the categories of threat are consistent, their relevance shifts depending on the industry. The risks that dominate one sector may barely register in another. For security leaders, recognizing these distinctions builds credibility with business stakeholders and keeps the conversation focused on what matters most to their organization.

In healthcare, ransomware and workplace violence rank high on the list because they directly impact patient safety and the delivery of care. In manufacturing, executives are more likely to emphasize sabotage, theft of intellectual property, and supply chain disruption that can bring production lines to a standstill. Financial institutions focus heavily on cyberattacks, insider fraud, and regulatory violations, where even a single breach can undermine customer trust and trigger significant legal exposure. Commercial real estate leaders, on the other hand, focus on tenant safety, workplace violence prevention, and infrastructure reliability, recognizing that an incident can impact both operational performance and long-term property value.

When adopting a risk-led security approach, threat assessments must always be tied back to the assets that drive business value in a particular context. Different industries experience the same categories of threat in very different ways, which is why relevance matters more than lists. Once that context is clear, the next step is to examine the actors behind those threats and understand how their intent and capability define the level of risk.

Threat Actors Underpin the Level of Threat

Chapter 2 introduced the concept of the risk triangle, where the intersection of asset, threat, and vulnerability determines the level of risk. To apply this in practice, we need to examine one of its core elements more closely: threat.

The actor behind it ultimately drives the level of the threat. Threat actors vary in their intent and capability, and these differences determine the probability of a successful attack. A casual intruder and a sophisticated criminal syndicate both represent threats, but not to the same degree. Not every type of threat actor exists in every environment, and not every potential adversary deserves the same degree of investment in controls.

To make this difference clear for both security teams and business leadership, we can evaluate each potential actor along two dimensions:

- Intent—How motivated are they to cause harm?
- Capability—How well-equipped are they to carry it out?

This creates a matrix useful for discussion, as shown in Table 4.2.

In real-world conversations, it often helps to map recognizable adversaries, such as vandals, thieves, fraudsters, or violent extremists, into these quadrants. Doing so helps asset owners understand why a highly capable and highly motivated adversary might require more urgent attention than an unmotivated or under-resourced actor.

TABLE 4.2 Threat Actor Characterization

	Low Capability	High Capability
High intent	Frustrated opportunist • May lash out when an easy gap appears • Needs only basic tools or insider help	Determined adversary • Has skills, funding, and patience • Will probe until a path opens
Low intent	Background noise • Idle curiosity or accidental exposure • Rarely escalates without a trigger	Sleeper threat • Possesses skills/resources but lacks motive for now • Can surge quickly if intent changes

This simple visualization also anchors the discussion in business terms. Controls should be prioritized for the scenarios where intent and capability intersect with the most capacity for harm and impact. By placing the focus on these high-potential-impact combinations, security leaders can explain why resources should be allocated to the threats most likely to succeed and cause material harm, rather than be spread thinner across every possible concern.

The question then becomes: how do we judge which actors are actually likely to act? Knowing that intent and capability matter is useful, but understanding how to evaluate these factors in practice is what enables leaders to translate theory into real-world, actionable assessments.

Pro Tip: Visual tools like intent–capability grids resonate with executives. They transform "what if" into "who and how," making it easier to justify why some actors demand urgent focus.

Measuring Intent

Intent reflects the degree of motivation a threat actor has to target a particular asset. This motivation may stem from ideology, financial gain, revenge, political goals, or personal grievances. A protestor angry at a company's public stance, a disgruntled employee seeking retribution, or an organized crime group looking for profit each represents very different forms of intent.

Two main factors help security professionals assess intent:

- Motivation—*Why would the actor want to cause harm?*

  For example, an organized crime group may be motivated by financial gain, while a former employee might be driven by anger or a desire for revenge.
- Opportunity—*Does the actor perceive a clear, viable path to achieving their goal?*

  A well-motivated attacker may still lack genuine intent if barriers to access appear insurmountable or if the detection risks outweigh the potential reward. Conversely, the perception of weak controls or easy insider access can dramatically raise intent.

Intent is dynamic. It can shift quickly in response to external pressures, emotional triggers, or sudden opportunities. For instance, a protest movement might remain peaceful until an incident escalates tensions, or a cybercriminal might ignore an organization until news of a weak vendor system surfaces.

This relationship between motivation and opportunity is well documented in rational choice theory, which describes offenders as decision-makers who weigh costs, benefits, and access when deciding to act.[5] Recognizing that thought process allows security leaders to explain intent to executives in practical, business-relevant terms: threat actors will act when the payoff looks worthwhile and the obstacles appear manageable.

Target Attractiveness—Why They Choose Your Asset

Intent is not shaped in a vacuum. The attractiveness of a potential target plays a significant role in determining whether an actor transitions from motivation to action. The same adversary who ignores one organization may actively pursue another, simply because one set of assets looks easier to access, more valuable, or more symbolic.

Threat actors weigh whether a target is "worth the effort." They consider both the payoff and the obstacles, asking whether the return justifies the risk. The most common cues of attractiveness include:

- Visibility & Symbolism—A high-profile brand, political stance, or frequent media coverage can make an asset a symbolic prize.
- Asset Value—Confidential data, cash equivalents, or proprietary intellectual property create direct financial or competitive gain.
- Operational Impact—The ability to halt production, disrupt a supply chain, or compromise life safety raises both attractiveness and leverage.
- Ease of Access—An open campus, porous cyber perimeter, or insider with privileged access makes a target more appealing.
- Potential Payoff—The likelihood of ransom being paid, resale value on illicit markets, or propaganda benefit influences adversary decisions.

A high-value, easily accessed target is highly attractive, whereas a low-value, difficult-to-reach target is far less compelling. Even within the same organization, different assets can appear very different to an attacker.

Consider in Table 4.3 how two different assets might have very different attractiveness ratings:

You can expand this analysis to consider a broader range of assets and scenarios. The categories in Table 4.4 provide a straightforward framework for classifying the appeal of a target to different adversaries.

Not all assets have equal appeal in the eyes of a potential adversary. A "trophy asset" draws consistent attention, while an "unlikely target" will rarely justify the effort. When evaluating threats with your internal partners, linking attractiveness to both motivation and opportunity creates a sharper, more realistic picture of intent.

Pro Tip: Just because a threat actor *wants* to cause harm doesn't mean they *can*. Always separate threat from vulnerability early in conversations. It keeps risk discussions focused and emotions out of the driver's seat.

Measuring Capability

If intent answers the question of *why* a threat actor might attack, capability explains *how well* they could do it. Capability is the actor's ability to carry out an attack successfully, based on the tools, knowledge, and support they can bring to bear.[6] Assessing this factor helps distinguish between adversaries who may want

TABLE 4.3 Rating Target Attractiveness

Asset	Threat	Attractiveness Rating	Why?
Customer payment data	Cyberattack	High	Direct financial value can be sold on black markets.
Employee breakroom TV	Theft	Low	Minimal resale value; not mission-critical.

TABLE 4.4 Target Attractiveness Examples

Rating	Description	Example Assets
Trophy target	This asset is a highly desirable target due to its exceptional value, ease of access, or the severe consequences of its compromise. Adversaries actively pursue it and pose a significant risk if attacked.	Customer financial data, top-secret intellectual property, high-profile executives, critical infrastructure (e.g., power grid control centers).
High value target	This asset is frequently targeted because it holds substantial value or operational importance. While not always the top priority for all adversaries, its compromise would have a significant impact.	Employee databases, high-value shipments, company trade secrets, executive offices, core IT systems.
Notable target	This asset has notable value and could be targeted by attackers with specific objectives. While not always the primary focus, it presents a viable opportunity for those with intent.	General employee workstations, non-executive leadership personnel, research & development projects, mid-tier financial accounts.
Opportunistic target	This asset has some level of attractiveness but is generally not a primary target unless opportunistic factors make it accessible. Attackers may bypass it for more valuable alternatives.	General office equipment, mid-level employee credentials, publicly available information with some operational relevance.
Unlikely target	This asset is of minimal interest to adversaries due to its low value, robust protections, or lack of meaningful impact if compromised. It is unlikely to be deliberately targeted.	Standard office furniture, publicly available information with no business sensitivity, minor inventory items.

to cause harm but lack the means, and those who combine both motivation and capacity into a genuine threat.

Several dimensions shape an actor's level of capability:

- Knowledge and Skills

  A lone amateur experimenting online does not typically present the same risk as a trained paramilitary team or a professional hacker-for-hire. The ability to conduct surveillance, breach defenses, and improvise under pressure determines how sophisticated the countermeasures must be. For example, opportunistic retail shoplifters may be deterred by cameras and guards, while organized cargo theft rings require coordinated intelligence, covert monitoring, and law enforcement partnerships.

- Tools and Resources

  Capability often scales with equipment and backing. From basic lock picks or pilfered credentials to drones, advanced malware kits, or insider accomplices, resources expand the reach of a threat actor. Well-funded adversaries—such as organized crime groups or nation-state actors—can sustain campaigns far longer than individuals acting alone.
- Operational Reach

  Geography and access matter. Some threats strike only within a local environment, such as vandalism or insider theft, while others can project force globally. A cybercriminal group operating overseas may compromise your data center without ever setting foot in the country. Understanding reach helps security teams balance protections across local sites, remote facilities, and digital assets that span borders.
- Experience

  Past success builds confidence and competence. An actor who has successfully carried out theft, sabotage, or cyber intrusions before is more likely to refine their tactics and adapt under pressure. Repeat attacks by the same groups in industries such as finance or energy show how experienced adversaries can escalate quickly and resist basic defenses.

Evaluating capability alongside intent allows security leaders to draw a sharper line between background noise and credible danger. An adversary with strong motivation but little skill may pose limited risk, while a highly capable actor, even if not immediately motivated, represents a sleeper threat that should be monitored closely.

Intent × Capability = Threat Level

When intent and capability are evaluated together, they provide a clear picture of the overall threat level posed by a potential adversary. The combination matters more than either factor on its own.

As seen in Figure 4.1, a highly motivated and well-equipped actor represents a significant danger because they possess both the reason and the means to act. At the opposite end, an unmotivated

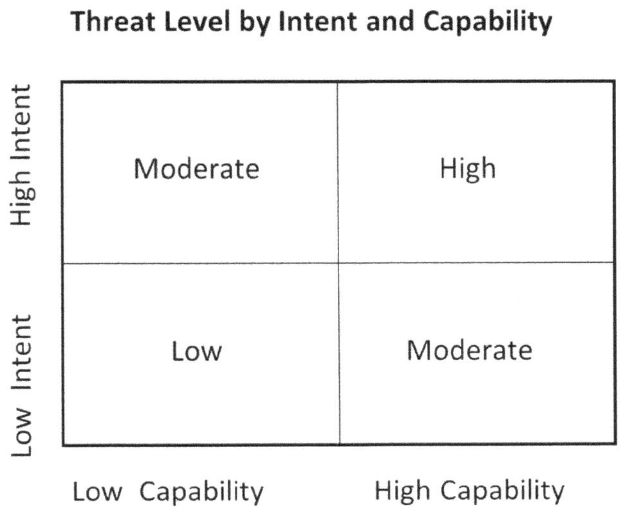

FIGURE 4.1 Threat Rating for Intent and Capability

or under-resourced actor still exists in the environment, but the probability of a successful attack is far lower. Most real-world adversaries fall somewhere between these extremes, and plotting known information against both dimensions helps separate credible risks from background noise.

This framework gives security leaders a straightforward way to explain threat levels in terms executives can understand. By showing where different actors land on the intent–capability scale, discussions about resource allocation shift from abstract probabilities to tangible scenarios: Which actors could realistically harm us, and which controls are most important for keeping them in check?

Understanding the Current Threat and Threat Actor Landscape

As evidenced by the factors discussed above, not all threats are equally likely to materialize.[7] Within an ESRM framework, one of the most valuable contributions security leaders make is helping stakeholders distinguish between theoretical risks and those with a credible chance of occurring. This clarity allows executives to allocate resources where they will have the greatest effect on protecting critical assets.

Earlier we discussed that threat truly arises only when intent and capability come together in a potential adversary. The next step is determining how many such actors exist in our environment, how interested they may be in our organization, and what probability they carry of acting. Business leaders do not simply want a list of possible dangers; they want a reasoned explanation of which are most likely to disrupt operations, compliance, or reputation.

To provide that explanation, security teams need data. Both historical evidence and forward-looking analysis can inform a realistic picture of the threat landscape. Reviewing past incidents, analyzing law enforcement and industry reports, and applying structured foresight all help convert vague concerns into concrete assessments. In real practice, a combination of rear-view metrics and horizon scanning gives the most balanced view: what has already happened, and what is coming next.

Historical Data to Assess Threat

Historical data is often the best starting point for evaluating the existence of any one type of threat. By reviewing what has already occurred, organizations can benchmark the frequency of specific threats, the damage they cause, and how those risks have evolved. Looking backward doesn't allow us to predict the future with certainty, but it can help us build a factual baseline that grounds risk discussions in evidence rather than speculation.

Key sources of historical threat data include:

- Internal Incident Reports

  Past breaches, workplace violence incidents, cyber intrusions, or infrastructure failures within the organization provide direct lessons. If the same type of incident has happened before, it deserves continued attention.
- Law Enforcement and Crime Data

  Local police reports and crime statistics can reveal external patterns such as rising theft, fraud, or violent crime near company sites. Retailers, for example, often reference local shoplifting or robbery rates when setting guard or patrol levels.
- Insurance and Actuarial Data

  Claims data across industries can highlight common points of loss. Insurance providers track cargo theft in logistics, slip-and-fall incidents in hospitality, and workplace accidents in construction, potentially offering a comparative benchmark.
- Industry-Specific Reports

  Security organizations and trade associations often publish annual assessments that highlight threats within particular sectors. Healthcare threat reports regularly show the persistence of ransomware and workplace violence, while financial services reports emphasize fraud and account compromise.

- Government Risk Assessments

  Many countries issue public reports on national security priorities, critical infrastructure risks, and cyber threat trends. These documents provide context for organizations that operate across jurisdictions.
- Academic and Think Tank Research

  Universities and research centers often conduct studies on crime trends, geopolitical risks, and emerging attack methods, offering insights that supplement operational data.

By combining these sources, security teams can establish a clear baseline for both the existence and the severity of common threats. For instance, healthcare and transportation organizations consistently report higher rates of workplace violence than other sectors, while financial institutions identify fraud and insider misuse as their most frequent risks. This differentiation allows security leaders to rate threat levels in ways that reflect the real operating environment rather than relying on generic assumptions.

Future Indicators of Threat

While historical data is valuable, it does not account for new and emerging patterns of threat. To avoid being caught off guard, organizations should supplement backward-looking analysis with active monitoring of forward-looking indicators. These signals help identify where risks may be building and when reassessment of threat levels is necessary.

Some key strategies for tracking emerging trends include:

- Threat Intelligence Feeds

  Cybersecurity platforms provide real-time updates on active campaigns, newly discovered vulnerabilities, and malware strains. For example, early warnings from industry threat-sharing groups have helped banks and hospitals patch critical systems before attackers could exploit them.
- Geopolitical Monitoring

  Political instability, trade disputes, sanctions, or regional conflict can signal risks to supply chains, workforce safety, or overseas operations. Manufacturers with single-source suppliers in politically volatile regions often rely on geopolitical scanning to anticipate disruptions.

- Economic and Market Analysis

  Economic downturns often coincide with an increase in fraud, workplace theft, and organized crime. Retailers and logistics providers, in particular, frequently experience spikes in shrinkage and cargo theft when economic pressure rises.
- Social Media and Open-Source Intelligence (OSINT)

  Monitoring online forums, social media, and underground markets can reveal early signs of emerging threats, from activist protests near corporate offices to criminal chatter about targeting a specific sector. Universities and event venues often use OSINT to gauge protest activity before major gatherings.
- Changes in Legislation and Regulation

  New privacy laws, data residency requirements, or environmental policies can introduce security challenges or create liability exposure. Financial institutions, for example, had to overhaul processes after the introduction of GDPR to avoid penalties.

By staying alert to these external indicators, security teams can anticipate patterns before they become imminent threats. This proactive stance shifts the conversation from reacting to incidents toward shaping preparedness strategies in advance, which strengthens both resilience and credibility with business leadership.

Pro Tip: When scary headlines take over executive brain-space, bring it back to the numbers. A simple side-by-side: "Here's what we've actually seen versus what's in the news," shifts the conversation from fear to facts.

Considering Emerging Threats

One of the most significant challenges in security risk management is evaluating emerging threats that lack a historical record. These are the risks that may not have occurred before, or that are just beginning to appear on the horizon. Because there is little past data to draw on, security teams must rely on predictive analysis, structured foresight, and scenario planning. The goal is not to guess the future but to anticipate where pressure is building and prepare before a disruption becomes critical.

Several structured methods can help frame emerging threat assessments:

- Horizon Scanning
  Monitoring signals of change that may be low in intensity today but carry the potential for high impact in the future. For example, early tracking of pandemic-related supply chain issues in Asia enabled some manufacturers to adjust their sourcing before global shortages occurred.
- Scenario-Based Modeling
  Creating "what if" scenarios based on technological shifts or geopolitical events. With quantum computing on the rise, many organizations are modeling how future decryption capabilities could render today's encryption standards obsolete.
- Trend Analysis
  Reviewing how similar risks have unfolded in other industries or regions. AI-driven cyberattacks, which first appeared in government espionage campaigns, are now surfacing in commercial sectors, highlighting how quickly advanced tactics migrate.
- Expert Consultation
  Engaging industry specialists, government analysts, or academic researchers to assess probability and impact. Expert panels often provide context that raw data cannot, such as identifying secondary effects on reputation, compliance, or operations.
- Red Teaming and Stress Testing
  Running simulations and penetration tests to probe whether an emerging threat could realistically affect the organization. Tabletop exercises around drone disruptions at airports, for instance, have revealed vulnerabilities long before an actual incident occurred.

Because these risks are uncertain, they must be evaluated across different time horizons: short-term threats that demand immediate mitigation, medium-term risks that require planned adaptation, and long-term possibilities that necessitate monitoring and strategic resilience. Treating them this way helps executives understand that emerging threats are not abstract speculation, but a structured part of ongoing risk management.

INSIGHT: PERCEPTION VS. REALITY IN THREAT MANAGEMENT

Emotions often drive security priorities more than data. Leaders, employees, and the public may focus on threats that feel immediate, such as active shooters or high-profile cyberattacks, because these events often dominate media coverage or personal experience. At the same time, statistically more probable risks, like internal fraud or business email compromise, may receive far less attention despite causing greater cumulative loss.

KEY DRIVERS OF SKEWED PERCEPTION

- Media Influence—Sensational headlines distort how often certain threats actually occur.
- Recency Bias—Recent events loom larger than long-term risks.
- Personal Experience—Past incidents cause some threats to be over-weighted compared to others.
- Social and Cultural Factors—Hot-button issues amplify specific fears within organizations.
- Fear of the Unknown—New or emerging threats feel outsized because they are unfamiliar.

The danger of perception-driven priorities is that resources can be pulled toward the most visible risks instead of the most consequential ones. By separating perception from reality, security leaders can redirect attention to the threats most likely to disrupt continuity, compliance, and resilience.

From Threat Level to Risk Level—Three Factors of Risk

The intersection of the first two ESRM questions—"What am I trying to protect?" (the asset) and "What does it truly need protection from?" (the threat)—begins to reveal the difference between a threat and an actual risk. A low-level-of-probability threat directed at a highly valuable asset, such as a violent attack against a CEO, may still demand substantial mitigation. In contrast, a high-probability but low-impact threat, such as minor employee negligence, may be more effectively addressed through training and policy reinforcement than through costly security investments.

This distinction highlights why identifying threats alone is insufficient. To determine whether there is a real risk, we must also ask whether a credible path exists for the threat actor to reach the asset. That pathway, whether a weakness in physical security, a gap in process, or a flaw in technology, is what we define as vulnerability, the third side of the risk triangle.

Vulnerability—The Last Piece of the Risk Rating Puzzle

The final piece of the risk triangle, vulnerability, determines how exposed assets are to the threats already identified. Without understanding vulnerability, organizations risk either overstating or understating the danger they face. This leads to two equally problematic outcomes: overspending on unnecessary security measures or leaving blind spots that can be exploited.

A vulnerability is a weakness or gap in security controls that a threat actor can exploit to cause harm to an asset.[8] Put simply, it is the pathway that allows the threat to reach the target.

For example, in the realm of data assets, if a company's most critical data is stored in a highly secured, encrypted, and access-controlled system, the practical risk of cyber compromise may be relatively low, even though cyber threats remain a global concern. On the other hand, considering physical issues, if employees consistently prop open secure doors in a facility, the vulnerability created by this behavior increases the likelihood of theft or harm, even if the perceived external threat of intrusion is considered low. The attractiveness of an open door becomes an invitation to opportunistic intruders.

Examples of vulnerabilities are easy to find across industries: in healthcare, outdated medical devices connected to hospital networks present exploitable gaps even when cyber defenses are strong; in retail, weak point-of-sale configurations have enabled credit card data breaches despite other solid protections; in transportation, failure to maintain perimeter fencing has allowed unauthorized individuals to access restricted areas of operation.

Recognizing vulnerabilities alongside assets and threats makes the risk picture complete. It also gives security leaders the most powerful lever for action: closing gaps that can be controlled.

Residual Risk—Why Vulnerability Assessment Comes First

Before we can answer the third ESRM question, "How do I most effectively and efficiently protect it?" (covered in Chapter 5), we need to understand the level of protection that already exists. Few organizations start from a blank slate. Most already have some measures in place, whether intentional or incidental. Even the most straightforward controls, such as locked doors, employee ID badges, or antivirus software, provide a baseline of protection.

Yet no matter how strong the safeguards, some level of risk always remains. This remaining exposure is known as residual risk. The more gaps uncovered in existing controls, the higher the level of residual risk. Recognizing and quantifying that risk is essential because it defines the starting point for all mitigation decisions.

An ESRM approach helps organizations determine how to manage residual risk. Options typically include:

- Accepting it—Acknowledging that the risk exists and choosing to live with it.
- Mitigating it—Reducing the likelihood or impact through additional controls.
- Transferring it—Using mechanisms such as insurance, outsourcing, or contractual agreements. While transfer can shift financial exposure, ultimate accountability almost always remains with the organization.

Examples of residual risk can be found in every sector. An energy provider may maintain robust cyber defenses but still tolerate some exposure to system downtime due to the need for continuous access to grid operations. A technology firm may accept occasional hardware theft as a low-probability event while setting a near-zero tolerance for intellectual property loss. A well-protected logistics company may still insure its high-value cargo against theft, recognizing that even the best supply chain security cannot entirely eliminate the risk.

Understanding residual risk is about making it visible and understood. By assessing existing control effectiveness and the vulnerabilities that remain, security leaders give their internal partners the clarity they need to decide which risks to accept, which to reduce, and which to transfer. Only with that clarity and transparency can the organization move forward into designing new protections.

To understand vulnerability in practical terms, organizations must take stock of the controls that already exist. This means asking a few key questions:

- What security controls are already in place?
- How do they align with the threats we have identified to our critical assets?
- How effective are those controls in practice?
- Where are the weaknesses or gaps?
- Are existing controls properly maintained and enforced?

This assessment matters because security is cumulative. Layers of protection build on one another, but gaps in even one layer can create pathways for exploitation. An effective risk-based approach prioritizes identifying and strengthening existing controls before recommending new investments. Strengthening weak points is often more impactful than adding new measures on top of a shaky foundation.

Pro Tip: Always frame residual risk as a business choice. Your role isn't to eliminate it, but to show leaders what they're accepting, and what it could cost.

Establishing a security control effectiveness baseline provides a snapshot of the organization's current state of protection. This baseline creates value in several ways:

- It offers a clear picture of how critical assets are being protected today.
- It highlights which vulnerabilities should be prioritized for mitigation.
- It provides justification for funding requests by linking new investments to identified gaps.
- It sets a benchmark for measuring improvement over time.

Organizations that skip this step can end up chasing short-term fixes, deploying new technologies or processes after incidents instead of building a deliberate, long-term program.

For example, a utility operator that invests in more surveillance drones to monitor transmission lines but fails to perform routine maintenance on the intrusion detection sensors along the fence line of a substation may still leave critical assets vulnerable. An accounting department might roll out new anti-fraud software but neglect to enforce separation of duties, creating the same insider risks that caused problems in the past.

By establishing a control effectiveness baseline, leaders can allocate limited resources to the vulnerabilities that matter most, aligning security with risk and ensuring that every measure contributes meaningfully to business continuity and resilience.

The Relationship between Controls and Threats

In the same way that assets are mapped to specific threats, controls must be matched to the risks they are intended to address. A measure that is highly effective in one scenario may be irrelevant in another.

For example, a canine detection team at a facility entrance may be the right choice to deter explosives or firearms, but it would do nothing to prevent property theft by an employee. The point is not that one measure is "good" and the other "bad," but that each only works when aligned with the threat it is designed to counter.

Organizations without a mature security/business relationship can fall into the trap of treating generic measures as a cure-all. Cameras and door locks are typical examples: they create a sense of security, but their protective value depends entirely on the type of threat. A camera cannot prevent fraud, and a locked door is no barrier to an insider with a key.

Controls only matter when they are mapped deliberately to the threats that put critical assets at risk. Chapter 5 will expand this idea by introducing the effects-based model of security planning, which organizes controls around the outcomes they create rather than the form they take. That approach ensures every dollar invested in security produces a measurable reduction in risk.

Putting It All Together: Rating Your Risks

So far, we have examined the three fundamental components of risk:

- Asset Value and Criticality
- Threat Level and Environment
- Vulnerability and Control Effectiveness

The next step is to bring these pieces together into a usable, repeatable, and *documentable* model. This allows security leaders to communicate risk clearly to business stakeholders and drive aligned, prioritized action.

Building Your Communications on What the Business Already Knows

In most risk-adjacent fields such as compliance, audit, insurance, or operations, leaders are familiar with the foundational formula:

Risk = Likelihood × Impact

This model is widely accepted and remains the backbone of enterprise risk management. It is not wrong, and in fact, it provides the basis for the approach we use here. ESRM does not reject this traditional formula. Instead, it refines it for security leaders by pulling out the element that matters most in practice: vulnerability. In doing so, it remains consistent with enterprise risk management standards while providing security teams with a more straightforward way to demonstrate their impact on outcomes.

In practice, likelihood is not just a number on a scale. It is the result of two distinct forces:

1. Threat Level—how likely it is that an adversary will attempt to act
2. Vulnerability—how likely it is that their attempt would succeed, given the current state of controls

Traditional models fold vulnerability *inside* the broader concept of likelihood. ESRM separates it on purpose. The reason is simple: vulnerability is the factor security leaders can directly influence.

We understand that:

- You cannot change the inherent value of a critical asset.
- You rarely control the external threat environment.
- But you can close a gap in defenses.

By showing business partners how vulnerabilities alter the real level of risk, and doing so in plain language, security leaders provide them with something actionable. It becomes a lever they can pull, a dial they can adjust, and a visible way to reduce exposure.

The model that follows is still grounded firmly in the logic of likelihood × impact, but it highlights the influence of security controls and makes strategy visible. This adjustment fosters real-world buy-in by first showing leaders how to measure risk and then how to reduce it.

An ESRM Risk Calculation Model to Understand and Demonstrate Risk

To prioritize risks effectively, organizations need a consistent method for rating them across all critical assets. Without a uniform approach, comparisons become subjective and conversations with asset owners turn into debates about opinion rather than evidence. Applying a clear, repeatable model like the one in Figure 4.2, based on the risk triangle, allows security teams to demonstrate risk in a way that is both structured and accessible.

At the end of this process, each risk is assigned a rating category, making prioritization straightforward. This enables both security leaders and their business partners to determine which risks require immediate action and which can be managed through routine controls.

There is no single "right" method for assigning scores. Risk professionals vary widely: some advocate for highly simplified models that classify risk as high, medium, or low, while others prefer complex methodologies that account for dozens of variables and require advanced software to reach an answer. Both approaches have merit, but in practice, most organizations need a middle ground.

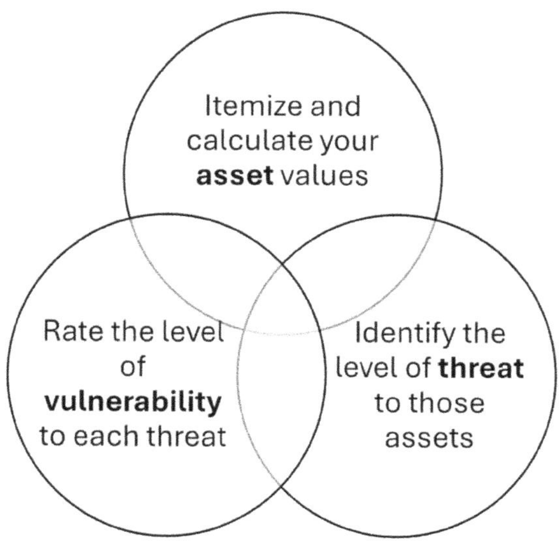

FIGURE 4.2 Calculating the Risk Triangle

The model presented here, developed through many hours of conversation with ESRM practitioners,[9] is *deliberately* simple. It provides enough detail to capture the three components of the risk triangle while remaining easy enough to apply in a spreadsheet or dashboard. More critically to the executive conversation, it makes the role of vulnerability visible, ensuring that security leaders can show how their actions directly influence risk reduction.

The model follows a structured four-step approach:

Step 1. Rate the Asset

Begin by rating each asset based on its importance to the organization. The goal is to understand which assets are indispensable to business continuity and which could be replaced with minimal disruption. This exercise should not be done in isolation. Use the conversations you've already had with stakeholders to guide your thinking, since they are the ones who know what is truly mission-critical.

Look at the rating scale in Table 4.5. A "5" rating (Indispensable) reflects an asset so central that the organization could not function without it. A "3" rating (Necessary) reflects something important but not irreplaceable. A "1" rating (Low Priority) indicates assets that can be replaced quickly or abandoned with minimal impact.

If you find that you cannot easily and confidently assign a ranking, that is a signal in itself. It may mean you need to revisit earlier activities, such as mapping assets to business operations and clarifying what matters most to your business partners. The purpose of this step is not just to enter numbers into a spreadsheet, but to achieve alignment on which assets truly drive the mission.

Step 2: Evaluate the Threat Level

Once assets are rated, the next step is to evaluate the level of threat they face. This means asking: *How likely is it that a threat actor would attempt to target this asset, and how frequently might such an attempt occur in our environment?*

To make threat levels actionable, use the scale seen in Table 4.6 to rate from 1 (Rare) to 5 (Almost Certain). A "5" does not mean guaranteed attack; it simply means the actor is both highly capable and highly motivated, with conditions that strongly favor an attack. A "1" reflects the opposite: a scenario that would require extraordinary circumstances or a major environmental shift.

TABLE 4.5 Asset Criticality Framework

Rating	Asset Category/Level of Impact	Description
5—Indispensable asset/ severe consequences	Your organization is highly dependent on this category of assets for nearly all essential operations, and replacing or restoring them quickly is almost impossible.	A significant disruption to this asset class would result in extreme operational and reputational damage.
4—Highly valued asset/ significant consequences	This asset category plays a crucial role in supporting many core functions, and its replacement would be difficult and time-consuming.	A major disruption to this area would create substantial operational and reputational harm.
3—Necessary asset/ noticeable consequences	These assets contribute to several critical and many important operations, and replacing them would be somewhat challenging.	A major issue affecting this asset category would cause disruptions that have a tangible impact on operations and branding.
2—Supportive asset/ limited consequences	A loss or compromise of this asset would create some challenges, but most key operations would remain functional.	The organization would experience a decrease in efficiency and productivity, but could adapt and continue most of its activities.
1—Low-priority asset/ minimal consequences	The organization does not depend heavily on this asset class, or it can be replaced with little effort or cost.	A sizeable impact in this area would have negligible effects on operations or branding.

Threat ratings should not be guesses. They should be informed by evidence, including the history of similar incidents, the behavior of known actors, patterns of targeting in your industry, and broader environmental conditions that may make attacks more or less likely to occur. This rating rubric provides executives with a common language for discussing the probability that a threat might manifest. Instead of debating whether something is "risky" or "unlikely," you can show where it falls on a scale that ties directly to observed patterns and data.

TABLE 4.6 Threat Level/Probability Framework

Rating	Threat Level Description	Potential Expected Frequency
5—Almost certain	The threat actor is highly motivated, highly capable, and current conditions strongly favor an attack. Past incidents have shown frequent and ongoing activity targeting similar assets.	Weekly to monthly
4—Likely	The threat actor or group demonstrates ongoing capability and intent, with recent incidents in similar organizations confirming active targeting patterns.	Annually to multiple times per year
3—Possible	The threat actor has demonstrated a known intent or capability, but barriers (logistics, defenses) or a lack of recent activity make the occurrence moderate.	Every 2 to 5 years
2—Uncommon	The threat is plausible but unlikely based on current intelligence. Actors with this profile show limited activity or infrequent success against similar targets.	Every 10 years
1—Rare	The threat would require exceptional circumstances (new geopolitical changes, major system failures) to materialize. Historical precedent is minimal or nonexistent.	Every 20 to 50 years

Step 3. Rate Controls to Find Vulnerability

The third step is to assess how effectively current security controls mitigate vulnerability. Controls exist to prevent, detect, or respond to threats, but their actual effectiveness varies widely. By rating each control on a consistent scale, you identify both where protection is strong and where weaknesses remain. This provides executives with a clear, evidence-based explanation of where resources should be directed.

Use the framework in Table 4.7 to guide this step. A score of "1" reflects an optimal control that is reliable, integrated, and leaves little room for exploitation. A score of "5" reflects an absent or ineffective control that provides no meaningful defense. Remember that on this scale, lower is better. A robust or optimal control reduces vulnerability, which in turn lowers the final risk rating.

TABLE 4.7 Control Effectiveness Framework

Rating	Revised Security Control Description	Example Interpretation
5—Absent control	This control is either entirely missing or exists in such a nonfunctional state that it provides no meaningful security benefit. There is no formal policy, procedure, or technology in place to address the associated risk.	A facility that houses sensitive data has no access control, allowing unrestricted entry.
4—Insufficient control	The control exists but is incomplete, poorly implemented, or unreliable. It may provide partial protection but fails to mitigate the associated risk consistently.	Security cameras are installed but are neither actively monitored nor properly maintained, rendering them unreliable.
3—Adequate control	The control is functional and generally effective in mitigating risk. However, it may have gaps, inefficiencies, or inconsistencies that limit its full effectiveness.	A door access system requires employee badges, but visitor access procedures are inconsistently followed.
2—Strong control	The control is well-designed, consistently applied, and provides a strong level of protection. Only minor refinements or optimizations could improve its effectiveness.	A monitored alarm system with motion detection and emergency response protocols protects a secure facility.
1—Optimal control	The control is fully effective, highly reliable, and seamlessly integrated into security operations. It provides maximum mitigation against the associated risk with no significant weaknesses.	A high-security vault has biometric access, multi-factor authentication, real-time monitoring, and intrusion-resistant construction.

Step 4. Calculate the Final Risk Score

Once you have assessed the criticality of assets, the threat level, and the effectiveness of controls, you can combine these factors to generate a Risk Concern Level. This score offers a structured way to compare risks across very different assets, ensuring resources are directed where they are needed most.

$$\text{Risk Concern Level} = \frac{\text{Asset Rating} + \text{Threat Rating} + \text{Vulnerability Rating}}{3}$$

FIGURE 4.3 A Basic Calculation of Risk

The calculation in Figure 4.3 is intentionally straightforward. Adapted and simplified from multiple standards,[10] it balances clarity with enough detail to be meaningful:

In this formula, the Vulnerability Rating is the average score of all controls applied to mitigate a specific threat (see Chapter 5 for more on how to rate controls). By separating vulnerability, you make visible the part of the model that security can most directly influence.

This approach gives us a quick and straightforward way to communicate risk to executives. It shows not just which risks exist, but which ones rise high enough to justify investment. That clarity helps align decisions with actual business risk rather than perceived concerns.

Important Note: *Use this qualitative model to frame priorities quickly. When an asset's potential loss crosses your organization's "material-impact" threshold, or when regulators require more rigorous analysis, you can escalate to quantitative methods such as Monte Carlo simulation, bow-tie analysis, or ISO 31010 techniques.*

INSIGHT: ADAPTING THE TRADITIONAL RISK MODEL FOR STRATEGIC CLARITY

The traditional Likelihood × Impact formula remains a cornerstone of enterprise risk management, and ESRM fully aligns with it. What ESRM adds is a more precise articulation for security decision-making. By pulling vulnerability out of the broader likelihood category, the model makes transparent what security leaders can actually influence. This clarity helps your business partners and stakeholders see which risk levels can be reduced through targeted controls and gives leaders a straightforward way to demonstrate how closing vulnerabilities directly lowers risk.

Far from departing from accepted standards, this refinement builds on them. It preserves consistency with enterprise models while giving security teams a more actionable pathway to align strategy with business priorities.

The example in Table 4.8 illustrates how even a basic spreadsheet model can effectively highlight which risks emerge as the most significant. For instance, ransomware against critical manufacturing equipment scores higher than theft of inventory, even though both may occur. That difference gives executives a data-driven reason to focus resources where the impact would be most severe.

INSIGHT: TABLE 4.8—TURNING RATINGS INTO PRIORITIES

This example shows how a simple formula makes risk prioritization visible. Even with different types of assets and threats, a consistent scoring model highlights which concerns rise above the rest. For instance, ransomware targeting critical manufacturing machinery rates higher than theft of inventory, not because theft is unimportant, but because the impact and vulnerability combine to create a more severe risk score. By using a uniform method like this, leaders can see why some risks demand immediate attention while others can be managed through routine controls.

Key Takeaways from Chapter 4

- Not all threats are created equal: Understanding which specific threats are most relevant to your critical assets, and how those threats evolve, keeps mitigation focused where it matters most.
- Threat level is shaped by people: Intent and capability are the two core drivers of human-caused threats. A motivated and well-equipped actor poses a fundamentally different level of risk than one who lacks the necessary tools or interest in acting.
- Assets and threats must be linked: Threats are only meaningful in context; tied to high-value or mission-critical assets, they require attention, but otherwise they remain background noise.
- Vulnerability makes the difference: Without a path to exploit, even a serious threat can remain theoretical. Separating vulnerability from general likelihood highlights residual risk and shows where it can be reduced.

TABLE 4.8 Calculating Risk

Name of Asset	Level of Criticality	Threat Category	Threat Rating	Control Rating	Equation	Risk Concern Level (1–5)
Skilled employees	4—Very important	Assault	2—Uncommon	1—Excellent	(4 + 2 + 1)/3	2
Manufacturing machinery & equipment	4—Very important	Ransomware attack	4—Likely	5—Unsatisfactory	(4 + 4 + 5)/3	4.3
Buildings and infrastructure	4—Very important	Destruction	4—Likely	3—Satisfactory	(4 + 4 + 3)/3	3.6
Inventory	3—Important	Theft	4—Likely	3—Satisfactory	(3 + 4 + 3)/3	3.3
Transportation assets	3—Important	Sabotage	3—Possible	1—Excellent	(3 + 3 + 1)/2	2.3

- Your risk model is your communication tool: Using a structured, transparent approach to rate assets, threats, and vulnerabilities helps security leaders explain residual risk, frame priorities, and gain support for aligned resource allocation.

Security Leader Toolkit: Chapter 4

ESRM Implementation Checklist

- Have I identified threats across all four categories: intentional, unintentional, environmental/infrastructure, and emerging?
- Have I mapped each threat category to the specific critical assets it targets?
- Have I distinguished between threats that are feared or visible and those that are actually likely and impactful?
- Have I built an Intent × Capability matrix to understand which adversaries are credible versus background noise?
- Have I assessed target attractiveness (visibility, value, accessibility, symbolism) for each of my top assets?
- Have I collected historical incident data (internal cases, industry reports, law enforcement data) and scanned for forward-looking indicators (regulatory changes, geopolitical instability, technological shifts) to inform my assessment of threat probability?
- Have I listed the existing controls currently protecting each asset?
- Have I identified the most significant vulnerabilities—weak or missing controls that could be exploited?
- Have I prepared a clear explanation for the leadership of:
  - Which risks are credible and require investment?
  - Which risks are overstated or perception-driven?
  - Which risks fall within tolerance and can be accepted or transferred?

Risk Calculation Template

This table ties the chapter's elements together: asset criticality, threat level, vulnerability (via controls), and overall risk concern. It is easily set up as a calculation in a spreadsheet.

Asset Name	Asset Criticality (1–5)	Threat Category	Threat Rating (1–5)	Control Effectiveness (1–5, Lower = Stronger)	Equation	Risk Concern Level (1–5)	Notes
Example: Manufacturing machinery	4—Highly Valued	Ransomware	4—Likely	5—Insufficient	(4 + 4 + 5)/3	4.3	Priority mitigation needed

How to Use

1. Rate Asset Criticality
2. Assign a Threat Category and Rating
3. Score Control Effectiveness
4. Average the three scores for a Risk Concern Level.
5. Compare across risks to decide which demand action, which are tolerable, and which can be accepted or transferred.

Notes

1 ASIS International, *General Security Risk Assessment Guideline* (Alexandria, VA: ASIS International, 2019); Federal Emergency Management Agency, *Threat and Hazard Identification and Risk Assessment Guide (CPG 201)* (Washington, DC: U.S. Department of Homeland Security, 2013); National Institute of Standards and Technology, *Guide for Conducting Risk Assessments*, NIST Special Publication 800–30, Revision 1 (Gaithersburg, MD: NIST, 2012).

2 Cybersecurity Ventures, "Ransomware Report: Latest Attacks and News," *Cybercrime Magazine*, accessed August 2025, https://cybersecurityventures.com/ransomware-report/.

3 World Bank, *Reshaping Global Value Chains in Light of COVID-19 and Geopolitical Shocks* (Washington, DC: World Bank, 2022), https://documents1.worldbank.org/curated/en/099454211022228485/pdf/IDU03cbebf2507975046f70a178034620f7de063.pdf

4 National Institute of Standards and Technology, *Post-Quantum Cryptography: NIST's Plan for the Future of Encryption* (Gaithersburg, MD: NIST, July 2022), https://www.nist.gov/news-events/news/2022/07/nist-announces-first-four-quantum-resistant-cryptographic-algorithms

5 Derek B. Cornish and Ronald V. Clarke, *The Reasoning Criminal: Rational Choice Perspectives on Offending* (New York: Springer-Verlag, 1986).

6 ASIS International, *General Security Risk Assessment Guideline*, Updated edition (Alexandria, VA: ASIS International, 2024).

7 National Institute of Standards and Technology, *Guide for Conducting Risk Assessments*, NIST Special Publication 800–30 Revision 1 (Gaithersburg, MD: NIST, 2012); International Organization for Standardization, *ISO 31010:2019 – Risk Management – Risk Assessment Techniques* (Geneva: ISO, 2019); ASIS International, *General Security Risk Assessment Guideline* (Alexandria, VA: ASIS International, 2019).

8 International Organization for Standardization, *ISO 31000:2018 – Risk Management – Guidelines* (Geneva: ISO, 2018).

9 Based on in-person conversations with Paul Mercer and Noah Price, and informed by additional discussions with Yannick DeSmit, Steen Bonke Sørensen, and Marko Sukilovic, conducted by the author over the course of professional engagements. The author's simplified interpretation is a useful heuristic for rating risk. More complex rating algorithms are available in commercial software solutions for risk assessment.

10 ASIS International, *General Security Risk Assessment (GSRA) Guideline* (Alexandria, VA: ASIS International, 2019); National Institute of Standards and Technology, *NIST SP 800–30 Revision 1: Guide for Conducting Risk Assessments* (Gaithersburg, MD: NIST, 2012); International Organization for Standardization, *ISO 31010:2019 – Risk Management – Risk Assessment Techniques* (Geneva: ISO, 2019).

CHAPTER 5

How Can We Most Effectively and Efficiently Protect It?—Choosing the Best Mitigations for Your Risk Profile

– In the last chapters, we covered identifying and assessing risks to our organization's assets by asking two key questions:

- What do I need to protect?
- What does it truly need protection from?

Now we face the final question that brings the ESRM approach to life:

- How do we most effectively and efficiently protect it?

This chapter bridges the gap between understanding the actual risks to your organization and implementing the best security measures to mitigate them. Assessing and prioritizing our risk gives us a clear picture of threats and vulnerabilities, but that understanding alone does not safeguard critical assets. The next step is turning insight into action by developing strategies that can be presented to asset owners and decision-makers. Security leaders must ensure that risks are addressed with controls aligned to the organization's priorities, risk tolerance, and budget.

The value of Enterprise Security Risk Management (ESRM) is that it keeps us moving from analysis to strategy to tactics without

DOI: 10.4324/9781003711346-9

losing sight of what matters most to the organization. By linking identified risks directly to proportionate, well-chosen mitigations, security teams avoid wasted effort and ensure that every investment contributes to stronger protection, better alignment, and lasting resilience.

Defining Effectiveness and Efficiency in Security

Every security program, regardless of the industry or maturity level, ultimately rests on two key principles: effectiveness and efficiency. Together, these two principles set the boundaries for every security decision.

- Effectiveness asks how well a control mitigates risk. Does it prevent a threat, reduce its impact, or enable a fast, informed response?
- Efficiency asks whether those outcomes are achieved without overextending people, budget, or time.

The goal when implementing a risk-based approach to security is to strike a balance between these two forces. Security measures must deliver solid protective effects, but they also need to be sustainable within the organization's operating environment.

This balance looks different in every organization. A biotech firm focused on intellectual property has different needs than a retailer focused on loss prevention or a healthcare provider balancing patient access and privacy. Even within the same sector, context matters: a mature program with strong governance will make different choices than a younger firm still developing its processes.

That diversity means the right question is not *What security controls exist?* But, *Which ones are right for us?*

A strong security program integrates three elements of protection:

- People—Trained staff who detect, prevent, and respond with judgment and agility.
- Process—Clear policies and repeatable procedures that drive accountability and consistency.
- Technology—Tools and systems—such as access control, surveillance, and cybersecurity platforms—that scale and automate protection.

Each of these comes with its own capabilities and associated cost. When these elements are intentionally chosen and balanced, they reinforce each other. Technology amplifies human capabilities, processes provide structure for decisions, and people supply the context machines cannot.

Prioritizing both effectiveness and efficiency leads to security programs that are resilient, business-aligned, and adaptable to change. This approach delivers stronger protection, smarter resource utilization, effective communication with stakeholders, and measurable business value.

Effects-Based Security: The Optimal Approach for ESRM Risk Mitigation

When designing optimal programs, ESRM provides a strategy: identify critical assets, assess risks, and set priorities for protection. However, although we lead with strategy, that strategy still requires action. The next step is translating risk insights into practical tactics that effectively reduce exposure.

Effects-Based Security (EBS) provides that bridge. It ensures that the controls chosen are directly tied to business risk and the outcomes leadership expects. Instead of beginning with a list of products, technologies, or categories of security services, EBS starts with the question: *What effect do we need this control to achieve?*

By focusing on outcomes such as deterrence, detection, or response, EBS keeps security efforts aligned with broader business objectives. The result is a program where every tactic contributes to reducing the risks that matter most, rather than adding tools that look impressive but do little to advance resilience.

A Brief History of Effects-Based Security and Its Application to ESRM

The idea of planning around outcomes rather than tools did not begin in corporate security. Effects-Based Operations (EBO) originated as a military doctrine, created to maximize operational effectiveness by prioritizing results instead of focusing only on tactics or resources. Developed and refined through institutions such as the RAND Corporation and the U.S. Department of Defense, EBO shifted the planning mindset. The goal was not simply to win battles but to disrupt an adversary's ability to function by targeting leadership, infrastructure, supply chains, and morale in combination.[1]

One of the earliest modern applications came from Colonel John A. Warden III, whose "Five Rings Model" guided U.S. airpower strategy during the 1991 Gulf War. Warden argued that striking centers of gravity such as leadership, infrastructure, systems, population, and deployed forces would have a far greater effect than focusing on direct combat alone.[2] This approach demonstrated that carefully chosen effects could change the course of conflict faster and with fewer resources than purely tactical engagements.

Over time, effects-based thinking migrated beyond the battlefield. Governments and national security agencies began applying the approach to counterterrorism, intelligence, and critical infrastructure protection. The United Kingdom's National Protective Security Authority adapted the concept directly to physical and operational security, showing how it could help organizations manage broad categories of threat with finite resources.[3]

From there, the logic carried naturally into corporate security risk management. Just as militaries sought to disrupt adversaries through carefully chosen effects, businesses facing diverse risks needed to achieve solid protective outcomes without overinvesting in tools that might not have the desired impact. The principle was the same: focus first on the effect you need to achieve, then select the combination of measures that deliver it.

Why Effects-Based Security Is an Ideal Framework for ESRM

Effects-based thinking fits naturally within ESRM because it provides a structured way to translate risk assessments into targeted, efficient security measures. Its value comes from four core advantages:

1. Focus on Outcomes, Not Tools

   Traditional security planning often begins with solutions like cameras, fences, or access control systems, without first asking what specific risks they are meant to reduce. EBS reverses that path. It begins with the question: *What effect do we need to achieve to protect this asset from this risk?* Once the desired outcome is clear, organizations can select the optimal combination of people, processes, and technologies to achieve it.

   Consider a university campus responding to a rise in bike thefts. The security team first considered expanding CCTV coverage, but realized that would only allow a response after a theft occurred. When they reframed the problem around the desired effect of controlling access to storage areas, they instead introduced secured racks with card-reader access for students and staff. The effect was more targeted than cameras alone, and theft rates dropped sharply.

2. A Proven Approach to Risk Mitigation

   The principles behind effects-based planning have been tested for decades in military, intelligence, and protective operations. Unlike solution-driven tactics that react to incidents, EBS allows security leaders to proactively design layered strategies using controls that have already been validated in real-world scenarios. When applied in a corporate setting, this discipline ensures that risk mitigation is both deliberate and defensible.

3. Better Use of Resources

   Balancing effectiveness with cost is one of the most challenging tasks in security. Budgets are limited, and security must compete with other business priorities. EBS helps maximize impact by ensuring every measure contributes meaningfully to risk reduction. Controls that do not produce measurable effects are quickly identified as low-value, thereby avoiding wasted spending and effort.

   A museum consortium offers this example. Facing limited funding, leadership debated whether to invest in costly biometric systems for researcher access to storage. Instead, by mapping the effect they wanted—delaying access and detecting unauthorized handling of artifacts—they chose to expand motion sensors and integrate video monitoring with existing access controls to allow for a visible audit trail of access. This combination provided similar protective effect at a fraction of the cost, preserving funds for conservation work.

4. Alignment with Business Priorities

   ESRM emphasizes that security must support the organization's mission and risk tolerance. EBS provides the mechanism for doing this by:

   - Translating risk discussions into well-defined effects that leaders can understand.
   - Allowing security professionals to communicate in business terms rather than technical jargon.

   Demonstrating, in measurable ways, how controls protect assets, continuity, and reputation.

Together, ESRM and EBS form a complete cycle. ESRM sets the priorities by identifying assets, threats, and vulnerabilities. EBS ensures that the chosen mitigations deliver real, efficient outcomes. The result is a program where analysis leads to action, and every control is directly tied to reducing a risk that matters to the enterprise.

INSIGHT: STANDING ON THE SHOULDERS OF SECURITY HISTORY

Modern security planning builds on decades of work by practitioners who recognized that no single measure could protect an organization on its own. Concepts such as Defense-in-Depth (DiD) and the NSA's D3R2 model (Detect, Delay, Deny, Respond, Recover)[4] became foundational because they highlighted a critical insight: protection must come from layers of complementary strategies, not from reliance on a single tool or tactic.

Neither framework has a single point of origin. Instead, they represent the collective experience of the security profession, distilled into simple, repeatable models that shaped how generations of practitioners approached risk. DiD emphasized the layering of barriers to frustrate adversaries and buy time for response. D3R2 provided a practical sequence of protective effects that security leaders could design into physical and operational environments. Both remain widely recognized today, not because they are complete in themselves, but because they gave the profession a common language to organize protective thinking.

EBS builds on this legacy. It takes the layering logic of DiD and the sequenced functions of D3R2 and applies them through the ESRM lens:

- What effect do we need?
- Against which risk?
- For which asset?

This evolution does not discard or discount earlier frameworks. It honors them by integrating their insights into a broader, outcome-driven approach that aligns directly with business priorities. In this way, EBS represents not a replacement but a next step in the progression of security thinking, connecting history to the practical needs of organizations today.

The Seven Security Effects: A Framework for Protection

Security is most effective when it focuses on the outcomes we need to achieve, not on the tools we might buy first. EBS provides a structure for that discipline, organizing protective measures around seven key effects that collectively manage risk across the life cycle of an incident.

Different models of these effects have circulated in the security field for decades. The version presented here is an approach inspired by the general approach of Thomas Norman's *Risk Analysis and Security Countermeasure Selection*,[5] which I then adapted and refined through years of practical application and discussions with security experts.[6] Understanding and applying these seven effects ensures that security leaders can design layered, outcome-focused programs that address risk with both precision and efficiency.

1. Deter

   Deterrence reduces the likelihood of an attack by convincing adversaries that the attempt is too risky, costly, or unlikely to succeed. It works on perception: when a target looks hardened, attackers often move on to softer alternatives.

   Example: An airport that places uniformed patrols and K9 units at entrances and visible checkpoints creates a powerful deterrent effect. Even before access controls or detection systems engage, the visible presence signals high likelihood of detection and interdiction to anyone considering a hostile act.
2. Control Access

   Access control restricts entry to critical assets, ensuring that only authorized individuals, vehicles, or digital identities may proceed. This effect is fundamental to preventing adversaries from reaching targets in the first place.

   Example: A global energy company uses badge-based systems with biometric verification at refinery gates. The layers of identity checks make it difficult for unauthorized personnel to enter hazardous or sensitive areas, reducing the chance of sabotage or theft.
3. Detect

   Detection provides early awareness of potential threats. It enables organizations to spot suspicious activity or ongoing incidents quickly enough to take action. Without detection, incidents may go unnoticed until damage is done.

   Example: A casino integrates AI-driven video analytics with its surveillance cameras. These systems detect abnormal behaviors, such as loitering near cash cages or restricted hallways, and alert staff before incidents escalate.

4. Delay

   Delay buys time. Slowing an adversary's progress gives responders critical minutes to act and reduces the chance of a complete breach. Delays are rarely sufficient on their own, but they amplify other effects.

   Example: A data center installs mantraps that require employees to pass through two secured doors, one closing before the next opens. This slows unauthorized entry attempts and gives security staff time to verify identities or intercept intruders.

5. Assess

   Assessment separates genuine threats from false alarms. It ensures resources are directed to the right problems at the right time, avoiding wasted response while still enabling rapid action when needed.

   Example: A port authority uses an integrated operations center to review radar anomalies flagged by detection systems. Operators assess whether a vessel poses a genuine threat or is simply off course, avoiding unnecessary deployments while still escalating real concerns quickly.

6. Respond

   Response is the active intervention that stops or mitigates harm once a threat materializes. It may involve security personnel, law enforcement, automated systems, or emergency protocols.

   Example: A hotel chain trains its staff to initiate lockdown procedures in the event of a violent incident. Doors can be secured remotely, local police are automatically alerted, and trained responders are dispatched to the affected area to protect guests and employees.

7. Communicate & Record

   This effect underpins every stage of security. Effective communication ensures that incidents are reported, escalated, and coordinated in real time. Accurate records provide evidence, accountability, and lessons for future improvement.

   Example: A manufacturing firm uses an incident management platform that records access logs, integrates CCTV footage, and pushes automated alerts to executives during crises. This ensures that decisions are made with accurate information and that post-event analysis has a reliable record to draw from.

Mapping Threats and Risks to the Best Mitigating Effects

In Chapter 4, we established that different assets inherently carry different levels of exposure to threats depending on their nature, use, and environment. A financial database is far more vulnerable to cyberattacks and fraud than to vandalism. A manufacturing plant, on the other hand, faces greater risk from unauthorized access, theft, or natural disasters than from insider misuse of digital credentials.

Just as threats align differently with assets, the way a threat unfolds determines which security effects are most valuable in reducing its impact. Matching the best effect to the aligned scenario is what turns analysis into protective action.

For example:

- Burglary is best mitigated by deterrence, access control, and detection. Visible cameras and lighting reduce the likelihood of an attempt, locked doors and barriers limit entry, and detection systems alert responders before losses mount.
- Ransomware is best mitigated by access control, detection, and delay. Strong authentication reduces unauthorized entry, detection tools quickly identify malicious activity, and delay mechanisms, such as multifactor authentication or separated network segments, slow attackers long enough for intervention.
- Terrorism requires a layered strategy that combines deterrence, delay, and response. Visible protective measures can discourage targeting, barriers and reinforced entry points slow escalation, and trained responders act to contain the incident and save lives.
- Natural disasters cannot be deterred, but they can be mitigated through assessment, response, and communication. Risk assessments identify vulnerabilities to hazards, emergency protocols support safety and continuity, and communication systems keep employees and stakeholders informed.

By focusing on the effects that matter most in each case, organizations can concentrate their resources where they deliver the most significant value. This ensures that mitigation is not generic but tailored to the way threats actually behave, which is essential for both efficiency and impact.

Pro Tip: Detection is essential, but only when paired with response. Without action, monitoring simply captures failure in high definition.

Table 5.1—continued from the presentation in chapter 4—systematically maps threat categories to the security effects that provide the most impact. Inspired in part by the approach described in *Integrated Security Systems Design* (once again, from the estimable Thomas Norman[7]), this model helps organizations employ the most impactful security strategies based on real-world threats and behaviors rather than generic security measures.

This matrix helps security teams direct resources to the countermeasures that matter most. Defenses can be tailored to how threats actually behave, ensuring that each effect applied has a

TABLE 5.1 Mapping Threat Type to Security Effect

Asset Type	Most Impactful Threat Category	Most Impactful Security Effect	Why This Effect Is Most Impactful
People	Assault	Detect, Respond	Early detection of aggressive behavior allows for intervention before escalation. A rapid response can minimize harm and protect individuals.
	Robbery	Deter, Control Access, Respond	Strong deterrence measures (visible security presence, signage) discourage criminals. Access control limits unauthorized entry, and a fast response mitigates losses.
	Workplace violence	Detect, Assess, Respond	Behavioral threat detection helps identify warning signs. Assessment ensures an appropriate response, and trained responders can intervene before violence escalates.

(Continued)

TABLE 5.1 (Continued) Mapping Threat Type to Security Effect

Asset Type	Most Impactful Threat Category	Most Impactful Security Effect	Why This Effect Is Most Impactful
	Sexual assault	Detect, Communicate & Record, Respond	Surveillance and reporting mechanisms help detect incidents. Communication ensures victims get immediate help. Response teams can act swiftly.
	Stalking	Detect, Assess, Communicate & Record	Continuous monitoring helps detect patterns of suspicious behavior. Assessment differentiates between harmless and threatening activity. Communication ensures threats are correctly reported and escalated.
	Harassment	Detect, Assess, Communicate & Record	Early detection of repeated inappropriate behavior allows intervention. Communication channels and records ensure proper documentation and corrective action.
	Targeted threats against executives	Deter, Control Access, Detect, Respond	Strong deterrence measures (executive protection, secure routes) reduce risk. Access control prevents unauthorized approaches. Detection tools track movement. An emergency response plan mitigates the risk.
	Active shooter incidents	Detect, Delay, Respond, Communicate & Record	Threat detection through surveillance and behavioral analytics is key. Delay mechanisms (locked doors, secure rooms) buy time for emergency response. Fast response and communication save lives.

(Continued)

TABLE 5.1 (Continued) Mapping Threat Type to Security Effect

Asset Type	Most Impactful Threat Category	Most Impactful Security Effect	Why This Effect Is Most Impactful
	Insider threats	Assess, Detect, Communicate & Record	Monitoring internal behaviors helps assess risks. Detection systems identify unauthorized activities. Communication ensures security teams respond to internal threats.
	Public health crises (pandemics, bioterrorism)	Assess, Respond, Communicate & Record	Continuous health monitoring and assessments detect outbreaks. A structured response minimizes spread. Communication ensures transparency and compliance with safety protocols.
Information	Data breaches	Control Access, Detect, Communicate & Record	Strong access control limits unauthorized access. Detection helps identify breaches early. Communication ensures swift incident response.
	Insider threats	Assess, Detect, Communicate & Record	Continuous monitoring detects unusual behavior. Assessment helps determine risks. Communication ensures timely response to prevent data loss.
	Cyber espionage	Detect, Control Access, Delay	Detection systems monitor unauthorized access attempts. Access controls protect sensitive data. Delay mechanisms hinder attackers' progress.
	Hacking	Control Access, Detect, Respond	Strict authentication controls prevent unauthorized entry. Early detection identifies intrusion attempts. Response actions stop ongoing cyberattacks.

(Continued)

TABLE 5.1 (Continued) Mapping Threat Type to Security Effect

Asset Type	Most Impactful Threat Category	Most Impactful Security Effect	Why This Effect Is Most Impactful
	Malware	Detect, Respond, Communicate & Record	Detection tools identify malicious software. Response mechanisms isolate threats. Communication ensures affected parties take action.
	Intellectual property theft	Control Access, Communicate & Record, Assess	Restricted access protects sensitive data. Communication ensures unauthorized activity is logged. Assessment determines internal/external threats.
	Social engineering	Assess, Detect, Communicate & Record	Behavioral analysis helps assess risks. Detection tools spot suspicious interactions. Communication ensures awareness and proper response.
	Accidental data exposure	Assess, Communicate & Record	Risk assessment helps identify weak data handling practices. Communication educates employees on security policies and records incidents for compliance.
	Unauthorized access	Control Access, Detect, Respond	Access control prevents unauthorized entry. Detection alerts security teams. Response mechanisms revoke or block unauthorized users.
	Third-party vendor data leaks	Assess, Communicate & Record, Detect	Risk assessment ensures vendor security compliance. Communication ensures response readiness, and detection tools monitor external data-sharing risks.

(Continued)

TABLE 5.1 (Continued) Mapping Threat Type to Security Effect

Asset Type	Most Impactful Threat Category	Most Impactful Security Effect	Why This Effect Is Most Impactful
	Regulatory non-compliance (GDPR, HIPAA, etc.)	Assess, Communicate & Record, Control Access	Compliance assessments prevent violations. Communication ensures policy adherence. Access control restricts sensitive data handling.
Infrastructure	Natural disasters (earthquakes, floods, hurricanes, wildfires)	Assess, Respond, Communicate & Record	Risk assessments help plan for disaster resilience. Response mechanisms ensure safety. Communication coordinates emergency actions.
	Sabotage	Detect, Control Access, Respond	Detection tools identify tampering. Strict access control prevents unauthorized modifications. Rapid response minimizes damage.
	Terrorism	Deter, Control Access, Delay, Respond	Visible deterrence reduces targeting risk. Strong access control and barriers delay attackers. Response measures neutralize threats.
	Cyber-physical attacks on industrial control systems	Detect, Control Access, Respond, Communicate & Record	Cybersecurity controls prevent unauthorized access. Detection tools identify anomalies, and response teams mitigate damage.
	Power outages	Assess, Respond, Communicate & Record	Risk assessments ensure backup power solutions. Response teams restore functionality, and communication keeps stakeholders informed.
	Telecommunications failures	Assess, Respond, Communicate & Record	Assessments identify critical vulnerabilities. Response efforts restore connectivity. Communication maintains operational continuity.

(Continued)

TABLE 5.1 (Continued) Mapping Threat Type to Security Effect

Asset Type	Most Impactful Threat Category	Most Impactful Security Effect	Why This Effect Is Most Impactful
	Water supply contamination	Detect, Assess, Respond, Communicate & Record	Detection tools monitor contamination. Assessments confirm risks. Response teams neutralize threats. Communication informs affected individuals.
	Transportation network disruptions	Assess, Communicate & Record, Respond	Risk assessments identify alternative routes. Communication ensures real-time updates. Response teams mitigate delays.
	Supply chain failures	Assess, Detect, Respond, Communicate & Record	Risk assessments ensure supply chain resilience. Detection tools identify disruptions. Response teams implement contingency plans. Communication maintains business continuity.
Reputation & Brand	Disinformation campaigns	Detect, Assess, Communicate & Record	Early detection prevents false narratives from spreading. Assessing credibility helps determine response strategy. Communication counters misinformation.
	Regulatory violations	Assess, Respond, Communicate & Record	Proactive assessments ensure compliance. Rapid response mitigates damage. Communication maintains transparency with stakeholders.
	Major fraud incidents	Detect, Assess, Respond, Communicate & Record	Detection tools identify fraud early. Assessment ensures proper escalation. Response mitigates financial and reputational damage.

(Continued)

TABLE 5.1 (Continued) Mapping Threat Type to Security Effect

Asset Type	Most Impactful Threat Category	Most Impactful Security Effect	Why This Effect Is Most Impactful
	Social media attacks	Detect, Assess, Communicate & Record	Continuous monitoring detects attacks. Assessing their impact guides responses. Communication protects brand integrity.
	Activist targeting	Deter, Detect, Communicate & Record	Visible security measures deter attacks. Detection tools identify risks. Strategic communication mitigates reputational harm.
	Exposure of unethical business practices	Assess, Respond, Communicate & Record	Internal risk assessments prevent ethical lapses. Response teams address issues. Communication shapes public perception.
	Product recalls	Assess, Respond, Communicate & Record	Risk assessments ensure compliance. Rapid response removes unsafe products. Communication maintains consumer trust.
	Customer data mismanagement	Detect, Assess, Respond, Communicate & Record	Detection tools prevent data mishandling. Assessing breaches ensures proper reporting. Response teams implement corrective actions.
	Corporate scandal leaks	Assess, Respond, Communicate & Record	Internal assessments identify risks before leaks occur. Response strategies contain damage. Communication restores public confidence.
	Media manipulation	Detect, Assess, Communicate & Record	Media monitoring detects false narratives. Assessing intent ensures the proper response. Strategic communication counteracts misinformation.

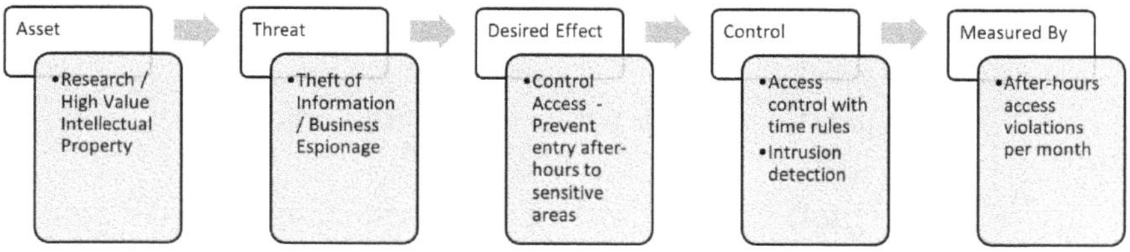

FIGURE 5.1 Mapping Effects-Based Security—Align Asset to Threat and Security Control with an Aligned Effect and a Way to Measure It

clear purpose in reducing risk. Figure 5.1 illustrates the path from the asset to the effect to the control.

Just as important, the table highlights common patterns across different threat types. Many risks can be mitigated by the same core set of effects, which allows organizations to invest in controls that provide protection on multiple fronts. This efficiency-driven approach ensures that budgets are spent strategically, maximizing both impact and sustainability.

While some threats will always require unique measures, most security challenges share overlapping needs. By designing multi-purpose solutions that address multiple effects simultaneously, organizations can achieve broader coverage, reduce redundancy, and develop programs that are both effective and cost-conscious.

Mapping Effects to Security Controls: Aligning Measures with Security Outcomes

Every security control contributes to one or more of the seven security effects described above. The key is selecting controls not for what they are, but for the outcomes they deliver. Each should be evaluated in terms of:

- Primary effect: the main security function it provides.
- Secondary/Tertiary effects: the additional benefits it delivers to risk mitigation.

By mapping controls to their effects in this way, security leaders can ensure investments are both effective and efficient. They can address the most pressing risks without creating waste or unnecessary redundancy.

Examples illustrate how this plays out in practice:

- A fence, gate, or locked door primarily controls access, but it also deters casual intruders and delays forced entry attempts.
- An emergency mass notification system primarily communicates urgent information, but it also supports response by directing people to safety.
- Security officers primarily provide response, but their visible presence deters threats and their judgment allows real-time assessment.
- CCTV cameras primarily detect and record incidents, but they also deter misconduct when placed in visible areas.

This approach enables leaders to compare options based on the actual effects they generate, rather than by product type or vendor promise.

Security Controls and Their Effects

Table 5.2 maps common security controls to their primary, secondary, and tertiary security effects, helping security leaders make targeted, evidence-based investment decisions. This framework keeps the focus on outcomes: how each control contributes to protection, and in what capacity.

- Primary effects (◆) drive strategy. Each control is assessed for the single most important outcome it delivers. This establishes its core purpose within the program and clarifies why it belongs in the security mix.
- Secondary effects (▲) extend value. Many controls support additional outcomes beyond their primary role(s). These secondary effects increase utility and strengthen risk mitigation when controls are layered.
- Tertiary effects (■) add flexibility. On their own, these contributions may not justify implementation. However, when combined with other measures, tertiary effects provide useful reinforcement and can even become primary in specific contexts.

TABLE 5.2 Mapping Security Controls to Effects Produced

Security Control	Deter	Control Access	Detect	Assess	Delay	Respond	Communicate & Record
Physical barriers & Access control ◆ = Primary effect | ▲ = Secondary effect | ■ = Tertiary effect							
Perimeter fencing	▲	◆			▲		
Barriers/bollards	▲	▲			◆		
Gated Entry/Access control perimeter	▲	◆			▲		
Turnstiles/Door locks access control interior	▲	◆	▲		▲		
Visitor management systems and controls	▲	◆	▲				■
Secure storage & Containers/safes	▲	◆			▲		
Identity & Biometric verification on control systems	▲	◆	▲	■	▲		■
Surveillance, Detection & Monitoring ◆ = Primary effect | ▲ = Secondary effect | ■ = Tertiary effect							
CCTV surveillance	■		◆	◆			◆
Intrusion detection system	■	▲	◆			▲	◆
Security lighting	▲		◆				
Alarm systems	◆					▲	◆
Automated security robotics & AI-based systems			◆	▲		▲	◆

(Continued)

TABLE 5.2 (Continued) Mapping Security Controls to Effects Produced

Security Control	Deter	Control Access	Detect	Assess	Delay	Respond	Communicate & Record
Remote video surveillance units			◆	▲		▲	◆
Security Personnel & Response ◆ = Primary effect | ▲ = Secondary effect | ■ = Tertiary effect							
On-site security personnel	◆	▲	◆	◆	▲	◆	◆
Canine detection services	◆	■	◆	▲		◆	
Emergency notification system				▲		▲	◆
Security operations center (SOC)			◆	◆		▲	◆
Cybersecurity & Information Protection ◆ = Primary effect | ▲ = Secondary effect | ■ = Tertiary effect							
Cybersecurity personnel			◆	◆	▲	◆	◆
Cyber access controls (MFA, Firewalls)	▲	◆	▲		▲		▲
Automated threat intelligence platforms	▲		◆	◆		▲	▲
Secure communication networks (Encryption, etc.)		▲			◆		◆
TSCM & Electronic surveillance protection (Bug sweeps, counterintelligence)		▲	◆		■		◆

(Continued)

TABLE 5.2 (Continued) Mapping Security Controls to Effects Produced

Security Control	Deter	Control Access	Detect	Assess	Delay	Respond	Communicate & Record
Policies, Training & Intelligence ◆ = Primary effect | ▲ = Secondary effect | ■ = Tertiary effect							
Security policies & procedures	■	■	■	◆		▲	▲
Background checks & employee vetting	▲	■	◆	◆		▲	
Security awareness & training programs		■	▲	▲		◆	◆
Business continuity & crisis response plans			▲	▲		◆	▲
Threat monitoring (Global threat intelligence)			◆	◆			▲
Supply chain security & Logistics tracking			◆	◆		▲	▲

Choosing the Right Security Measures for Maximum Impact and Value

Once threats are mapped to effects, the next challenge is selecting the measures that make the best use of limited resources. Without disciplined planning, security investments may be spread across too many options with not enough impact. ESRM + EBS provides the discipline by requiring that every control be evaluated for both effectiveness and efficiency before it is adopted. The goal is to assemble the right mix of people, processes, and technology that together provide the greatest protection for the business.

Prioritizing High-Value Security Controls

Not all controls provide equal value. Some deliver broad coverage across multiple effects, while others address only a narrow threat at high cost. When selecting controls, prioritize those that:

- Deliver multiple security effects—Controls that serve more than one purpose provide higher value. For example, security officers deter threats through visible presence, detect suspicious behavior, assess unfolding situations, and respond directly to incidents.
- Address the most probable and impactful threats—Limited budgets must focus on the scenarios most likely to occur and those that would be most damaging if they did. Access control that blocks unauthorized access to a sensitive research area is a choice that has a higher likelihood of daily impact than a rarely used specialty sensor, such as gunshot detection, that only applies to what is often an unlikely hazard.
- Complement existing security measures—Strong programs look for gaps rather than duplications. If CCTV already provides excellent visibility, the better investment may be improved analytics or incident reporting rather than adding more cameras to the same coverage area.
- Maximize technology's role in cost reduction—Automated monitoring, alerting, or AI-assisted analysis reduces repetitive workload and frees personnel to concentrate on high-value decisions.
- Scale with business needs—Modular solutions, such as access control platforms that can be expanded across multiple facilities, offer long-term adaptability, whereas fixed or standalone devices may quickly become obsolete.

- Demonstrate a clear return on investment—The strongest controls measurably reduce risk exposure relative to their cost. For instance, intrusion detection tied to rapid response provides clear, defensible value compared to a cosmetic feature with little practical impact.
- Account for maintenance requirements—A control with low upfront costs can still create long-term strain. Systems that require constant software patching, specialized service contracts, or heavy energy use may be less efficient than alternatives that achieve the same effect more sustainably.

By applying these criteria, security leaders can focus on measures that deliver the most protection per dollar spent, while ensuring the program is both resilient and financially sustainable.

Pro Tip: Not every risk requires a new tool. Sometimes, a well-crafted policy delivers more value than a high-cost solution.

Effects-Based Design in Action

To see how these criteria play out in real decisions, we can map different assets and threats to the effects they require and the controls that deliver them. The exercise illustrates how the same measure can be applied across multiple situations.

Asset: **People**

- Threat: **Assault**
- Needed Effects: Detect, Respond
- Potential Controls:
  - CCTV Surveillance: Detect ◆, Assess ◆, Communicate & Record ◆
  - On-Site Security Personnel: Respond ◆, Detect ▲, Communicate & Record ◆
  - Alarm Systems: Detect ◆, Respond ▲

Asset: **Executive Leadership**

- Threat: Targeted Threats Against Executives (including active assailant scenarios)
- Needed Effects: Deter, Control Access, Detect, Respond

- Potential Controls:
  - On-Site Security Personnel: Deter ◆, Detect ▲, Respond ◆, Communicate & Record ◆
  - Identity & Biometric Verification on Control Systems: Control Access ◆, Detect ▲, Communicate & Record ■
  - CCTV Surveillance: Detect ◆, Assess ◆, Communicate & Record ◆

Asset: **Manufacturing Equipment**

- Threat: **Sabotage**
- Needed Effects: Detect, Control Access, Respond
- Potential Controls:
  - Intrusion Detection System: Detect ◆, Control Access ▲, Respond ◆, Communicate & Record ◆
  - Turnstiles/Door Locks (Interior Access): Control Access ◆, Detect ▲, Delay ▲
  - Business Continuity & Crisis Response Plans: Respond ◆,
  - CCTV Surveillance: Detect ◆, Assess ◆, Communicate & Record ◆
  - On-Site Security Personnel: Respond ◆, Detect ▲, Assess ◆

Asset: **Reputation & Brand**

- Threat: Social Media Attacks
- Needed Effects: Detect, Assess, Communicate & Record
- Potential Controls:
  - Automated Threat Intelligence Platforms: Detect ◆, Assess ◆, Communicate & Record ▲
  - Security Policies & Procedures: Assess ◆, Communicate & Record ▲, Detect ■
  - Business Continuity & Crisis Response Plans: Assess ▲, Respond ◆, Communicate & Record ▲
  - Secure Communication Networks (Encryption, etc.): Communicate & Record ◆, Assess ■

Notice how CCTV surveillance recurs across scenarios. In an assault case, it serves as a primary detection tool, while in executive protection, it assumes a supporting role alongside deterrence and access control. Similarly, on-site security personnel span multiple contexts: they deter and respond in executive threats, assess incidents in sabotage attempts, and act as the decisive response in assaults. Even policies and crisis plans extend beyond paper: in sabotage, they guide response and continuity, while in brand attacks, they structure communication and protect reputation.

By mapping controls in this way, you can identify which measures consistently deliver value across a wide range of asset–threat combinations. These multi-effect tools "punch above their weight," sometimes taking the lead, other times reinforcing other layers.

This is the essence of an efficient ESRM + ESB approach: build first around the measures that provide outcomes across domains, then fill specific gaps with targeted controls. The result is a layered, adaptable program demonstrably aligned with business priorities.

Measuring and Validating Security Effects

Designing a program around effects is only half the job. Security leaders also need to determine whether the chosen controls are delivering the expected outcomes. Validation ensures that effectiveness and efficiency are not assumed, but proven.

As discussed in Chapter 2, baselining and measuring risk exposure is essential to knowing whether new controls change the picture. Without a baseline, improvements in detection speed, response time, or incident reduction cannot be demonstrated. Likewise, as Chapter 6 will explain, continuous monitoring and performance metrics are essential for sustaining a mature program over time.

There are several ways to validate whether a control is achieving its intended effect:

- Testing effectiveness—Penetration tests, red team exercises, and tabletop scenarios expose whether deterrence, detection, or response functions actually hold under pressure.[8]
- Monitoring performance—Data from access logs, incident reports, and system alerts can confirm whether controls are working as intended or drifting over time.
- Comparing against baselines—Establishing a pre-control benchmark allows leaders to track measurable improvements in outcomes.
- Gathering feedback—Employees and front-line officers can often identify where a process is failing or where a tool is slowing operations unnecessarily.

Validation is not about proving perfection. It is about understanding threat, identifying gaps, understanding residual risk, and demonstrating to leadership that every measure is accountable. A control that cannot show a measurable effect quickly becomes a liability, either wasting resources or creating a false sense of security. The principles of continual improvement, explored in Chapter 6, build directly on this process, ensuring that validation becomes part of ongoing governance rather than a one-time exercise.

Layering Security: The Power of Combined Effects

Security is most effective when multiple effects reinforce one another. No single control or effect can mitigate every threat on its own, which is why Defense-in-Depth (DiD) strategies are essential.

DiD refers to the practice of layering complementary security measures so that if one fails, another compensates.[9] This philosophy has long roots: it was used in military fortifications, later adapted in cybersecurity, and now stands as a guiding principle across physical and organizational security.[10] The central idea is simple: a determined adversary should never encounter a single point of failure that, once bypassed, opens unrestricted access to critical assets.

In practice, this layered approach acknowledges that every control can fail through human error, technical malfunction, or simple chance. By overlapping effects, organizations increase the odds that a weakness in one layer is caught by another. The result is a program that is both more resilient and more credible to executives, who understand that risk can never be entirely eliminated, only managed.

Defense-in-Depth across Domains

DiD is not limited to one type of risk. The same layered logic applies whether the challenge is physical or digital, human or systemic. Every control can fail. Doors can be forced, credentials can be stolen, technology can malfunction, and people can make mistakes. Resilient programs accept that reality and plan for it by overlapping protective effects.

Consider how a determined adversary might attempt to breach both a physical facility wall and a digital barrier. In each case, the attacker must confront a series of obstacles: visible deterrents, restricted access, detection systems, and response mechanisms. Even if one measure falters, another is ready to slow progress or stop the intrusion altogether. Layers of effects shape each encounter, and together those effects create a system that is far stronger than the sum of its parts.

TABLE 5.3 Comparing Defense-in-Depth Across Domains

Security Effect	Physical Intrusion Example	Cyber/Insider Threat Example
Deter	Security signage, visible patrols, and lighting discourage attempts.	Insider threat policies and awareness training discourage misconduct.
Control Access	Locked doors, gates, and biometric scanners restrict entry.	Role-based access limits who can view or download sensitive files.
Detect	Motion sensors and CCTV alert security teams.	Automated alerts flag unusual account activity or data transfers.
Delay	Bollards, fencing, and reinforced doors slow intruders.	Multifactor authentication and encryption slow unauthorized access.
Assess	Security staff review camera feeds or alarms to confirm a threat.	SOC analysts evaluate alerts to confirm intent.
Respond	Security personnel or law enforcement intervene.	Accounts are suspended; IT, HR, and Legal act to contain the impact.
Communicate & Record	Alarms trigger notifications; video footage provides evidence.	Incident logs, system alerts, and case documentation support investigation.

Table 5.3 illustrates how the seven effects of security can play out in two very different contexts: a physical intrusion attempt and a cyber or insider threat scenario.

By comparing these two domains, it becomes clear that DiD is a universal principle. The specific controls vary, but the effects are consistent. A well-designed program ensures that, regardless of where an adversary attempts to penetrate, whether through a physical barrier or a digital system, they encounter multiple layers of resistance that make success difficult, slow, and costly.

How Combining Multiple Effects Strengthens Security

Some security measures naturally deliver several effects at once, which makes them especially valuable in a DiD program. These high-impact controls increase coverage while reducing redundancy, ensuring that every dollar spent works across multiple risks.

- Security personnel provide perhaps the clearest example. Their presence deters misconduct, they detect and assess suspicious activity in real time, they respond directly to

incidents, and they record observations for later analysis. Few other measures combine so many protective effects.
- CCTV and surveillance systems do more than detect incidents. They allow security teams to assess events as they unfold, provide recorded evidence for investigations, and deter unwanted behavior when cameras are visible.
- Cybersecurity firewalls and access controls prevent unauthorized entry, detect anomalies in traffic, and delay intruders through multifactor authentication or layered defenses.
- Alarms and intrusion detection systems identify incidents, trigger assessments, summon responders, and generate records that strengthen investigations and compliance.
- Emergency notification systems contribute both to immediate response and to communication, guiding people to safety while keeping leadership informed.

By emphasizing multi-effect solutions, security leaders can achieve stronger protection with fewer tools. This does not mean doing more with less; it means doing more with the same resources by choosing controls that serve multiple functions simultaneously.

Effects-based implementation ensures that investments are effective in mitigating risk and efficient in sustaining operations. When threats evolve, multi-effect controls provide the flexibility to adapt, proving their worth repeatedly.

For executives, this approach provides clear value. It shows that the security program is designed for resilience, efficiency, and adaptability, rather than for activity alone. Controls can be justified in business terms. Each one delivers multiple outcomes, aligns with risk priorities, and provides a strong return on every dollar spent. This framing lays the groundwork for conversations with leadership about program maturity, resource requirements, and long-term strategy.

Key Takeaways from Chapter 5

- Start with the effect. Every control should be tied to a clear outcome, rather than being chosen for its appearance or novelty.
- Balance impact with cost. The strongest programs reduce risk while staying sustainable for the business.
- Layer for resilience. DiD ensures that if one measure fails, others still provide protection.

- Choose multi-effect controls. Measures that deliver several outcomes, such as trained personnel, provide the best return.
- Leverage policy as well as technology. Sometimes a procedure or standard delivers more value than an expensive tool.

Security Leader Toolkit: Chapter 5

ESRM Implementation Checklist

- Have I introduced the seven core effects (deter, control access, detect, delay, assess, respond, communicate & record) to my stakeholders?
- Have I mapped threat types to the effects that provide the strongest mitigation?
- Have I identified controls in place that achieve multiple effects (e.g., access control that both delays and records)?
- Have I validated whether existing controls are still functioning as intended, or if "control drift" has set in?
- Have I documented the business case for chosen controls, showing risk reduction and resource alignment?
- Have I ensured that residual risk after mitigation is visible and acceptable to leadership?

Control Layering Worksheet (Template)

Use this template to design layered mitigations across multiple effects for each prioritized risk.

Asset	Threat	Desired Security Effects (Choose from 7)	Controls in Place	Additional Controls Needed	Notes/ Residual Risk
Example: Data Center	Ransomware	Control Access, Detect, Respond	MFA for admin accounts (control access)	Endpoint monitoring (detect), IR playbook (respond)	Residual risk: vendor patch cycles
Example: Executive Suite	Workplace Violence	Deter, Control Access, Delay, Respond	Guard presence (all effects), ID badges (control access)	Panic alarms (respond), lockdown drills (delay)	Residual risk: reliance on officer response time

How to Use It

1. Pick one critical asset and its most relevant threat.
2. Select the effects that matter most (from the seven).
3. Document what controls already exist.
4. Add any new controls needed to strengthen layers.
5. Note the residual risk that remains even with controls in place.

Notes

1 RAND Corporation, *Effects-Based Operations: A Grand Challenge for the Analytical Community* (Santa Monica, CA: RAND Corporation, 2001), https://www.rand.org/content/dam/rand/pubs/monograph_reports/2006/MR1477.pdf.

2 David S. Fadok, *John Boyd and John Warden: Air Power's Quest for Strategic Paralysis* (Maxwell Air Force Base, AL: Air University Press, 1995), https://media.defense.gov/2017/Dec/27/2001861508/-1/-1/0/T_0029_FADOK_BOYD_AND_WARDEN.PDF.

3 National Protective Security Authority (NPSA), *Protecting Your Assets*, accessed July 2025, https://www.npsa.gov.uk/protecting-your-assets.

4 CyberArk, "What Is Defense in Depth?" *CyberArk*, accessed August 25, 2025, https://www.cyberark.com/what-is/defense-in-depth/.

5 Thomas L. Norman, *Risk Analysis and Security Countermeasure Selection*, 2nd ed. (Boca Raton, FL: CRC Press, 2016).

6 Based on personal conversations with Noah Price, Paul Mercer, John Petruzzi, and General William J. Walker, conducted by the author over the course of professional engagements.

7 Thomas L. Norman, *Integrated Security Systems Design*, 2nd ed. (Waltham, MA: Butterworth-Heinemann, 2012).

8 NIST, *Security and Privacy Controls for Information Systems and Organizations*, NIST Special Publication 80053 Revision 5 (Gaithersburg, MD: National Institute of Standards and Technology, 2020), control CA8, https://csf.tools/reference/nist-sp-800-53/r5/ca/ca-8/.

9 National Institute of Standards and Technology, *Security and Privacy Controls for Information Systems and Organizations*, NIST Special Publication 800–53, Revision 5 (Gaithersburg, MD: NIST, 2020), Control PL-8; ASIS International, *Physical Asset Protection*, 2nd ed. (Alexandria, VA: ASIS International, 2018).

10 U.S. Nuclear Regulatory Commission, "Defense in Depth History," Last modified August 23, 2018, https://www.nrc.gov/reading-rm/basic-ref/students/history-101/defense-in-depth.html.

SECTION 2
CLOSE AND TRANSITION

Section 2 explored how the three guiding questions of ESRM provide a structured way to turn strategy into action. Chapter 3 showed how security begins with identifying the assets that matter most to the business, including intangible ones such as data, brand reputation, and customer trust. Chapter 4 demonstrated that those assets face very different threats, each shaped by intent, capability, and organizational vulnerability. Chapter 5 translated this analysis into practice, showing how security leaders can align controls to effects, layer protections, and make investments that deliver both effectiveness and efficiency.

Taken together, these chapters remind us that acting in ways that are misaligned with business reality can derail a security program. Overvaluing physical assets while ignoring intellectual property, obsessing over a single visible threat while overlooking others, or buying impressive controls that do little to mitigate real vulnerabilities are all common errors that waste resources without reducing risk.

Field Lesson: Misaligned Priorities, Missed Protection

The Situation

A global technology company was preparing for the major product launch of a brand-new piece of hardware, which they expected to leapfrog the competition. Leadership approved a significant

DOI: 10.4324/9781003711346-10

budget to "lock down" the corporate campus and reassure investors. Security upgrades included expansions to the perimeter fence, biometric access to ultra-sensitive areas, and expanded guard coverage at the main entrance. The improvements were visible, expensive, and applauded in the boardroom.

The Overlooked Risks

While attention was fixed on the campus perimeter, critical vulnerabilities inside the business went unaddressed. Development servers storing unreleased product designs were accessible to too many contractors. No clear policies governed how sensitive data could be printed, shared, or taken offsite, and while entry was heavily controlled, there was limited outbound screening of personnel. Additionally, the public relations team had no monitoring in place for disinformation campaigns already circulating online.

The Consequences

- A contractor with legitimate access downloaded design files and leaked them to a competitor.
- Confusion in the market drove investors to question the company's ability to protect its intellectual property.
- The security budget was spent on measures that, while extensive, did little to address the actual risks that materialized.

What ESRM Would Have Changed

1. **What are we trying to protect?**
   Beyond the campus itself, the product designs and brand reputation were the assets most critical to business success.
2. **What does it truly need protection from?**
   Insider misuse, uncontrolled data sharing, and reputational manipulation, not forced entry through the front gate.
3. **How can we most effectively and efficiently protect it?**
   Role-based access controls for servers, secure printing policies, contractor credential audits, and social media threat monitoring—all at a lesser cost than the perimeter investment.

The Lesson

Security programs fail when priorities are established based on fear, visibility, or executive preference rather than risk. ESRM shifts the focus back to assets, threats, and vulnerabilities, ensuring that resources are targeted at what truly matters. By grounding decisions in outcomes, organizations avoid the trap of misaligned priorities and deliver protection where it counts most.

From Effects to Strategy

By grounding decisions in effects, security leaders ensure that the measures adopted in an ESRM program are not only technically sound but also strategically aligned with business priorities. The value lies in the clarity of this structure: risk is assessed, priorities are established, and actions are directly tied to measurable outcomes.

With this, ESRM moves from concept to practice. Security is no longer defined by the tools an organization owns, but by the outcomes it achieves.

Section 3 takes the next step: sustaining this alignment over time through continual improvement, governance, and culture.

Section 3

SUSTAINING ESRM—IMPROVEMENT, OVERSIGHT, AND CULTURE

With the core ESRM questions answered, the next step is to ensure that Enterprise Security Risk Management (ESRM) endures over time. Security cannot remain effective if treated as a one-time project; it requires a cycle of reflection, adjustment, and reinforcement. Section 3 examines how to maintain ESRM programs in alignment with shifting business priorities, evolving threats, and the daily behaviors that determine whether security principles are successful or ineffective.

In Chapters 6 and 7, we examine the disciplines that sustain ESRM beyond its initial implementation. Chapter 6 focuses on continual improvement, showing how structured reviews, metrics, and after-action learning ensure controls remain effective and relevant. Chapter 7 explores culture, illustrating how values, incentives, and leadership behaviors integrate ESRM into everyday decision-making throughout the enterprise. Together, these chapters emphasize that ESRM is not just a framework to be built, but a system to be lived.

DOI: 10.4324/9781003711346-11

Here's how the following two chapters extend the ESRM model:

- **Chapter 6: Continual Improvement Strategies**
  Shows how to monitor controls, measure effectiveness, and adapt programs through structured feedback loops, ensuring resilience in a changing environment.
- **Chapter 7: Required for Success—Making the Shift to a Security-Driven Culture**
  Explains how employee mindsets, incentives, and leadership modeling transform ESRM from a strategy on paper into a daily practice that drives resilience.

CHAPTER 6

Continual Improvement Strategies

Enterprise Security Risk Management (ESRM) cannot be treated as a one-time project. It requires a continuous, evolving approach that must adapt to new internal and external threats, shifting business environments, and the critical lessons that emerge from both successes and failures in the security program. Just as in other cycle-driven disciplines, such as Six Sigma's quality management or ITIL's continual service improvement (CSI) cycle, the work of implementing ESRM never reaches a permanent finish line. These disciplines are built on the understanding that excellence is a pursuit, not a destination.

Six Sigma,[1] for example, emphasizes reducing variation and defects by continuously measuring performance, identifying inefficiencies, and applying data-driven corrections to improve outcomes. The underlying philosophy is that no process is ever truly perfect; there are always hidden weaknesses waiting to be uncovered and improved.

Likewise, ITIL's CSI cycle[2] is based on the principle of aligning technology services with the evolving needs of the business. It requires organizations to monitor performance, review outcomes, and implement enhancements on a regular cadence, not just in reaction to failure. CSI stresses that value is created by constantly asking: *Is this service still meeting the business's needs today, and how can it be improved for tomorrow?*

These philosophies map easily into the security domain and are examples of highly adopted business frameworks that require continuous improvement to stay relevant. Risk-led security programs under the ESRM methodology cannot rely on past successes,

DOI: 10.4324/9781003711346-12

unreviewed implementations, or static policies. We must continuously measure, assess, identify gaps, and refine security controls to remain effective. A security program that ignores this improvement mindset is in danger of becoming the equivalent of any once-innovative business process that has calcified over time; still nominally in place on paper, but quietly drifting out of alignment with its environment.

A static security program is like a car that never gets maintenance. The tires may hold air, and the engine may still run, but small failures, like worn brakes, an oil leak, or a dead headlight, compound over time until the vehicle becomes unsafe or breaks down entirely. In the same way, controls and processes that are never updated can lull organizations into a false sense of security, masking vulnerabilities that only reveal themselves when an incident occurs.

Continuous improvement of security is a factor in every industry. In healthcare, regulatory requirements and patient safety expectations are constantly evolving, forcing security programs to keep pace with both compliance and care delivery. In retail, theft tactics evolve season by season, requiring fresh deterrents and investigative approaches. In banking and financial services, the threat landscape shifts rapidly as cybercriminals devise new forms of fraud, account takeover, and digital intrusion, while regulators continually raise the bar for data protection and anti-money laundering controls. In manufacturing and logistics, global supply chains introduce daily risks—from cargo theft and counterfeit parts to geopolitical disruptions and natural disasters—that demand flexible, resilient security solutions. In critical infrastructure, the stakes are higher still, with nation-state adversaries continually developing new ways to probe and disrupt essential services. Across all sectors, the risk landscape is dynamic, and security leaders and teams must be equally dynamic to remain effective.

This chapter explores ways you can sustain and strengthen your organization's ESRM program through structured incident response, ongoing risk assessments, updates in response to change, and deliberate, embedded cycles of evolution. The goal is to create a security program that expects change, then adapts to it, and grows stronger with every iteration. By treating continual improvement as a built-in discipline, part of the ongoing ESRM cycle, security leaders can ensure that security remains aligned with business priorities, responsive to emerging threats, and resilient in the face of disruption. This mindset sets the stage for understanding why the ESRM cycle never truly stops, and why improvement must be woven into every phase of security management.

The ESRM Cycle: Improvement Never Stops

While understanding *why* continual improvement is essential, it's equally (or more) important to know *how* that improvement happens inside the ESRM framework. ESRM is designed as a continuous cycle. It isn't something you finish and put away. Each pass through the cycle brings security leaders back to the same three core questions:

1. What am I trying to protect?
2. What does it truly need to be protected from?
3. How can we most effectively—and efficiently—protect it?

When asked regularly, these questions can expose how quickly conditions shift. Assets gain or lose criticality, threats adapt and evolve, and mitigation strategies that made complete sense when implemented may no longer be cost-effective or aligned with the business. The ongoing discipline of ESRM in a real-world program is in returning to these questions again and again, ensuring that assumptions are revalidated and priorities remain current.

The true strength of risk-based security, though, lies in what needs to happen next. The fourth, often overlooked step is reflection and improvement. Deliberately evaluating whether the chosen controls and strategies delivered the outcomes they were meant to provide. Did the access control *actually* prevent unauthorized entry? Did the awareness training *measurably* reduce phishing clicks? Did the incident response plan restore operations within the *expected* time? Reflection closes the loop, turning each cycle into a learning process rather than an end state.

This post-mitigation reflection is where the most significant long-term value is created for a security program, because it tests whether our controls and strategies are working as intended. When the cycle functions as designed, it becomes a continuous conversation between the business, the risk environment, and the security team. And while asking these questions repeatedly is part of the discipline, the real value comes from testing whether our answers still hold.

Monitoring Security Control Effectiveness

Improvement begins with the basics. A security control's job is to achieve a specific protective effect. That might be deterrence, access control, detection, or response. However, simply having the control in place doesn't guarantee that it's delivering the effect you expect. Two years past installation, a badge reader might still lock and unlock doors, but if its database includes hundreds of active credentials for former employees, it's failing in its primary role of restricting access. A detection tool that works 95% of the time but has false positives that overwhelm the response team may technically "function" but still fail to support effective mitigation.

Continuous improvement requires us to ask (over and over) a crucial question:

Are our controls still doing what we need them/designed them to do?

To answer that question, every control needs a baseline that allows the security team to understand and document:

- The threat it is meant to address
- The standard of performance it must meet
- The way its performance will be measured.

Over time, controls must be reassessed for technical function and continued relevance to the current environment. Without this discipline, organizations risk "control drift," where measures that once made sense slowly lose effectiveness or alignment until they provide little real protection.

Pro Tip: Don't mistake activity for progress. If a control isn't still tied to an actual risk, it isn't improvement.

Identifying Signs of Control Drift

Examples of control drift can be found in almost every area of security:

- A video surveillance system that still records, but whose expired warranty means critical updates are no longer available, leaving it vulnerable to cyber intrusion.

- Evacuation drills that follow the same routine year after year, even though floor layouts, staffing levels, or tenant populations have changed, making the plan less effective in practice.
- Overgrown landscaping that blocks camera sightlines or creates hiding spots near entrances, undermining both deterrence and detection.
- A visitor management process that logs entries faithfully but is rarely cross-checked against watch lists, leaving a false sense of security.

Measuring effectiveness should include both quantitative and qualitative methods. Quantitative approaches include metrics such as error rates, uptime, and compliance with service-level agreements. For example, tracking the percentage of successful badge swipes at access points can highlight whether a system is functioning as expected. But qualitative feedback is equally important. Interviews with staff, security officers, and end users can reveal whether a control is actually changing behavior or if workarounds are undermining it. For instance, employees propping open secured doors to move equipment may indicate that a physical barrier, while technically functional, is operationally ineffective.

Table 6.1 illustrates examples of common categories of security controls, the protective effects they are designed to achieve, methods for evaluating their effectiveness, and warning signs that signal drift. These examples are not exhaustive, but they provide a framework that you can adapt to your organization's unique environment.

INSIGHT: TABLE 6.1—FRAMEWORK FOR IDENTIFYING CONTROL EFFECTIVENESS DRIFT

This framework serves as a reminder that controls should be evaluated by their *function* rather than their form. Too often, organizations report on whether a control exists rather than whether it is doing the job it was meant to do. Security leaders also need to recognize that drift doesn't usually happen all at once. Controls degrade slowly, with slips like an expired credential here and a blocked camera sightline there, until their protective value has eroded almost entirely. Table 6.1 helps organizations examine both the technical aspect (is the control functional?) and the operational aspect (is it working as intended in practice?).

TABLE 6.1 Example Framework for Identifying Control Effectiveness Drift

Category of Control	Intended Function	Evidence of Effectiveness	Signs of Drift/ Concern
Access controls	Restrict entry and movement to authorized individuals	Audit logs, % of invalid attempts denied, credential reviews	Large number of inactive/expired credentials still active; tailgating incidents
Surveillance & detection	Monitor and record activity in key areas	System uptime reports, usable footage, alarm response times	Cameras offline or obscured; excessive false alarms overwhelming staff
Emergency preparedness	Enable safe response to crises (fire, active shooter, natural disaster)	Drill completion rates, after-action reviews, compliance checks	Staff confusion, outdated floor plans, lack of participation in drills
Visitor & third-party management	Track, screen, and control external individuals and vendors	Visitor logs reconciled with access lists; % of ID verifications completed	Bypassed check-in processes; logs maintained but never analyzed
Training & awareness	Reduce human error and improve response to threats	Phishing test results, knowledge assessments, post-training surveys	Staff ignoring procedures, low training completion, outdated content

Finally, it's also critical to remain mindful of common blind spots that can erode effectiveness over time. One of the most frequent is overreliance on vendor assurances. A manufacturer or service provider may certify that a system meets all technical specifications, but only operational testing within your own environment will reveal whether it performs as intended under real-world conditions. Another blind spot lies in overlooking integration points between controls. A camera may record flawlessly, but if its footage is never cross-checked against access logs, a key layer of deterrence and investigative value is lost. Finally, many organizations fall into the trap of assuming that "no news" is a sign of success. The absence of reported incidents does not necessarily mean a control is effective; it may simply indicate that a particular threat has not yet materialized, or, more concerning, that it has gone undetected.

By layering these perspectives, combining technical checks, operational validation, blind-spot checks, and cultural feedback, organizations can build a more accurate picture of control effectiveness. This, in turn, fuels the continual improvement cycle, ensuring that the security program both maintains controls and actively tests and adapts them against evolving risks.

Measuring Control Effectiveness Against the Baseline

As discussed, measuring control effectiveness begins with a baseline; however, sustaining that effectiveness requires a consistent method for rating and revisiting performance. In Chapter 4, we introduced the control scoring matrix as a tool for objectively evaluating vulnerabilities. Scores range from optimal performance (1) to absent or ineffective (5). That model helps with initial prioritization. With continued use, it can also provide a common language for measuring whether controls remain effective over time.

When applied as part of security improvement, the scoring matrix becomes a monitoring mechanism. Instead of simply asking whether a control exists, security leaders can ask: *Where does this control sit today on the spectrum of effectiveness, and has its score changed since the last review?*

A camera that scored a solid "2" last year because it was functional but lacked redundancy may now deserve a wavering "3" if it has become outdated and can't be patched, or a stellar "1" if it has been upgraded with analytics and monitoring integration. These shifts tell a story about the control itself, and about your organization's evolving risk posture.

To make these reviews actionable, you can connect control scores to Key Performance Indicators (KPIs) that can be tracked and reported regularly. Table 6.2 offers examples of the kinds of dashboard metrics that translate technical evaluations into business insights.

Keep in mind, though, controls don't drift in a vacuum; changes in the business and the world around it constantly reshape their relevance. To keep pace, security leaders must scan both the organization itself and the world in which it operates.

Monitoring the Internal and External Environment

Keeping your security program within your organization's risk tolerance means staying attuned to changes in the environment. Internal changes, such as workforce shifts, reorganizations, or new business strategies, can significantly impact your security posture. Additionally, you need to monitor the external threat

TABLE 6.2 Example Dashboard KPIs

Example KPI	Why It Matters
% of controls mapped to current top 10 risk scenarios	Confirms that control resources are aligned to today's most pressing threats, not outdated or irrelevant ones.
% of controls with clear linkage to a documented mitigation strategy	Highlights strategic intent behind each control, reducing waste and ensuring every measure has a defined purpose.
% of controls outdated based on last review date (>1 year old)	Flags controls that may no longer reflect the current threat landscape, risk environment, or organizational structure.
% of controls passing technical or operational health checks	Identifies controls that are performing as intended, helping to prioritize remediation for those that are not.
MTBF (Mean Time Between Failure) for physical or technical controls	Provides insight into reliability and helps inform proactive maintenance and capital replacement planning.
% of controls with active maintenance plans or Service Level Agreements (SLAs)	Demonstrates long-term sustainability of controls and ensures accountability for upkeep through vendor or internal commitments.
% of controls tested against real-world incident scenarios (e.g., tabletop, red team, drills)	Shows whether controls function as expected under realistic conditions, not just in theory.
Average time to remediate a failed control	Tracks responsiveness to control degradation and highlights whether fixes are keeping pace with operational demands.
% of control owners submitting timely performance reports	Reinforces accountability and demonstrates whether monitoring is embedded in governance structures.

landscape, encompassing cyber tactics, geopolitical instability, and new forms of criminal innovation. A control applied a year ago may already be ineffective if it hasn't kept pace with these developments. Continuous improvement depends on deliberate, structured monitoring of both internal and external factors that influence risk. Monitoring needs to happen across multiple factors to keep pace with the environment.

Tracking New Business Models

When organizations grow through mergers, acquisitions, global expansion, or digital transformation, the asset landscape can change almost overnight. New facilities, employees, and technologies introduce fresh vulnerabilities, while integration pressures often stretch existing controls. A merger might consolidate physical offices but leave two parallel IT systems operating, creating duplicate access points for attackers. Expansion into new markets can expose the business to unfamiliar regulations, cultural norms, and geopolitical risks. To keep the security program relevant and in line with the organization's risk profile and tolerance, security leaders must proactively map how each business shift affects asset value, threat exposure, and resource prioritization, and re-baseline controls accordingly. Sadly, many organizations treat growth as "business as usual" and fail to reassess their security posture. This complacency is one of the fastest ways a program drifts out of step with reality.

Understanding Technology Adoption

From artificial intelligence and cloud adoption to Internet of Things (IoT) and Operational Technology (OT) integration, new technologies present both opportunities and risks. Remote work infrastructures, for instance, can extend an organization's attack surface far beyond traditional boundaries. Without intentional alignment, legacy controls may not cover the new environment. Consider the possibility of a firm deploying IoT sensors across its supply chain: the sensors improve efficiency, but potentially introduce thousands of potential cyber access points. A mature ESRM program evaluates these innovations for operational benefits and to understand how they reshape the threat landscape. Unfortunately, many organizations rely too heavily on vendor claims of security, only to discover later (after costly incidents occur) that integration testing and independent validation would have revealed hidden vulnerabilities.

Pro Tip: Never rely solely on vendor assurances. Make sure to test new technology in your environment to prove it works under real conditions.

Maintaining Cross-Department Collaboration

Security cannot operate in isolation. Effective ESRM requires ongoing collaboration with HR, IT, Legal, Compliance, Operations, and Communications. Each function owns assets and risks that intersect with security outcomes. Operations owns the risk of loss of product or service, HR manages insider threat risks,

Legal monitors regulatory obligations, and IT safeguards digital assets. By embedding security monitoring into these relationships, organizations ensure that security decisions reflect business priorities and regulatory mandates. More importantly, they create resilience across the enterprise. No single team holds all the company's risk knowledge, but together they form a complete picture. However, collaboration won't happen by default. Without structured forums like risk committees, cross-department reviews, or joint exercises, security can easily slip back into a silo and lose connection with the broader business.

Watching the Externals

External forces can reshape the risk landscape just as dramatically[3] as those inside the organization. A helpful framework for scanning the external environment is the PESTEL analysis, which includes Political, Economic, Social, Technological, Environmental, and Legal factors.[4] Political changes may alter the regulatory landscape or shift the security implications of operating in certain regions. Economic trends can affect crime rates or resource availability. Social movements may create reputational risks or civil unrest near company sites. Technological advances introduce both opportunities and new threats. Environmental issues, from extreme weather to climate-related migration, can strain security infrastructure. And evolving legal requirements, from data privacy laws to critical infrastructure mandates, can render existing controls inadequate or non-compliant instantly.

Organizations that monitor only the most recent crisis or today's headlines risk being blindsided by developments in other areas. Effective environmental monitoring necessitates scanning across all six PESTEL dimensions, even those that may seem less urgent, to ensure that nothing important is overlooked.

INSIGHT: TABLE 6.3—SCANNING THE EXTERNAL ENVIRONMENT WITH PESTEL

The PESTEL model expands environmental monitoring beyond the latest crisis or technical feed, reminding leaders that risks rarely emerge in isolation. By scanning across all six PESTEL categories, organizations build a broader view of how seemingly distant changes may converge on their operations. The key is discipline. Many companies overemphasize the "T" in PESTEL, tracking technological risks in detail, while neglecting social, political, or legal shifts that can be equally disruptive. The strength of this approach lies in its balance. It provides a framework that prevents blind spots and ensures scanning is systematic, not ad hoc. When applied consistently, PESTEL scanning helps security leaders identify weak signals early and bring a strategic perspective to leadership conversations.

Anticipating Future Threats

Continual improvement requires reacting to today's incidents *and* anticipating tomorrow's. This means applying structured foresight methods such as scenario analysis, tabletop simulations, and participation in industry threat-sharing groups (such as ISACs or ISAOs). For example, enterprises that monitored ransomware trends years ago and joined peer-sharing groups were able to pre-stage recovery playbooks, while others that ignored early warnings paid millions in ransom and lost public trust. But foresight must be disciplined: collecting every available threat feed without context can overwhelm teams and dilute focus. The key is turning intelligence into actionable insight, not accumulating more data for its own sake.

TABLE 6.3 Scanning the External Environment with PESTEL

Factor	Relevance to Security	Examples of Impact
Political	Government stability, policy changes, conflict, regulation	Shifts in export controls; instability affecting global operations
Economic	Market conditions, inflation, resource availability	Increased theft during downturns; supply chain delays from cost pressures
Social	Demographics, activism, public sentiment	Civil protests near facilities; reputational risks from social movements
Technological	Innovation, adoption rates, vulnerabilities	Rapid adoption of AI/IoT; new cyber exploits; obsolescence of legacy systems
Environmental	Climate, disasters, resource constraints	Extreme weather disrupting operations; increased costs for resilience
Legal	Laws, compliance mandates, liability frameworks	New privacy regulations; stricter reporting requirements for critical infrastructure

When the ESRM cycle becomes an integrated function of how the security function operates, it forms a continuous value loop. Each insight, incident, or change feeds into the next round of risk identification, prioritization, and mitigation. Constant adjustment is not a sign of uncertainty; it's a mark of maturity. Organizations that embrace this feedback cycle are more secure, more agile, and better positioned to navigate disruption. Of course, monitoring the landscape is only part of the effort. Another factor is how you monitor and how those insights are turned into action.

Methods for Effective Program Monitoring

In the previous section, we examined the factors that need to be monitored, including the internal and external forces that constantly reshape the security landscape. The next question is *how* to monitor those factors in a way that produces actionable insight rather than just more data. Organizations need structured methods that confirm whether controls are performing, reveal where they are not, and guide the next round of improvements.

Regular Risk Assessments

Risk assessments are key to security program monitoring. By regularly reevaluating asset criticality, threat likelihood, and control effectiveness, organizations can track how their risk profile evolves over time. Using the same scoring model across assessments enables long-term comparisons and trend analysis, making it possible to see whether risks are truly shrinking, growing, or simply shifting shape. A review, for example, might reveal that while theft incidents have declined due to improved access controls, the likelihood of cyber disruption has increased as operations have moved online. Without repeating assessments, such a shift would remain invisible until a disruption actually occurred.

Security Audits and Penetration Testing

Audits and penetration tests provide the reality check that every program needs. These activities go beyond paperwork reviews to actively probe the resilience of physical and cyber defenses. Physical walkthroughs may reveal that evacuation routes are blocked by furniture, or that turnstiles can be easily bypassed or jumped if a security officer is out of sight, while cyber red team exercises can uncover how easily attackers could move laterally once inside the network. A bank that believes its systems are "locked down" may discover through a penetration test that an overlooked integration point with a vendor system has created a backdoor for attackers, or that a physical access point can be accessed if a careless employee fails to fully latch a door or a magnetized switch is out of alignment. These exercises are not about assigning blame; they are about exposing vulnerabilities before adversaries do.

Threat Intelligence and Industry Benchmarking

Monitoring must also look outward. We looked at the factors of PESTEL above. Threat intelligence offers a forward-looking perspective by identifying the tactics, techniques, and procedures that adversaries employ across the industry. Participation in Information Sharing and Analysis Centers (ISACs) or Information Sharing and Analysis Organizations (ISAOs) allows companies to benefit from the collective experiences of their peers. Benchmarking against industry peers can also reveal whether a program is leading, lagging, or simply average in performance. An organization that compares itself against others in its sector might discover it spends less on security defense per facility than its peers, highlighting a potential exposure. Intelligence and benchmarking ensure that organizations are not blindsided by threats that are already visible to others.

RESOURCE

ISACS, ISAOS, AND GLOBAL INFORMATION-SHARING BODIES

Participation in industry-specific intelligence-sharing groups helps organizations stay ahead of emerging threats by pooling insights across peers. These groups allow members to share real-world incidents, emerging threat intelligence, and best practices that no single organization could see alone. Participation strengthens foresight, coordination, and resilience across industries.

INDUSTRY ISACS AND ISAOS

- **National Council of ISACs (U.S.):** Umbrella organization linking multiple sector-specific ISACs across critical infrastructure. Website: https://www.nationalisacs.org/
- **FS-ISAC (Financial Services, Global):** The largest international ISAC, sharing timely intelligence on cybercrime, fraud, and systemic risks in the financial sector. Website: https://www.fsisac.com/

- **A-ISAC (Aviation, Global):** Provides intelligence sharing on threats to airlines, airports, and aviation manufacturers. Website: https://www.a-isac.com/
- **H-ISAC (Health, Global):** Focused on healthcare providers, pharma, and medical device security. Website: https://h-isac.org/
- **E-ISAC (Electricity, North America):** Operated by NERC, shares grid-focused intelligence with utilities and regulators. Website: https://www.eisac.com/
- **Automotive ISAC (Automotive, Global):** Collaboration hub for automakers and suppliers on vehicle cybersecurity. Website: https://automotiveisac.com/
- **RH-ISAC (Retail & Hospitality, Global):** Shares threat intelligence across retail, restaurants, and hospitality organizations. Website: https://rhisac.org/
- **PT-ISAC (Public Transit, U.S.):** Supports threat and security information sharing across U.S. public transportation systems. Website: https://www.apta.com/
- **ONE-ISAC (Oil and Natural Energy, North America):** Shares threat intelligence among upstream, midstream, and downstream energy operators. Website: https://oneisac.org/

GOVERNMENT AND INTERNATIONAL BODIES

- **OSAC (Overseas Security Advisory Council, U.S. State Department):** Public–private partnership providing security risk reporting and guidance for U.S. organizations overseas. Website: https://www.osac.gov/
- **FIRST (Forum of Incident Response and Security Teams, Global):** International consortium of CSIRTs fostering global collaboration and response coordination. Website: https://www.first.org/
- **ENISA (European Union Agency for Cybersecurity, EU):** EU agency offering guidance, best practices, and coordinated cyber defense initiatives. Website: https://www.enisa.europa.eu/
- **NCSC (UK National Cyber Security Centre, UK):** Provides public and private sector organizations with actionable cyber defense intelligence and best practices. Website: https://www.ncsc.gov.uk/

Security Metrics and Key Performance Indicators

Monitoring metrics provides the necessary evidence that shows whether a security program is actually working. By converting raw monitoring data into actionable awareness, metrics enable leaders to identify trends and detect drift before a minor issue becomes a significant vulnerability.

Without metrics, monitoring remains anecdotal. With them, security teams can demonstrate impact, compare performance over time, and link improvements directly to reduced risk. Some of the most widely used include:

- Mean Time to Detect—Shows how quickly the organization identifies incidents, a leading indicator of detection capability.
- Mean Time to Respond—Measures the speed of containment and mitigation, reflecting the maturity of incident response.
- Recovery Time Objective—Defines the maximum acceptable downtime for critical systems and highlights resilience targets.
- Recovery Point Objective—Indicates how much data loss is tolerable, often setting expectations for backup and restoration.
- Access Control Validation Rates—Demonstrates whether authentication systems are functioning as intended by tracking successful versus denied attempts.
- Unresolved Policy Exceptions—Flags gaps between written standards and daily operations, signaling where compliance or practicality may be failing.
- Training Completion and Comprehension Scores—Gauge whether the workforce is both receiving and retaining essential security knowledge.

Monitoring Incidents and Residual Risk Remediation

Security programs in the real world operate under one unavoidable truth: Some risk will always remain.

As discussed in Chapter 4, residual risk refers to the level of exposure that persists even after mitigations have been applied.[5] Whether due to resource constraints, control limitations, or business tolerance, not every threat can be entirely eliminated, nor can every incident be prevented. Residual risk is also highly contextual. A manufacturing operation may tolerate greater exposure to cyber intrusion and delay updates if it means keeping critical systems continuously available for busy operational periods, while a bank will often set near-zero tolerance for data compromise due to regulatory scrutiny and reputational stakes. What counts as "acceptable" in one enterprise may be intolerable in another.

Because of this reality, every security program (ESRM or not) must include robust incident response capabilities. Beyond the immediate reactive capability to interrupt an incident as it occurs, these structured processes enable organizations to contain damage, protect assets, and recover quickly from security failures. Just as importantly, the way an organization responds becomes a key driver of continual improvement. Every breach, near miss, or crisis provides insight into how residual risk behaves in the real world, and where additional controls, training, or adjustments may be necessary.

Pro Tip: A near miss is free intelligence! Capture and act on it before it becomes tomorrow's full-blown incident.

When an incident occurs, response execution should follow predefined protocols while remaining adaptable to the specifics of the event. During an event, the primary goals are universal: minimize harm, safeguard life and assets, preserve evidence, and restore operations.

Once the immediate threat is contained, recovery begins. This phase focuses on restoring business functions, but needs to then go further in extracting strategic value from the incident. That value comes in the form of learning. Incidents are business disruptions. But they are *also* data points that reveal how risk manifests in practice. A phishing attack that slipped past filters highlights gaps in awareness and detection. An insider fraud scheme that went undetected for months shows the need for stronger monitoring and separation of duties. Each event, however unwelcome, provides clarity about how well the security program performs under real-world stress.

Post-Incident Reviews: Lessons Learned for Stronger Security

In a risk-based security model like ESRM, post-incident reviews utilize disruption to drive progress. Being a resilient organization doesn't mean you will never have an incident. What makes resilience is the act of learning from incidents and making a change. A structured review ensures that lessons learned become part of the ongoing ESRM cycle, closing the feedback loop between planning, implementation, response, and adjustment.

Importantly, reviews also reinforce an organization's stance on risk tolerance. As discussed in Chapter 2, different industries accept different levels of residual risk. Post-incident reviews provide leaders with the opportunity to assess whether their actual responses align with their stated tolerance—and to recalibrate if necessary.

Conducting an Effective Security Post-Incident Review

A well-conducted post-incident review should not be about finding fault with individuals. It's about uncovering the truth about your program's capacity to respond and creating clarity around future needs. The purpose is to understand the chain of events as accurately as possible, identify both strengths and weaknesses in the response, and translate those insights into practical improvements.[6] Reviews that devolve into finger-pointing often discourage candor and obscure the real lessons, while reviews that focus on facts and solutions foster trust and build resilience.

A proper review asks *what happened* and *why it happened in that particular way*. It examines how people, processes, and technology interacted under stress and whether those interactions aligned with established plans. For example, a review might highlight that while an intrusion was detected promptly, delays in escalating to decision-makers slowed the response. These are not failures of individuals but indicators of where procedures or training should be refined.

Equally important is who participates in the review. Limiting the discussion to the security team risks missing critical perspectives. A comprehensive review typically involves representatives from IT, facilities, human resources, legal, communications, and business operations. Any function that was affected by or contributed to the incident should be part of a review. Each brings a unique lens: HR may highlight gaps in employee readiness, IT may flag integration issues, and communications may point to delays in stakeholder messaging. This cross-functional approach prevents blind spots and ensures that recommendations are practical and aligned with business priorities.

Many organizations also designate a neutral facilitator to guide the review. This could be an internal audit professional, a risk manager, or an external consultant. The facilitator's role is to maintain an objective discussion, ensure that all voices are heard, and prevent the review from devolving into defensiveness or accusations. In particularly complex or high-impact cases, bringing in an outside observer can also add credibility and impartiality, which may be essential for leadership buy-in.

TABLE 6.4 Key Questions to Guide a Post-Incident Review

Question	Purpose
What happened?	Create a clear and factual timeline of the event. Identify the initiating event, all escalation points, and the resolution. Include perspectives from all stakeholders involved (security, IT, facilities, HR, communications, and leadership).
What went right?	Recognize which controls, procedures, or behaviors helped reduce harm or enabled a successful response. Capturing these successes validates investments and reinforces good practices.
What went wrong?	Identify breakdowns in detection, delays in response, communication gaps, or misalignment between teams. Pay special attention to signs of latent vulnerability that might have gone unnoticed until the incident occurred.
What should change?	Translate the findings into practical recommendations. This might include procedural revisions, new training requirements, policy changes, or the introduction of new technologies.

To maximize learning, the review should be formalized and repeatable, following a structured process rather than improvisation. Whether triggered by a real incident or a planned exercise, this discipline ensures consistency and comparability across events. Over time, a series of reviews can build a library of lessons learned, patterns of recurring vulnerabilities, and a record of how the security program has matured in response. Table 6.4 illustrates the kinds of guiding questions that make reviews both systematic and constructive.

INSIGHT: CREATING PSYCHOLOGICAL SAFETY IN REVIEWS

For post-incident reviews to be successful, people must feel safe in admitting mistakes or flagging problems. If individuals fear punishment, critical details will be withheld, and the organization will learn little. Encouraging candor requires leadership to explicitly frame reviews as opportunities to strengthen the system, rather than as a means to critique individuals. Some organizations use neutral facilitators to promote objectivity and open dialogue. Others anonymize specific feedback to allow brutal truths to surface. Whatever the method, the goal is to foster a culture where learning from failure is valued as highly as celebrating success.

After-Action Reports: A Tool for Embedding Lessons

Post-incident insights must be formally captured to have a lasting value. Verbal debriefs and informal discussions can spark good ideas in the moment, but without a written record, those lessons often fade or fail to reach the people who need them most. A well-structured After-Action Report (AAR) ensures that lessons are documented, with actions tracked, assigned, and acted upon. The AAR is the mechanism that turns an incident into an improvement.[7]

A consistent but straightforward structure makes AARs usable across different incident types, regardless of whether the event was a cyber breach, a natural disaster, a workplace violence incident, or a planned drill. Consistency also enables the organization to build a library of reports over time, allowing for comparison across incidents and the identification of recurring patterns.

Sample Outline for an After-Action Report

1. Executive Summary—High-level description of the incident and its overall impact.
2. Timeline of Events—Chronological detail from detection to containment and recovery, including key decisions.
3. Impact Assessment—Effects on people, assets, operations, finances, and reputation.
4. Response Analysis—What worked well; what failed or lagged under stress.
5. Root Cause Analysis—Underlying factors that contributed, including human, technical, or procedural elements.
6. Recommendations—Procedural, technological, or cultural changes needed to prevent recurrence or reduce impact.
7. Ownership and Deadlines—Clear accountability for implementing changes, with timeframes for completion.

The report should be viewed as a living document that informs future planning and governance. For higher-impact events, the AAR should be presented to executive leadership and, when appropriate, shared with external stakeholders such as regulators, insurers, or industry partners. When tracked systematically, AARs become your program's historical record, tracing the roadmap of the organization's resilience journey.

INSIGHT: COMMON PITFALLS IN INCIDENT REVIEW

Even well-intentioned reviews can miss the mark if certain traps aren't avoided:

- Finger-pointing over fact-finding. Reviews that devolve into blame discourage honesty and miss systemic issues.
- Too narrow a lens. Limiting participation to the security team excludes valuable perspectives from IT, HR, operations, and communications.
- Vague recommendations. Reports that conclude with "do better training" or "improve communication" lack accountability and rarely lead to change.
- No follow-through. Even strong recommendations lose impact if ownership, deadlines, and progress tracking are absent.
- Assuming silence means success. A lack of reported incidents doesn't always indicate effectiveness; it may signal threats are slipping through undetected.

Avoiding these pitfalls ensures the post-incident process remains credible, constructive, and connected to genuine improvement.

The ultimate test of a post-incident process is whether it drives meaningful change. Capturing insights is valuable, but only if those lessons are translated into concrete adjustments in policy, training, controls, and governance. Continual improvement means moving beyond reflection to action, so that what was learned becomes what is done. This brings us to the next step: adjusting the security program in response to environmental change.

Adjusting Your Security Program in Response to Environmental Change

Control reviews are only valuable if they lead to measurable change. Security leaders must ensure that insights and lessons are translated into tangible improvements. This is where many teams falter: reports are written, findings are logged, but little actually changes. In a mature ESRM environment, every lesson learned carries forward into a visible adjustment, whether in policies, training, technology, or governance.

Think of it as a "before-and-after" continuum.

Before, a fire drill might reveal that staff are unsure of their evacuation routes.

After, new signage, updated instructions, and targeted refresher training close that gap.

Before, a workplace violence exercise may expose slow escalation paths.

After, updated communication protocols and tested escalation trees improve response time.

The value of continual improvement lies in transforming weaknesses revealed in practice into strengths for the future.

Pro Tip: Always ask, "What's different now because of this incident?" If the answer is "nothing," you didn't improve.

To ensure this process doesn't stall, improvements must be tracked with the same discipline applied to incident response. Assigning clear owners for each change, setting deadlines, and reporting progress through governance dashboards or risk committees ensures accountability. Without these follow-up mechanisms, even the best recommendations risk fading into "shelfware."

Table 6.5 outlines common areas where lessons learned can be applied, along with their purpose and practical examples of how changes can be operationalized.

TABLE 6.5 Examples of Applying Lessons Learned to Strengthen the ESRM Program

Action Area	Purpose	Practical Application
Strengthen policies and procedures	Ensure rules and protocols are clear, actionable, and effective.	Clarify ambiguous language, adjust escalation thresholds, revise approval workflows, and update protocols that failed during the event. Redistribute updated documents to all affected stakeholders.
Enhance training programs	Address knowledge or behavior gaps that contributed to the incident, or reinforce behaviors that reduced harm.	Refine onboarding and refresher modules, adding targeted drills to address identified weaknesses, and ensure content reflects current risks and best practices.

(Continued)

TABLE 6.5 (Continued) Examples of Applying Lessons Learned to Strengthen the ESRM Program

Action Area	Purpose	Practical Application
Upgrade or fine-tune controls	Improve performance of existing security measures and reallocate resources to higher-impact areas.	Address underperformance caused by integration issues, poor configuration, or incomplete coverage. Utilize post-incident data to justify targeted investments in technology or processes.
Improve communication and escalation paths	Reduce delays and confusion during incident response.	Update contact lists, escalation trees, and messaging templates as needed. Reassess emergency communication platforms to ensure timely, accurate information flow.
Track implementation of changes	Ensure recommendations lead to measurable improvements.	Build an implementation plan with assigned owners and deadlines. Track progress and report updates through ESRM governance or relevant business unit reviews.

By embedding a culture of post-incident analysis and proactive refinement, organizations demonstrate that continuous learning is a fundamental component of their risk management philosophy. Over time, this leads to a more resilient security posture, where every failure is an opportunity to strengthen defenses, build trust, and reduce the likelihood of future incidents.

Operationalizing Continuous Improvement

For monitoring and adjustment to be effective, activities must be operationalized appropriately and integrated into the organization's change and risk management processes. Risk identification and review cycles must become a steady rhythm that blends into the regular cadence of both the security team and the business. Continual improvement is less about "big moments" and more about sustained discipline that is baked into everyday management, not as an annual afterthought.

Assign and Document Responsibilities

A practical starting point is to assign clear ownership over security controls. Every critical security control should have a designated owner responsible for its health, performance, and maintenance. In a small organization, this might be one person for all of them, but the responsibility must still be clear. This step improves accountability, ensures timely updates, and prevents the "no one's job" problem that allows degradation to go unnoticed.

Tie Into Existing Governance

From there, the program must be deliberately linked to governance structures that already carry weight in the enterprise. Control reviews can be embedded into risk committee agendas, enterprise audit cycles, and business unit performance reviews. This integration keeps security from being sidelined as a "technical" issue and instead frames it as part of the organization's overall risk posture and resilience strategy.

For example, control reviews can be reported as part of:

- Board Risk Committees—Reporting key ESRM metrics (e.g., % of controls tested, incident review outcomes) alongside financial and compliance risks ensures leadership sees security as part of strategic risk management.
- Audit Processes—Aligning ESRM reviews with internal audit cycles validates that controls are in place and functioning as intended, and highlights gaps before external auditors or regulators do.
- Enterprise Performance Reviews—Embedding ESRM metrics into operational reviews makes security a shared business responsibility beyond the security function. Business unit leaders then see their own performance as tied to resilience outcomes.

Pro Tip: Tie ESRM updates to existing governance meetings. You'll get leadership attention without adding new bureaucracy.

Build a Flexible Improvement Plan

Reassessment should be both trigger-based and calendar-based. Scheduled reviews (quarterly, semi-annual, or annual) are important, but also, certain events should automatically prompt reevaluation of controls, such as: A failed test, incident, or near miss. A significant emerging threat trend that could undermine the control's effectiveness. A material change to the protected asset, such as expansion, relocation, or a significant technology upgrade.

When operationalized in this way, monitoring becomes a constant, adaptive feedback loop. Security stays aligned with evolving threats, shifting business priorities, and the realities of daily operations. More importantly, it ensures that continual improvement is a measurable, visible process that is embedded in enterprise governance.

Continuous improvement is what transforms ESRM from a project into a culture, from a task list into a leadership mindset. Through post-incident reviews, performance monitoring, and strategic alignment activities, the ongoing improvement cycle ensures that the security function remains relevant and resilient.

INSIGHT: THE ASIS INTERNATIONAL ESRM MATURITY MODEL

Continual improvement in ESRM is supported by defined frameworks and professional guidance. ASIS International has developed a formal ESRM Maturity Model to help organizations assess their current security program status and chart a course toward more integrated, strategic practices. The model acknowledges that not every organization starts from the same point and that meaningful progress often occurs in incremental steps.

The ESRM Maturity Model assesses five domains of security integration:

- Culture—the degree to which ESRM principles are understood and embraced throughout the organization.
- Context—how well security integrates the organization's values, environment, and regulatory obligations into decision-making.
- Stakeholders—the strength of collaboration between security professionals, asset owners, and leadership.
- Risk Management—the rigor and consistency with which ESRM processes are applied to assets, threats, and vulnerabilities.
- Governance—the extent to which ESRM is institutionalized within enterprise oversight and decision-making structures.

Each domain progresses through five maturity levels, which mirror other business improvement frameworks (Table 6.6):

ASIS also provides a free self-assessment tool[8] that enables organizations to answer five high-level questions and receive a maturity profile, along with guidance on next steps. This makes the model practical for organizations of any size.

TABLE 6.6 The ASIS ESRM Stage of Maturity

Level	Description
1. Initial	ESRM is ad hoc and inconsistent. Security operates reactively, with limited alignment to the business.
2. Repeatable	Early ESRM practices are gaining traction. Security begins introducing risk-based policies and basic training.
3. Defined	ESRM is documented and consistently applied. Processes and controls are standardized across the organization.
4. Managed	ESRM is proactive and integrated. Security collaborates actively with asset owners and leadership on shared risk decisions.
5. Optimized	ESRM is embedded at the enterprise level. Security acts as a trusted strategic advisor, and continuous improvement is a natural part of governance.

One of the strongest insights from the maturity model is the emphasis on culture as the foundation for success.[9] Without cultural adoption, it is challenging to sustain improvements in other domains. As organizations climb the maturity ladder, security leaders shift from being enforcers of rules to being strategic advisors who help the business make informed risk trade-offs.

For organizations seeking to operationalize continual improvement, the ESRM Maturity Model provides both a diagnostic and a roadmap. It helps answer the critical question: *How far along are we on the journey to making ESRM an optimized, enterprise-wide discipline?*

Key Takeaways from Chapter 6

Continual improvement in ESRM means building a program that measures performance, learns from incidents, and adapts to change. These core lessons illustrate how monitoring and adjustment maintain security effectiveness over time.

- ESRM is a cycle, not a finish line. Programs must be revisited, tested, and refined to stay effective in changing environments.
- Controls require proof. Measuring against baselines and tracking drift ensures that they continue to deliver their intended effect.

- Incidents are data points. Post-incident reviews and AARs turn disruption into lessons that strengthen the program.
- Improvement must be embedded. Integration with governance, ownership, and reporting turns change from ad hoc to systematic.
- External change matters. Business shifts, new technologies, and global threats all reshape risks. Mature programs adapt to them early.

Security Leader Toolkit: Chapter 6

ESRM Implementation Checklist

- Have I established a regular cadence for reviewing the effectiveness of security controls (monthly, quarterly, or annually)?
- Have I created a process to detect control drift (controls that exist but are no longer functioning as intended)?
- Have I designed an incident review process and tied after-action reviews into program updates?
- Have I aligned my reviews with business resilience objectives (continuity, compliance, trust)?
- Have I established a continuous improvement backlog (listing fixes, owners, and deadlines)?
- Have I created or adopted KPIs and metrics to measure ongoing security performance?
- Have I scheduled periodic risk reassessments to catch environmental and organizational changes?
- Have I documented how improvements will be reported to leadership in business language?
- Have I established a process to close the loop—confirming that corrective actions were implemented and effective?

After-Action Review Template

Purpose: Use this template after any security incident, exercise, or disruption to capture lessons, ensure accountability, and strengthen future resilience.

How to Use It

- Complete (or begin) this template within 72 hours of any incident or exercise.
- Involve all stakeholders who were part of the event.
- Keep the tone learning-focused, not blame-focused.

Section	Prompts	Notes
Event summary	What happened? When and where did it occur? Which assets were involved?	
Response actions	What actions were taken immediately? Who was involved in the response?	
What worked well	Which controls, processes, or responses were effective?	
What failed or fell short	Which controls, processes, or responses failed, were slow, or were absent?	
Root causes	Were vulnerabilities exploited? Was it a human error, process gap, technology failure, or external factor?	
Business impact	What was the operational, financial, regulatory, or reputational effect?	
Improvement opportunities	What could have prevented or reduced the impact?	
Action plan	Specific improvements to implement. Who owns them? By when?	
Residual risk decision	What risks remain after improvements? Were they accepted, transferred, or mitigated further?	
Follow-up review date	When will this be revisited to confirm that changes were effective?	

- Document action items and assign ownership with deadlines.
- File AARs in a centralized repository to build an organizational lessons-learned library.

Notes

1 "Six Sigma Continuous Process Improvement," *Six Sigma Online by Aveta Business Institute*, accessed August 16, 2025, https://www.sixsigmaonline.org/six-sigma-continuous-process-improvement/.

2 "Atlassian ITSM: ITIL Continual Service Improvement," *Atlassian*, accessed August 16, 2025, https://www.atlassian.com/itsm/itil/continual-service-improvement.

3 "The PESTEL Framework and Its Variants for Analysing the Strategic Environment," *SSRN*, September 9, 2020, https://ssrn.com/abstract=5266562.

4 Washington State University Libraries, "What is a PESTEL Analysis," *Business LibGuides*, accessed August 16, 2025, https://libguides.libraries.wsu.edu/c.php?g=294263&p=4358409.
5 International Organization for Standardization, *ISO 31000:2018 – Risk Management – Guidelines* (Geneva: ISO, 2018), 2–3.
6 Federal Emergency Management Agency, *Homeland Security Exercise and Evaluation Program (HSEEP)* (Washington, DC: FEMA, January 2020), https://www.fema.gov/sites/default/files/2020-04/Homeland-Security-Exercise-and-Evaluation-Program-Doctrine-2020-Revision-2-2-25.pdf.
7 ASIS International, *Security Incident Management in 2025: Research on How Security Professionals Prepare for, Respond to, and Recover from Security Incidents* (Alexandria, VA: ASIS International, 2025), https://www.asisonline.org/globalassets/publications-and-resources/security-issues-research/2025/incidentmanagement/security-incident-management-report-webinar-version.pdf.
8 ASIS International, "ESRM Maturity Model Self-Assessment," *ASIS International*, accessed August 2025, https://www.asisonline.org/security-news/esrm-maturity-model-self-assessment/.
9 ASIS International, "Influence in ESRM Maturity," *Security Management Magazine*, September 2023, Available at: https://www.asisonline.org/security-management-magazine/articles/2023/09/esrm/influence-in-esrm-maturity/.

Chapter 7

Required for Success

Making the Shift to a Security-Driven Culture

Enterprise Security Risk Management (ESRM) provides a robust framework for aligning security activities with business priorities. But even the most well-designed and well-resourced ESRM program can falter if the organization's culture isn't aligned with its goals. Without cultural reinforcement, policies go unread, training is ignored, and controls are bypassed. None of this happens due to malice; it happens because security hasn't been internalized as part of how the organization operates.

Culture Is Critical

Security Culture is what transforms ESRM from a theoretical model into a human one.

Consider three quick scenarios in very different operations:

Staff Awareness

At a major urban hospital, a nurse at a floor desk noticed a visitor's badge was missing a colored date stamp. Without hesitation, she politely redirected the visitor to the security desk. Later, it was discovered that the visitor had been attempting to access a restricted patient area. That small, instinctive action averted a potential safety incident and possible HIPAA violation.

Information Security Awareness

In a busy manufacturing plant, a phishing email disguised as an urgent shipping order was stopped within minutes because a

DOI: 10.4324/9781003711346-13

warehouse supervisor remembered a recent security briefing and reported it immediately. IT was able to block the domain before the malware reached production systems.

Facility Awareness

On the other hand, a suburban corporate office suffered a significant loss of property when an employee propped open a side door "just for a smoke break" to avoid badge swipes. The door stayed open long enough for an unauthorized individual to enter and steal unsecured laptops and personal property in a training room that was temporarily unoccupied.

The examples given demonstrate that security culture isn't a "nice to have" or something that non-security professionals can overlook. Security Culture is the difference between a program that is written on paper and one that actually works in real life.

Security Culture Across Industry

A security-driven culture is about employee mindset: the shared values, beliefs, and daily habits that influence how people think about and engage with security risk. In organizations where culture is strong, employees instinctively pause before clicking on suspicious links, report lost badges or digital equipment without fear of reprisal, and factor security considerations into their routine decision-making. In weaker cultures, these behaviors are inconsistently practiced—or worse, seen as obstacles to productivity.

What this looks like can vary by industry or location:

- Healthcare—Staff treat patient privacy and facility safety as inseparable from patient care. They fully understand the need to integrate both access control and infection prevention into their daily routines.
- Manufacturing—Production teams understand that safety procedures and equipment lockouts protect uptime, but so do cybersecurity controls. They act accordingly, even under schedule pressure.
- Corporate environments—Employees see both physical and digital access controls as part of safeguarding client trust, proprietary data, and company reputation, not simply extra steps to inconvenience them.
- Retail—Store associates recognize that steps and processes to prevent theft also help ensure customer safety, brand integrity, and a welcoming shopping environment.

- Transportation & Logistics—Drivers, dispatchers, and warehouse staff follow route security protocols and cargo checks as rigorously as delivery schedules, knowing that both speed and safety protect the supply chain—and the people moving the goods.
- Energy & Utilities—Field crews and control room operators understand that cyber hygiene, physical access restrictions, and safety checks are all as critical to keeping essential services running without interruption as equipment maintenance is.

Culture is the long-term amplifier of security governance, policy, and training. You can have the right metrics, processes, and policies in place, but without a culture that supports them, those efforts won't stick. As the saying goes, "Culture eats strategy for breakfast."[1]

Shifting to a security-driven culture is a long-term project. It is more than a single awareness campaign or a new set of rules. It's creating an environment where security is seen as everyone's responsibility, modeled from the top down, reinforced at every level, and integrated into how business gets done.

Understanding the Security Culture Landscape

Like everything else related to ESRM, before you can shift your organization's culture, you must first understand it. Security culture refers to the emotional and behavioral environment in which risk decisions are made every day, often consciously, but sometimes unconsciously. It reflects how people view their role in protecting the organization, how they interpret risk, how they behave when on "auto-pilot," and how they respond to security messaging.

Unconscious decision-making plays a significant role in security that many people may not realize. A finance associate who simply shreds a suspicious letter with the rest of the day's mail without thinking of reporting it is acting on habit, not stated policy. A maintenance worker who automatically double-checks that a service entrance door latches behind them, even when their hands are full, is following a mental script that has been built over years. These "default" responses, whether risky or protective, are the foundation of your real-world security posture. If they align with your security policies and principles, they reinforce resilience. If they don't, they create silent vulnerabilities.

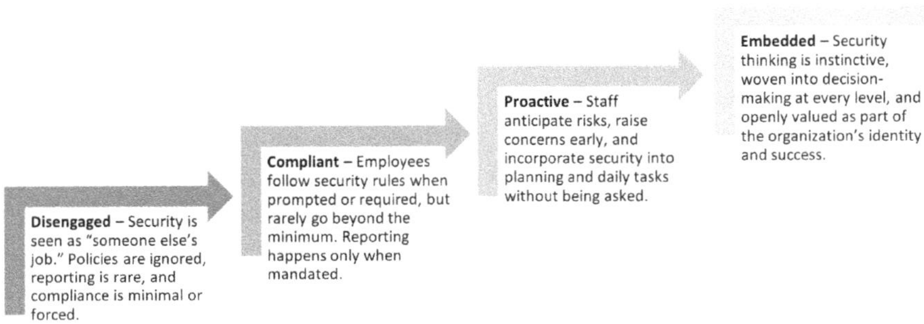

FIGURE 7.1 A Simple Cultural Maturity Framework

In the context of ESRM, security culture is the connective tissue between strategic governance and day-to-day execution. It's what determines whether people follow procedures, report anomalies, and make informed decisions in moments of uncertainty. It helps identify new opportunities for improvement through engaged employee reporting rather than through multiple security incident reviews. As we have discussed throughout this book, ESRM emphasizes shared ownership of risk, which means cultural alignment is not optional.

A helpful way to understand your current security culture state is to assess your cultural maturity, along with the other factors you are seeking to understand, at the very beginning of the ESRM cycle. You have further to go with implementing your new or updated security program if there is no existing (or even a resistant) security culture. Still, it's much better to understand where you are starting from. One simple framework for measuring your current position is illustrated in Figure 7.1.

Where an organization sits on this spectrum isn't static. Your maturity can ebb and flow over time. It can shift forward with consistent leadership and reinforcement, or slide backward if priorities change or trust erodes. Recognizing your current position is the first step in charting a deliberate path toward an embedded, resilient security culture that supports your ESRM program.

Diagnosing Your Current Culture

To effectively influence your security culture, you need to begin with a baseline. But how do you measure something as complex and human as culture?

The answer lies in combining a view of attitudes and behaviors across the enterprise. Metrics can help show whether awareness is increasing, whether secure behavior is becoming a habit, and whether people believe security is part of their everyday role.[2]

A strong diagnostic effort can be founded on three complementary sources:

1. **Surveys**

   Surveys provide a broad, quantifiable view of perceptions and priorities. An example of questions you might consider is shown in Table 7.1.

TABLE 7.1 Example Security Culture Survey

Question	Answer Options
1. I feel that the security of my workplace is part of my job responsibilities.	• Strongly Agree • Agree • Neutral • Disagree • Strongly • Disagree
2. If I notice a potential security issue, I know how to report it.	• Strongly Agree • Agree • Neutral • Disagree • Strongly • Disagree
3. I trust the security team to respond appropriately to my reports.	• Strongly Agree • Agree • Neutral • Disagree • Strongly • Disagree
4. Security processes support me and help me do my job effectively.	• Strongly Agree • Agree • Neutral • Disagree • Strongly • Disagree
5. My manager encourages secure practices in our team's work.	• Strongly Agree • Agree • Neutral • Disagree • Strongly • Disagree

(Continued)

TABLE 7.1 (Continued) Example Security Culture Survey

Question	Answer Options
6. The security training I've received is relevant to my role.	• Strongly Agree • Agree • Neutral • Disagree • Strongly • Disagree
7. I believe my department integrates security practices into our work without creating unnecessary obstacles.	• Strongly Agree • Agree • Neutral • Disagree • Strongly • Disagree
8. I feel comfortable reporting security concerns without fear of negative consequences.	• Strongly Agree • Agree • Neutral • Disagree • Strongly • Disagree
9. I see leaders in my organization modeling secure behavior.	• Strongly Agree • Agree • Neutral • Disagree • Strongly • Disagree
10. Security is discussed regularly in team meetings or planning sessions.	• Strongly Agree • Agree • Neutral • Disagree • Strongly • Disagree

This survey can be adapted to suit your organization's preferred format—using either descriptive labels ("Strongly Agree" to "Strongly Disagree") or a numerical scale (1 to 5, where 1 = strongly disagree and 5 = strongly agree). Other questions might be added with a more "yes"/"no" dynamic, but beware of survey fatigue and keep the survey concise, focusing on something that can be completed in only a few minutes.

Once you have collected the data, segmenting the results by department, location, or role type can highlight pockets of cultural strength and those that require more attention. Comparing scores over time also provides a clear indicator of progress, or an early warning if engagement begins to slip.

2. **Conversations**

Through conversational focus groups or one-on-one interviews, you can gain a deeper understanding and uncover more nuanced insights into security culture barriers, leadership tone, and conflicting incentives. Some examples of questions you could consider for these interviews are:

For Focus Groups *(encourage discussion and shared ideas)*

- What's the biggest obstacle to following security processes in your role?
- What might make it easier for you to report suspicious activity?
- Can you recall a time when you had to make a quick decision with a security impact? What happened?
- What's one thing leadership could do to make security feel more relevant to your team?
- In your view, what's one "everyday" action we could take that would make the organization safer?

For One-on-One Interviews *(encourage candor and detail)*

- Have you ever seen a security policy that conflicted with getting your work done? How did you handle it?
- When you think about past security incidents here, what stands out to you about how they were handled?
- How do you usually hear about security changes or updates, and how effective is that communication for you?
- What would make you more likely to participate in optional security training or activities?
- Can you think of a time when someone modeled good security behavior and it influenced what you did?

For focus groups, select open-ended questions that encourage dialogue and allow participants to build upon each other's responses. Aim for a mix of operational and cultural topics so you hear both "how we work" and "how we think" perspectives.[3]

For one-on-one interviews, select questions that may touch on sensitive issues such as conflicts with leadership priorities or past mistakes. The privacy of a one-on-one interview can encourage honesty. Record themes, not just quotes, and compare results across teams, departments, or regions to identify cultural strengths, blind spots, and inconsistencies. Make sure that you let people know that their feedback will not be attributed if they are pointing out negative aspects of the program.

Behavioral Evidence

What people do often matters more than what they say or what questions they answer correctly on a form. Observing and tracking real-world behavior provides an unfiltered view of how security is actually practiced in day-to-day operations, regardless of the written policies. These metrics will first help you validate whether policies are being followed, but more importantly, they can reveal habits, pain points, and levels of engagement that surveys or interviews might miss.[4]

Examples of useful behavioral evidence include:

- Incident Reporting Patterns
  - Percentage of phishing simulations reported in a cyber program (including how quickly reports come in).
  - Ratio of reported near-misses to those discovered later by investigation for all incident types. High reporting can signal vigilance, while low reporting may indicate gaps in awareness or a lack of trust.
  - Time-to-report for security concerns or suspicious activity.
- Training Engagement
  - Percentage of security training completed without reminders or managerial prompting.
  - Voluntary participation in optional training, awareness campaigns, or simulations.
  - Post-training follow-up activity, such as increased reporting or policy adherence.
- Access Control Compliance
  - Number of physical access violations (e.g., tailgating, propped doors, sharing access cards).
  - Percentage of visitors correctly signed in and escorted.
  - Frequency of badge or credential replacements due to loss.
- Technology & Data Protection Habits
  - Instances of devices found unattended and unlocked during spot checks.
  - Compliance with secure file-sharing and data storage protocols.
  - Use of approved communication channels vs. shadow IT or personal accounts.

- Engagement in Security Programs
  - Participation in voluntary security initiatives like champion programs, safety committees, or cross-department drills.
  - Attendance and active involvement in tabletop exercises.
  - Contributions of security-related suggestions or process improvement ideas.
- Response & Recovery Actions
  - Employee adherence to procedures during drills (e.g., evacuation, shelter-in-place, cyber incident response).
  - Speed and accuracy of role execution during incident simulations.
  - Post-incident cooperation and follow-through on assigned corrective actions.

When reviewing behavioral data, it's critical to consider context. For example, a sudden drop in phishing reports could indicate that vigilance is slipping, or it could mean that technical controls are blocking more malicious emails before employees see them. Similarly, a high number of access violations might indicate careless behavior, or it might reveal that a physical layout makes compliance impractical.

The goal of measuring metrics isn't to punish individuals based on what they are doing, but to use the numbers as leading indicators: signs of where culture is strong, where it's at risk, and where targeted interventions can drive improvement.

INSIGHT: KEY TAKEAWAYS FOR CULTURE MEASUREMENT

- Don't rely on a single method; combine perception, conversation, and behavior.
- Phrase survey questions to reveal both attitudes and confidence in taking action.
- Use focus groups to uncover local variations in culture.
- Track behaviors that indicate habits, not just compliance.
- Segment results by business unit, region, or role to find hot spots or blind spots.

Reassess regularly to spot cultural shifts (positive or negative) before they take root.

One note of caution: culture measurement can backfire if employees see it as a trap. Avoid leading questions that make people feel judged, surveys that lack anonymity, or data collection that seems disconnected from action. Also, if you ask for feedback, be prepared to act on it. If you do not, participation and honesty will drop sharply in future assessments.

Just as ESRM emphasizes evidence-based risk decisions, a cultural shift must also be grounded in real data to track and manage it properly. This first diagnostic step establishes the baseline, providing you with a starting point for measuring growth and adjusting your course over time.

Common Cultural Barriers to Security Engagement

Shifting culture in response to your initial findings will not be as easy as flipping a switch. Many organizations encounter similar roadblocks when attempting to integrate security into their everyday behavior. Recognizing some of the barriers listed in Table 7.2 and addressing them with practical countermeasures can accelerate your shift to a security-driven employee culture.[5]

Overcoming these barriers will never be a one-time fix or project. Change is an ongoing process of identifying friction points, reinforcing desired behaviors, and making course corrections as the organization changes.

TABLE 7.2 Common Cultural Barriers and How to Address Them

Barrier	Real-World Example	What Works
"It's not my job" mindset	A warehouse worker notices a propped-open dock door but assumes "security will handle it." Hours later, an inventory discrepancy is traced to that entry point.	Build shared risk ownership into job descriptions and onboarding; recognize quick actions by non-security staff.
Resistance to change	Office staff bypass a new badge reader by tailgating because it "slows them down."	Explain the "why" in relatable terms; remove friction by integrating controls into natural workflows.
Lack of visible leadership support	A manager talks up security but skips required training, signaling it's not a priority.	Require leaders to model secure behaviors, join exercises, and publicly support security initiatives.

(Continued)

TABLE 7.2 (Continued) Common Cultural Barriers and How to Address Them

Barrier	Real-World Example	What Works
Conflicting incentives	Call center staff avoid verifying caller identity to hit speed targets.	Align performance metrics so secure behavior is rewarded alongside productivity.
Overreliance on "common sense"	A fake invoice is paid because it looked routine, despite "obvious" red flags.	Replace assumptions with documented procedures and regular training refreshers.
Security fatigue	After years of phishing simulations, staff ignore them or treat them as a nuisance.	Vary awareness tactics; use storytelling/gamification; involve staff in shaping content.
Perceived lack of feedback	Staff report suspicious activity but never hear the outcome, reducing engagement.	Close the loop—thank reporters and share outcomes to build trust and reinforce action.

INSIGHT: TABLE 7.2—COMMON CULTURAL BARRIERS AND HOW TO ADDRESS THEM

This table highlights a core truth about shifting to a security-driven culture: most barriers are behavioral rather than technical in nature. Barriers to adoption live in habits, perceptions, and incentives that shape daily decisions. Addressing them likely will not require massive budgets or new tools. It will require making security expectations visible, aligning them with how people actually work, and reinforcing them in ways that feel relevant and rewarding. The most effective countermeasures replace friction with accessibility and isolation with shared ownership. This helps turn one-time reminders into lasting cultural shifts.

Influencing Organizational Behavior: The Psychology of Change

Creating a security-driven culture requires changing behavior, arguably one of the most challenging things an organization can do at scale. People are creatures of habit. They prefer routines, resist disruption, have seen programs come and go, and often view change with skepticism or fatigue.

Security leaders don't need to be psychologists or certified change consultants, but we do need to understand that a culture shift requires planning, patience, consistency, and empathy. Most security initiatives that fail to gain traction do so more often because the change was mishandled rather than because the controls were technically flawed.

ESRM is a cycle-driven set of activities, and change management is a key component of the continuous improvement of the security program. Just as ESRM follows a model, to implement a large-scale change in security properly, it's beneficial to leverage another standardized model.

Modeling Change

Pro Tip: You don't have to launch every change step at once. It's often more effective to pick one or two high-impact steps and execute them well before moving on.

One of the most widely used change models in business is John Kotter's 8-Step Process for Leading Change.[6] It offers a practical roadmap for moving personnel from their current mindset and behaviors to a more aligned and engaged state. When adapted to ESRM, Kotter's steps can be applied to security-specific actions:

1. Create a Sense of Urgency

   Demonstrate why a stronger security culture is essential now. Use relevant data, incident examples, or industry case studies to highlight risks and opportunities. Avoid fear-only messaging; focus on protecting what matters to the business. This can all be based on the same information you've been gathering all along about critical risks, but tailored to a broader audience.
2. Build a Guiding Coalition

   Form a cross-functional team of respected leaders, influencers, and security champions who will advocate for security principles and model desired behaviors. This can be the same group of stakeholders that you have already identified to support your security program. Your stakeholders in

ESRM already understand their ownership of the risk, and this is a natural extension of their need to mitigate risks that might impact them.

3. Form a Strategic Vision and Initiatives

   Define what a security-driven culture looks like in your organization. Tie it directly to business priorities so it feels integral, not optional. This fits nicely into the role of the oversight and governance team that you may have implemented already for your ESRM effort. If not, this step is a great place to start advocating for the need for that strategic governance.
4. Enlist a Volunteer Army

   Just as when you were identifying your stakeholders and partners for security, go beyond formal roles. Recruit employees at all levels to contribute ideas, share success stories, and reinforce positive security actions. The biggest change drivers in your organizations might not be the executives, but the person at the reception desk who knows everyone and sees everything!
5. Enable Action by Removing Barriers

   Identify and address processes, policies, or conflicting incentives that hinder secure behavior. Make it so the right choice is also the easy choice. This can be especially difficult in security, but if the adoption of a security change is slow or conflicted, it may be worth revisiting how complex or time-consuming it is.
6. Generate Short-Term Wins

   Start with achievable, visible changes that show progress quickly. For example, an improvement in incident report rates in one department can be celebrated enterprise-wide.
7. Sustain Acceleration

   Use early wins to build momentum for larger changes, such as integrating security metrics into leadership scorecards or aligning security key performance indicators (KPIs) with operational objectives. Embedding your security metrics and information into the regular flow of executive reporting will keep the program at the forefront.
8. Institute Change

   Embed security practices and compliance into performance reviews, onboarding, and leadership development so they survive turnover and shifting priorities.

In change management, as with everything in ESRM, sequencing matters. Begin with actions that eliminate obvious friction and deliver small wins before tackling complex, enterprise-wide changes. Making the reporting process simpler and faster, for example, can yield visible results that build momentum for later, more complex cultural shifts.

When adapted thoughtfully, change management gives ESRM practitioners a tested structure for moving from intent to action, helping us turn strategic direction into daily habit, and daily habit into organizational identity.

INSIGHT: ESSENTIAL CHANGE MANAGEMENT RESOURCES FOR SECURITY LEADERS

While this chapter offers a security-specific lens, many of the best insights on driving behavior change are drawn from broader business and leadership literature. These titles are highly respected and widely used by change leaders across industries (Table 7.3):

TABLE 7.3 Change Management Resources

Title	Author(s)	Key Concept
Leading Change	John P. Kotter	Describes the classic 8-step framework for organizational transformation.
Switch: How to Change Things When Change Is Hard	Chip & Dan Heath	Balances emotion and logic to drive sustainable change.
Influencer: The New Science of Leading Change	Patterson, Grenny et al.	Identifies six sources of influence that drive behavioral change.
The Power of Habit	Charles Duhigg	Explains the habit loop and how leaders can replace old behaviors with better ones.

Behavioral Science in Practice

Several psychological principles[7] are especially relevant to the task of creating, promoting, and embedding a strong security culture. Understanding these principles helps security leaders design initiatives that people are more likely to adopt, repeat, and internalize.

- **Social Proof and Norms**

  People look to their peers to understand what is considered acceptable behavior, especially in situations where expectations aren't explicitly stated. If team members routinely see others locking screens, challenging unescorted visitors, reporting anomalies, or pausing to assess potential problems before acting, those behaviors become normalized. For instance, you might choose to highlight positive examples of secure behavior in team communications, such as quick incident reporting or effective safety actions, to reinforce a proactive security message.
- **Framing and Narrative**

  Language plays a decisive role in shaping identity. Instead of framing security actions as compliance tasks ("You must report all suspicious emails"), connect them to a positive identity ("We protect our customers' trust every time we report something suspicious"). In ESRM, we start with the question of "What do we need to protect?." This reframing can echo the importance of that question and boost the role of all employees in answering the "How do we most effectively protect it?" question. This can help you transform security from being another task to complete into a point of pride. Engaged teams stop asking, "Do I have to?" and start thinking, "Of course I will, this is what we do here."
- **Inertia and the Status Quo Bias**

  People tend to default to doing what they've always done, even when a better option is available. Overcoming this bias means making the secure behavior easier than the insecure one, explaining why it matters, and reinforcing it until it becomes a habit. One example of reducing improper/insecure file sharing might be to integrate a secure document transfer tool directly into a common workflow, such as email, so that the secure choice is also the simplest and fastest option available.

These factors are useful and practical tools for shaping how security is perceived and practiced. They're especially powerful when combined with structured change management efforts.

Engaging Leadership to Model Security Mindsets

In any organization, culture flows from the top. No matter how well-designed your policies are or how engaging your training

TABLE 7.4 Leadership Signals: Visible Support vs. Undermining Behavior

Visible Support	Undermining Signals
Joins annual tabletop exercise alongside managers and frontline staff.	Skips mandatory training while requiring others to complete it.
Brings up security considerations in strategic planning meetings.	Treats risk or incident reports as distractions from "real work."
Publicly recognizes a team's secure behavior during a town hall.	Ignores or downplays policy violations by senior staff.
Aligns department goals with security KPIs.	Pushes for exceptions that bypass security controls for convenience.

materials might be, if leadership isn't modeling secure behavior, the broader workforce is unlikely to follow suit.

Leadership behavior is one of the most powerful accelerants (or inhibitors) of security culture. When executives and department heads visibly support risk management principles and the security program, they send a strong message that security is a shared business priority.

Research and experience demonstrate that employees draw behavioral cues from their leaders.[8] If leaders ignore security protocols, delegate all responsibility to the security team, or treat risk discussions as irrelevant, employees will follow suit; often unconsciously, but also often as a result of resenting leadership's exemption from policy. But when leaders model secure behavior, participate in training, and connect security to business outcomes, they signal that security is a shared business priority and set the tone for the rest of the organization (Table 7.4).

Even small leadership behaviors create ripples. A director who challenges a tailgater in the lobby sends a stronger message than a dozen security posters. On the flip side, a senior manager propping open a secure door for convenience can undo weeks of awareness efforts.

Tactics for Leadership Engagement

To embed a culture of security, leaders need opportunities and tools to actively demonstrate their commitment. This means intentional visibility, consistent messaging, and participation in key moments. If your leaders really want to help embed your security culture, encourage them to enact some of the following behaviors.

- Participate in training and tabletop exercises—When executives participate in security awareness sessions or incident response simulations, they demonstrate that security is not just an operational issue, but a leadership concern.
- Speak publicly about security values—A brief comment at a town hall, an internal blog post, or a short video message can reinforce that security is integral to how the organization defines success.
- Incorporate security into team goals and business reviews—Leaders can embed security KPIs into departmental dashboards or incorporate readiness discussions into regular performance check-ins.

INSIGHT: ONBOARDING NEW LEADERS INTO A SECURITY-DRIVEN CULTURE

Leadership transitions can either strengthen or weaken security culture. New leaders often arrive with their own priorities, and without deliberate onboarding, security may fall out of view. To maintain cultural momentum:

- Provide an ESRM orientation that explains the organization's security priorities, governance structure, and the leader's role in cultural reinforcement.
- Share recent successes and challenges so they see security as a living, active part of operations.
- Pair them with a security champion or senior leader who can answer questions and model desired engagement behaviors.
- Encourage early participation in a visible security event, whether it's a tabletop exercise, safety walk-through, or recognition of a team's secure actions.

When leaders visibly participate, address security in business terms, and integrate it into their own goals, they normalize the expectation that security is part of everyone's job. Over time, this alignment at the top creates consistency throughout the organization. So secure behavior isn't something employees do for the security team, but something they do because it's part of how the business operates.

Establishing Security Champions across the Business

Another way to scale leadership influence is by creating a network of security champions.[9] These should be respected individuals embedded in departments who act as advocates for secure behaviors, serve as first-line communicators of policy updates, and act as feedback channels between business units and the security team.

Champions don't need to be security experts; they need to be credible, communicative, and committed. In a software development group, for example, a champion might share secure coding reminders during sprint planning, flag risks early, and connect the team with security resources. Over time, these habits can normalize secure decision-making without slowing the pace of work.

Two common pitfalls can undermine a champion program: burnout and role confusion. Champions are often high performers, so without clear expectations and recognition, they may become overextended. Similarly, if their role isn't well-communicated, peers may mistake them for policy enforcers or decision-makers. Both issues can be avoided by setting a manageable time commitment, clarifying that the champion is a connector, not a rule-maker, and keeping them engaged with regular updates and visible wins.

When supported and recognized, security champions become trusted peers who translate leadership vision into everyday action, making security a visible, shared responsibility across the organization.

INSIGHT: TIPS FOR A SUCCESSFUL SECURITY CHAMPION PROGRAM

- Recruit volunteers from departments with higher-risk exposure (e.g., Finance, HR, and R&D).
- Offer tailored briefings and recognition to keep champions engaged and motivated.
- Provide simple communication tools—FAQs, slide decks, infographics—so they can share consistent messages.
- Meet regularly to exchange updates, gather feedback, and address cultural friction points before they grow.
- Pair new champions with experienced ones for informal mentoring and faster onboarding.
- Involve champions early in new initiatives so they can help shape messages and spot potential adoption challenges.

Security champion networks work because they extend cultural influence beyond the formal leadership structure. A risk-based security culture takes root when both trusted peers and executives reinforce expectations and behaviors. Champions give Security a local voice. People have someone in the room who can connect policies to daily realities and keep secure practices visible between formal training sessions. When champions are supported, recognized, and connected to both leadership and their peers, they help turn security from an occasional focus into a daily habit.

INSIGHT: WHEN LEADERSHIP ENGAGEMENT NEEDS FORMALITY

For many organizations, leadership engagement with ESRM occurs through partnerships, dialogue, and shared accountability, rather than a formal governance structure. However, in larger companies, heavily regulated industries, or areas with high risks, creating formal oversight can help keep ESRM visible, consistent, and effective.

When security risk affects compliance, reputation, or strategic continuity, structure adds clarity. Consider these formal approaches if your organization is scaling or subject to regulatory scrutiny:

- Appoint an executive ESRM sponsor (C-suite or board level) to champion risk alignment and secure resourcing.
- Establish a cross-functional risk review group with representation from security, compliance, IT, HR, and operations.
- Integrate ESRM into existing enterprise governance processes like risk committees, business continuity reviews, or strategic planning cycles.
- Track ESRM KPIs at the leadership level, such as residual risk trends, incident time-to-detect metrics, or culture engagement indicators.
- Document decision authority for risk acceptance, mitigation, or escalation, especially for high-impact business units.

Not every organization needs this formality. However, when ESRM must scale, span global operations, or align with regulators, structure provides the necessary staying power. It makes leadership support visible, repeatable, and aligned with enterprise risk priorities.

Designing Security Awareness for Behavior Change: Training That Sticks

Security culture can't exist without awareness, but "awareness" alone isn't enough. Too often, security training is treated as a

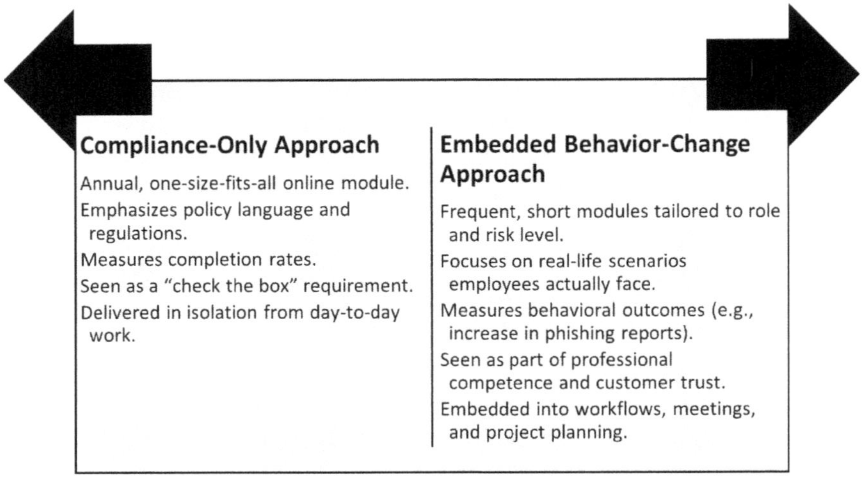

FIGURE 7.2 Compliance Training vs. Behavior-Change Training

compliance exercise. We roll out a once-a-year, one-size-fits-all module designed to check a regulatory box. People may pass the quiz and collect a completion certificate, but their daily decision-making remains unchanged.

The ultimate goal of security awareness is to effect behavioral change. That means helping employees automatically make safer choices in their daily tasks, without stopping to remember "what the training said." It means replacing one-off sessions with an impactful and ongoing approach[10] that keeps security visible, relevant, and tied to real work (Figure 7.2).

Pro Tip: One annual training session won't build culture. Ongoing, visible awareness efforts turn security into everyday behavior.

Core Elements of Effective Security Awareness Programs

To design training that drives lasting behavior change, you need more than a list of policies or a set of generic slides. The most effective security training programs take a modern, human-centered approach that recognizes how people actually learn, form habits, and make decisions under real-world conditions. Designing effective training requires thinking beyond "what information do we want to share?" and focusing on "what behaviors do we want to see?," then determining a path to make them the natural choice. The key training design principles[11] outlined in Table 7.5 provide a framework for developing training that is relevant, memorable, and seamlessly integrated into the everyday workflow, rather than being treated as a standalone event.

When awareness training is designed with the learner in mind, reinforced regularly, and connected to real-world work, it is more likely to become part of the organization's operational rhythm. Employees are more likely to make secure choices instinctively

TABLE 7.5 Core Elements of Effective Security Awareness Programs

Principle	How to Apply It
Role-Specific Content	Tailor training to the specific audience. A receptionist needs different scenarios than a network engineer, and a warehouse supervisor faces different risks than a sales manager. Use realistic examples drawn directly from their work environment, like phishing attempts for office staff, visitor screening for reception, and secure equipment handling for plant operations. The more relevant the example, the more likely the behavior will stick.
Repetition & Reinforcement	One-off training fades quickly. Use multiple touchpoints throughout the year to refresh key concepts. Outputs like email tips, brief "security moments" in meetings, short video reminders, or intranet banners. The goal is to keep security visible and top of mind, without overwhelming staff or pushing it into background noise.
Learning in the Flow of Work	Integrate security tips and prompts into daily tasks so they appear at the moment of need. Examples include a pop-up reminder before sending an email with sensitive attachments, or an in-app guide the first time someone uses a secure file transfer system. This just-in-time approach enables employees to connect training to action immediately.
Engaging Formats	People remember what captures their interest. Use storytelling, interactive simulations, gamification, or visual "spot the risk" challenges to bring content to life. Phishing simulations followed by supportive coaching turn mistakes into learning opportunities without damaging trust.
Behavior-Based Objectives	Define the specific behaviors you want to see more often, such as reporting suspicious emails, locking unattended devices, and challenging unknown people in the environment, and build training around reinforcing those actions.

because they've practiced them in realistic contexts, received timely reminders, and seen those actions valued by their peers and leaders.

Measuring and Evolving Security Culture

In the first section of this chapter, we mentioned gathering data to set a security culture baseline. Still, like any aspect of the ESRM program, culture needs to be measured, monitored, and continuously refined. Organizations that take culture seriously treat it not as a "soft" or intangible concept, but as a strategic asset with real indicators of progress and areas for improvement.

No single number defines security culture, but using the methods described already in this chapter, certain indicators can signal growing maturity:[12]

- Percentage of employees who believe "security is part of my job."—This sentiment is foundational. When people believe they have a role in protecting the organization, their behavior tends to follow.
- Near-miss reporting rates—A rise in reported near-misses (e.g., attempted phishing, misplaced devices, and unlocked doors) often reflects increased vigilance—not increased failure.
- Voluntary participation in security activities—Are employees signing up for extra training, joining security committees, or nominating team security champions? Engagement beyond what's required is a strong sign of cultural buy-in.
- Reduction in policy violations due to negligence or apathy—Fewer careless errors often signal a growing sense of accountability and awareness.
- Security as a topic in team discussions or planning sessions—When employees raise security considerations unprompted—during meetings, project planning, or tool selection—it suggests that secure thinking is embedded in decision-making.

Turning Metrics into Action

Metrics are only valuable if they drive change. High participation rates in training certainly look good on paper, but if policy violations persist, the training likely needs reevaluation. Similarly, if near-miss reporting is low, that may indicate fear of repercussions or uncertainty about the reporting process.

Consider these actions for an effective use of your metrics:

1. Identify what the metric is telling you: is it measuring behavior, perception, or both?
2. Determine the root cause behind changes in the metric.
3. Translate findings into specific actions. For example, low reporting rates could trigger an awareness campaign clarifying the "no penalty" policy for honest mistakes, or a redesign of reporting tools to make them easier to use.
4. Track post-action impact to see if interventions are working.

Just as with the other types of metrics we discussed in Chapter 6 on Continuous Improvement, culture maturity metrics are critical diagnostic tools for program improvement. In the same way that incident data or control performance results help identify technical or procedural gaps, culture metrics can reveal human and behavioral gaps that require program adjustments. If the data indicates that awareness is high but behavior change is lagging, the program may require more workflow integration or leadership modeling. If enthusiasm is strong in some departments but absent in others, targeted outreach or tailored messaging can close the gap. Measuring culture, like any other ESRM element, is part of the ongoing cycle of assess → adjust → re-measure, ensuring the human side of security evolves alongside technical controls.

Key Takeaways from Chapter 7

- Culture makes ESRM real. Without cultural reinforcement, even strong policies and processes won't stick.
- Leaders set the tone. Employees watch leadership behavior closely and take their cues from it.
- Change needs structure. Applying change management and behavioral science helps overcome resistance to change.
- Champions scale influence. Trusted peers extend security culture beyond formal leadership channels.
- Training must build habits. Role-specific, ongoing learning creates lasting behavior change.
- Measure to improve. Cultural metrics expose blind spots and guide continuous refinement.

Security Leader Toolkit: Chapter 7

ESRM Implementation Checklist

- Have I measured the current state of security culture (through surveys, focus groups, or interviews)?
- Have I identified the most significant cultural barriers (e.g., "not my job," compliance-only mindset, resistance to change)?
- Have I built a coalition of allies (champions in other departments who support ESRM)?
- Have I communicated a clear vision for security as a business enabler?
- Have I developed quick wins that demonstrate value and build credibility?
- Have I embedded security expectations into policies, processes, and incentives?
- Have I created a feedback loop to measure cultural shifts over time?
- Have I aligned ESRM with existing change management efforts (digital transformation, compliance, resilience initiatives)?
- Have I given leadership talking points so they model the behavior publicly?

Security Culture Survey Template (10 Questions)

Use this short survey to gauge your organization's baseline security culture. Rate each statement on a scale of **1 = Strongly Disagree** to **5 = Strongly Agree**.

1. I understand why security is important to our organization's success.
2. My manager communicates that security is part of how we do business.
3. Executives in this company model secure behavior.
4. I know what the most critical security risks are in my role.
5. I believe security policies and procedures are reasonable and practical.
6. If I see a security concern, I know how to report it.
7. When I report a concern, I believe it will be taken seriously.
8. Following security procedures makes it easier for me to do my job well.

9. I feel accountable for protecting company assets (physical, digital, and reputational).
10. Overall, I believe this organization values security as part of its culture.

How to Use It

- Distribute via survey tool or paper form.
- Calculate averages by department and overall.
- Look for low scores (≤3) as signals of cultural barriers.
- Repeat yearly to track improvements.

Security Culture Focus Group Discussion Guide

Use these open-ended questions in small group discussions to uncover cultural barriers:

1. When you hear "security" in this company, what comes to mind first?
2. What helps you follow security procedures, and what gets in the way?
3. Do you feel leadership sets the right example when it comes to security? Can you give examples?
4. How easy is it to report a security concern? What would make it easier?
5. If you could change one thing to make security feel more like a part of our culture, what would it be?
6. Do you see differences in how various departments or teams approach security?

How to Use It

- Run sessions with six to ten participants across different functions.
- Capture themes (barriers, motivators, role of leadership).
- Share insights with executives alongside survey results or instead of them.

Notes

1 While often attributed to Peter Drucker, the phrase "culture eats strategy for breakfast" is likely apocryphal. The true origin is unclear, though it reflects themes found in the work of both Peter Drucker and Edgar Schein. See, for example, discussions in business leadership literature and organizational culture commentary.

2 Larkin Anders, “Guide to Measuring Your Security Awareness Training Program Culture,” *Hook Security*, accessed August 15, 2025, https://www.hooksecurity.co/blog/guide-to-measuring-your-security-awareness-training-program-culture.
3 Beverly Peters, “Designing Your Focus Group Questions and Questioning Route,” *AEA365* (blog), American Evaluation Association, January 22, 2021, https://aea365.org/blog/designing-your-focus-group-questions-and-questioning-route-by-beverly-peters/.
4 Living Security, “Cybersecurity Metrics That Matter: Measuring Behavior, Engagement & Motivation,” *Living Security Blog*, June 15, 2023, https://www.livingsecurity.com/blog/cybersecurity-metrics-that-matter-measuring-behavior-engagement-motivation.
5 Christina Lekati, “How Psychology and Behavioural Science Can Help You Build Your Cybersecurity Culture,” *Cyber Risk GmbH*, accessed August 15, 2025, https://www.cyber-risk-gmbh.com/How_Psychology_and_Behavioural_Science_Can_Help_You_Build_Your_Cybersecurity_Culture.html.
6 John P. Kotter, *Leading Change* (Boston, MA: Harvard Business Review Press, 1996).
7 Daniel Kahneman, *Thinking, Fast and Slow* (New York: Farrar, Straus and Giroux, 2011).
8 Edgar H. Schein and Peter A. Schein, *Organizational Culture and Leadership*, 5th ed. (Hoboken, NJ: John Wiley & Sons, 2017).
9 Security Compass, “Why You Need to Create an Effective Security Champion Program,” *Security Compass Blog*, September 21, 2021, https://www.securitycompass.com/blog/why-you-need-to-create-an-effective-security-champion-program/.
10 Digital Learning Institute, “Microlearning: The Benefits,” *Digital Learning Institute*, accessed August 15, 2025, https://www.digitallearninginstitute.com/blog/microlearning-the-benefits.
11 National Institute of Standards and Technology, *Building a Cybersecurity and Privacy Awareness and Training Program*, NIST Special Publication 800–50 Revision 1 (Gaithersburg, MD: NIST, 2023), https://doi.org/10.6028/NIST.SP.800-50r1.
12 KnowBe4, *Security Culture Maturity Model* (Clearwater, FL: KnowBe4, 2022), https://www.knowbe4.com/security-culture-maturity-model.

SECTION 3

CLOSE AND TRANSITION

Section 3 explored how security implementations remain effective over time by embedding improvement and culture into daily practice. Chapter 6 demonstrated that continual improvement maintains the relevance of controls through structured reviews, lessons learned, and performance monitoring. Chapter 7 showed that culture is what makes a security program effective: without shared values, visible leadership, and everyday reinforcement, even well-designed programs drift into irrelevance. Together, these chapters reinforced that sustaining ESRM requires discipline, oversight, and above all, human engagement.

Field Lesson: When Metrics Meet Meaning

The Situation

A multinational manufacturing company spent a year building its new risk-based security program. It had all the correct elements—asset inventories, risk registers, mitigation plans—and it reported regularly to leadership. On paper, it was a textbook rollout. But on the ground, business units weren't engaged. Plant managers dismissed it as something "corporate" was doing. Reports were distributed but rarely read. Training was rolled out but seldom reinforced. Even the security team knew the program wasn't landing.

DOI: 10.4324/9781003711346-14

The Friction

That disconnect came into sharp relief after a small fire at a flagship facility caused two days of downtime. Losses climbed into six figures, shipments were delayed, and customers were irate. In the post-incident review, the regional facilities director challenged the security team:

"You've been talking about this new risk-based model for months. So where was it when this happened? What good are your metrics if they don't help us stop this?"

The Wake-Up Call

The team realized they had built their program around theory rather than operational relevance. They were tracking risk counts, proposed mitigations, and training hours delivered—none of which addressed uptime, maintenance costs, or compliance risk.

The Shift

Instead of defending the program, the CSO invited the facilities director to reshape it. Together, they established shared operational metrics, including downtime avoided, near misses investigated, mitigation response time, and cross-team participation in drills. Ownership shifted as well. Local leaders took responsibility for site-level risks, with security acting as facilitator rather than enforcer. Within a year, not only did metrics improve, but trust did too.

What ESRM Got Right (Eventually)

1. **What are we trying to protect?**
   Business continuity, operational resilience, and customer satisfaction—not just abstract data points.
2. **What does it truly need protection from?**
   Gaps in ownership, siloed thinking, and misaligned priorities.
3. **How can we most effectively and efficiently protect it?**
   By aligning measurement with what plant managers cared about and co-building the program in operational language.

The Lesson: Metrics Don't Matter If No One Believes Them

Security culture doesn't come from dashboards, reports, or quarterly reviews; it comes from shared accountability. Security succeeds when you listen more than lecture, adapt more than defend, and build programs with your partners instead of for them.

From Sustaining to Evolving

Section 3 completes the cycle of sustaining ESRM through improvement and culture. These two chapters can be summarized as:

- **What do I need to sustain?** (Chapter 6: controls tested, lessons embedded, improvement cycles reinforced)
- **What must be embedded to last?** (Chapter 7: culture, leadership modeling, and shared accountability across the enterprise)

With these elements in place, ESRM stops being a one-time project and becomes part of the organizational fabric.

Looking Ahead

With continual improvement and culture embedded, ESRM becomes more than a framework; it becomes part of the organization's DNA. Yet sustaining today's program is only part of the challenge. Security leaders must also look beyond the present, anticipating how global turbulence, emerging technologies, and converging risks will reshape the landscape.

The final chapter turns to that future. Chapter 8 examines what lies ahead for ESRM, from the impact of AI and automation to the expanding scope of risk leadership. It shows how investing in ESRM today builds the resilience organizations will need tomorrow, and why the future of security belongs to leaders who can adapt, align, and evolve.

SECTION 4

WHAT'S NEXT FOR ESRM?

With the foundations of ESRM established and the program sustained through continual improvement and culture, the final step is to look ahead.

Security leaders cannot afford to treat any security implementation as a static achievement; the risk environment is evolving too quickly. Emerging technologies, converging threats, and geopolitical volatility all demand that programs be able to adapt at hyperspeed.

Section 4 turns to the future, showing how ESRM provides the structure and discipline needed to navigate an environment defined by acceleration, convergence, and uncertainty.

Chapter 8 explores how the enduring principles of asset value, risk ownership, and business alignment equip organizations to integrate artificial intelligence and automation into their programs and respond to new threat vectors without losing strategic focus.

- **Chapter 8: The Future of ESRM—Adapting to an Accelerating World**

  Explains how ESRM enables organizations to embrace innovation, manage convergence, and sustain resilience in a risk environment where disruption is constant, technology is transformative, and trust is the most valuable security outcome.

DOI: 10.4324/9781003711346-15

Chapter 8

The Future of ESRM

Adapting to an Accelerating World

From Execution to Evolution

With the foundations of Enterprise Security Risk Management (ESRM) established through risk-based implementation, strategic governance, and cultural integration, we have covered the essential components of building a modern, sustainable security program. The preceding chapters have walked through what it takes to operationalize ESRM in today's organizations: aligning security with business goals, embedding it into enterprise structures, and enabling people at all levels to participate in managing risk.

But the work doesn't end there. The future of security risk management will demand even greater agility, foresight, and integration. This final chapter turns our attention forward, to the next frontier of ESRM, where artificial intelligence, automation, digital convergence, and geopolitical volatility will test the resilience of every organization.

Amid all this flux, one thing remains constant: the core principles of ESRM will endure. Siloed departments, reactive models, and static controls will be unable to keep pace with the expected rate of change. Security organizations need a framework that anticipates, adapts to, and integrates change. ESRM provides that framework, offering us a foundation for navigating tomorrow's volatility.

Pro Tip: Great security programs earn trust in calm times. That way, when rapid change hits, we are the first call, not an afterthought.

DOI: 10.4324/9781003711346-16

AI, Automation, and the Changing Face of Risk

Emerging technologies like artificial intelligence (AI), machine learning (ML), operational technology (OT), and the Internet of Things (IoT), in years past abstract concepts on the horizon, are now woven into the daily operations of our modern enterprises. The rapid adoption of tools that were only recently considered "cutting edge" shows how quickly technology and AI are reshaping security functions from top to bottom.[1] Predictive analytics can identify many threats before they fully materialize. Advanced video systems flag suspicious behaviors in real time. ML algorithms sift through millions of data points to uncover hidden fraud patterns. Natural language processing tools monitor communications for early signs of insider risk. In many organizations, AI already operates like an additional "team member," scanning logs, monitoring networks, analyzing physical security feeds, and alerting decision-makers to anomalies they might otherwise miss.

Unfortunately, the very technologies that extend reach and speed also expand exposure. AI systems can be poisoned with false data, manipulated into deceptive outputs, or exploited to bypass controls. Technology may be repurposed for unintended surveillance, profiling, or even outright weaponization by malicious actors. The rise of deepfakes,[2] AI-generated phishing campaigns, polymorphic malware,[3] and the numerous paths to exploiting OT and IoT devices illustrate a threat environment that spans multiple domains. The line between digital and physical is becoming increasingly thin.

For many organizations, the adjustment will be most jarring in the tempo of this new risk environment. AI-enabled threats evolve in near real time, learning from defenses and adapting in response. Security cannot treat them as isolated events to be studied one at a time; risk management must become a continual exercise, a living process rather than a periodic review.

This is the context in which ESRM thrives. Its emphasis on ongoing assessment, cross-domain visibility, and alignment with business priorities enables security leaders to keep pace with rapid change. At the same time, Technology and AI remain a double-edged sword. Capable of overwhelming traditional defenses, but also of augmenting security programs when applied with discipline. As the future unfolds, organizations that take a risk-led approach to security can leverage these technologies to become true enablers rather than unmanaged risks.

Key Forces Shaping the Future Risk Environment

Key Force 1. Acceleration of Complexity and Change

Businesses are evolving at breakneck speed, driven by the combined forces of digital transformation, global expansion, and rapidly shifting workforce models, including remote, hybrid, and gig-based employment structures. In this environment, the old idea of a "five-year plan" seems almost quaint. Static roadmaps are quickly outpaced by real-world disruption. As the AI era moves forward, organizations must learn to operate in cycles of constant reassessment, where strategic and operational priorities may shift multiple times within a single fiscal year. Speed of change is visible even in the pace at which the concepts written about here may already have come to pass in the time it takes to go from writing to publishing a book. Technologies like AI-enabled automation, data-driven decision-making platforms, decentralized operations, and even early-stage quantum computing are driving this shift. They offer immense opportunities for efficiency and growth. A manufacturer might integrate AI into predictive maintenance systems to keep production lines running without interruption, while a global retailer may use automation to personalize customer experiences in real time. But each of these advances introduces new operational dependencies and creates security blind spots. Systems become more interconnected, and a failure or compromise in one area could have cascading effects across the enterprise.

Traditional control sets, designed for the more stable and slower-moving environments of the past, will be pushed beyond their limits in the new security environment. These legacy approaches may still function for certain routine risks, but they will not be able to keep pace with dynamic, interlinked threats that play out in weeks or even days. Static incident response plans, periodic risk assessments, and inflexible compliance checklists will no longer be sufficient to protect the enterprise in an era where competitors, regulators, and threat actors alike are leveraging rapid technological advancements.

Pro Tip: In fast-changing environments, shorten your feedback loop. Monthly or quarterly risk reviews may overlook shifts that occur in days or hours. Utilize ongoing horizon scanning to stay ahead of the curve.

Key Force 2. Convergence of Cyber and Physical Threat Domains

The boundary between physical, cyber, and operational risk is increasingly diffuse,[4] and in many cases, it has all but disappeared. Threats that once existed in separate silos now overlap, reinforce, complicate, and amplify one another. Attacks, now and increasingly as technology adapts, will frequently span multiple domains simultaneously: a ransomware campaign might not only encrypt core business data but also shut down building access systems[5] and disrupt environmental controls, creating both operational chaos and safety hazards. A carefully staged social engineering attack could lead to the theft of IT credentials while simultaneously manipulating an employee into granting unauthorized physical access. In highly connected environments, the effects will be much more problematic to contain. They will expand and cascade, multiplying the damage and extending recovery timelines.

This interconnectedness will be further driven in the coming decades by the very technologies designed to make operations more efficient. Smart city and building systems, industrial control networks, cloud-hosted business platforms, and IoT-enabled devices will become more deeply integrated into both physical and digital infrastructure than they are currently. While this integration delivers efficiency, speed, scalability, and convenience, it also creates new avenues for exploitation. A compromise in one system may provide a foothold into others, turning what might have been a localized event into an enterprise-wide crisis.

These cascading effects demand a security model that sees the big picture, connecting the dots across domains and timeframes as the technology and security ecosystems evolve and grow. Enterprises will no longer be able to afford to treat physical security, cybersecurity, and business continuity as separate disciplines managed by independent teams with limited communication. The risks are too interdependent, and the speed of escalation too great. Integrated visibility to systems that allows data from access control systems, intrusion detection platforms, network monitoring tools, and operational performance dashboards to be aggregated and analyzed holistically will become a baseline requirement.[6] Joint response capabilities, where physical and cyber teams train together, rehearse shared playbooks, and coordinate decision-making in real time, will be essential for managing complex, multifaceted threats.

In the future, as AI-driven attacks target multiple systems simultaneously and global interconnectivity deepens, the organizations that embed a risk-led posture into their DNA will be the ones capable of identifying early warning signs, mobilizing unified responses, and restoring stability with minimal disruption. ESRM, by design, fosters this level of integration. It makes convergence of approach, if not organizational structure, part of how security risks are assessed, prioritized, and mitigated across the enterprise, ensuring that a breach in one domain triggers a full-spectrum review of potential downstream impacts.

Key Force 3. Rise of Hybrid Threats and Non-Traditional Actors

In the future risk environment, threat actors will continue to become more diverse, adaptive, sophisticated, and complex to categorize.[7] Nation-states, organized crime syndicates, hacktivist collectives, and insider threats will increasingly blur together, both in capability and intent. In many cases, these groups will not operate in isolation; they will share intelligence, exchange tools, or even collaborate and partner when objectives align. The result will be a threat environment in which attribution becomes murky, and the same set of tactics can be deployed for wildly different ends.

Hybrid threats that blend multiple forms of attack into a single, coordinated campaign will become the norm rather than the exception. A single attack might combine a cyber intrusion by professional hackers to disable security cameras, a disinformation campaign to manipulate public perception, physical sabotage from flash-mob-style threat actors to disrupt operations, and targeted social engineering to compromise key personnel. The intent may be any one of many outcomes, from strategic disruption to economic leverage, political influence, or reputational harm, but the path to achieving it will cut across multiple vectors in ways that are carefully synchronized to maximize impact.[8]

As these tactics evolve, they will likely be amplified by emerging technologies, possibly ones we have not yet even foreseen. AI-generated deepfakes are already used for social engineering. As technology evolves, they might be used to impersonate executives well enough to fool more complex biometrics, potentially issue fraudulent directives, or initiate costly breaches. Autonomous drones with self-correcting behavior might be deployed for stealth surveillance or physical disruption, and compromised IoT devices could serve as entry points for larger-scale cyber operations. What once required months of planning and significant resources will increasingly be executed with speed, precision, and a fraction of the cost by outsourcing or joining forces across various threat communities.

This complexity means organizations will no longer be able to plan around a single "type" of threat actor or rely on narrow playbooks designed for isolated incidents. Instead, they will need to defend against a spectrum of actors, motives, and tactics, often without knowing which combination they will face until an attack is underway.

Key Force 4. Geopolitical Instability and Global Uncertainty

The global operating environment will be defined by persistent instability, where geopolitical tensions, regulatory fragmentation, climate pressures, and fragile supply chains combine to create a complex and often volatile risk landscape.[9] For multinational organizations, this means the question will not be *if* disruption will occur, but *when* and *where*. The current and future challenge lies in the unpredictability. Risk may emerge from an unexpected quarter, and seemingly unrelated events might intersect to produce cascading impacts on operations.

In the future security environment, security and compliance obligations will continue to shift rapidly from one jurisdiction to another. Regulatory divergence, whether driven by competing political agendas, regional economic priorities, resource scarcity, or shifting alliances, will demand constant monitoring and rapid adaptation. A policy or leadership change in one country could trigger contractual breaches, technology restrictions, or operational delays in multiple others. Meanwhile, the business continuity landscape will be shaped by a broader range of threats, including civil unrest, political upheaval, severe weather events, and climate-driven resource scarcity.

The supply chain, once managed as a predictable, often *boring*, series of transactions, is predicted to become a dynamic and fragile web.[10] Disruptions could stem from armed conflict that shuts down critical shipping lanes, cyberattacks targeting logistics networks, sanctions that cut off access to essential components, or environmental events that halt production in key manufacturing regions. Each disruption may ripple through the enterprise faster than traditional contingency plans can accommodate.

Looking ahead, organizations will need to operate as if uncertainty is the default condition. Decision-making will need to account for overlapping risks, rapid escalation, and the potential for simultaneous crises in multiple regions. This will require robust monitoring and intelligence capabilities, as well as governance structures that can translate complex, cross-border risk data into timely and coordinated action.

ESRM can provide a stabilizing framework in this context by focusing on impact and prioritization rather than rigid adherence to geographic or departmental boundaries. It enables leaders to view risks through the lens of enterprise value, ensuring that resource allocation, mitigation efforts, and contingency planning remain consistent even when the external environment is anything but.

Key Force 5. Expanding Attack Surfaces through Technology

The explosion of connected devices, cloud infrastructure, intelligent building systems, and remote work platforms has already dramatically and permanently expanded the surface area available to threat actors. As technology continues to permeate every aspect of physical existence, every additional sensor, application, and integration point becomes both an enabler of efficiency and a potential vector for exploitation. As technology ecosystems grow, the distinction between internal and external perimeters blurs, giving way to a complex web of systems, vendors, partners, and endpoints that must all be secured in real time.

In the coming years, the attack surface will only widen. Technologies such as ubiquitous 5G-enabled IoT networks, autonomous industrial systems, and AI-powered customer interfaces will bring unprecedented capabilities, and with them, new vulnerabilities that are not yet fully understood. Security teams will face the mounting challenge of managing increasingly complex interdependencies between systems, vendors, and business processes. A compromise in a third-party SaaS provider could expose sensitive corporate data; a vulnerability in a building automation system could be exploited to disrupt operations; an insecure API could serve as a bridge between unrelated networks, allowing attackers to move laterally without detection. The interconnected nature of modern infrastructure means that securing individual components is no longer enough. Protection must be designed into the entire ecosystem.

The growing scope and complexity of this challenge will make reactive approaches unsustainable. Threat actors are not only targeting more endpoints, but they are also leveraging automation to probe and exploit weaknesses at scale. This creates a scenario in which organizations without integrated, continuously adaptive security programs will struggle to keep pace with evolving threats.

ESRM offers a future-ready alternative. By embedding governance, risk prioritization, and cross-functional coordination into the adoption and management of technology, it ensures that every new device, platform, or integration is evaluated through a risk lens before deployment.

Pro Tip: Treat every new integration as both an opportunity and a potential risk. Apply the same due diligence to internal projects that you require from external vendors.

Key Force 6. Challenges and Opportunities

The rapid evolution of AI and other emerging technologies will present both formidable challenges and transformative opportunities[11] for the security profession. On one side, the sheer scale and complexity of digital ecosystems, combined with the adaptive nature of AI-enabled threats, will stretch traditional security methods beyond their limits. On the other, these same tools, when applied within a disciplined risk framework, can significantly enhance security's speed, scope, and accuracy.

When part of the ESRM program, AI becomes a technical upgrade and a strategic multiplier. AI can take on the heavy lifting of data analysis, enabling continuous scanning of vast data streams for anomalies, patterns, and early indicators of emerging threats. It can accelerate risk visibility, reduce time-to-detection, and support decision-making that is both more agile and more evidence-based. Automation can streamline repetitive, time-consuming processes such as log reviews, credential audits, and incident triage, freeing human professionals to focus on higher-order tasks that require context, judgment, and ethical consideration.

But leveraging these opportunities requires a deliberate approach. Without robust governance, AI deployments can introduce bias, reduce transparency, and create dependencies that are difficult to unwind. Overreliance on automation risks dulling human skills, while fragmented adoption of tools without integration into a unified risk framework can lead to gaps and inconsistencies.

Here, the ESRM model proves invaluable. Its future-ready foundation ensures that AI and other technologies are adopted in a way that is:

- Cross-functional—Breaking down silos to connect security processes directly to operational and business objectives.
- Risk-informed—Prioritizing action based not only on threat type, but on potential impact to critical assets and enterprise value.
- Adaptive—Encouraging ongoing reassessment and refinement of controls, rather than treating compliance as a static endpoint.

The organizations that internalize these ESRM principles today will be best positioned to turn tomorrow's challenges into opportunities. They will meet volatility with resilience, speed with strategy, and uncertainty with clarity.

These opportunities are already shaping the way people and technology work together in real security operations. Understanding this partnership is critical because the ability to harness AI's capabilities while preserving the strengths of human judgment will define the most successful security programs of the future. The following section examines how this partnership is evolving and its implications for decision-making in the era of AI.

Human + Machine: The Future of Security Decision-Making in ESRM

As organizations move deeper into an era defined by automation, speed, and complexity, the role of the security professional will undergo a profound transformation. The security functions of the future cannot and will not be a choice between human and machine. They will be a partnership, where each component amplifies the strengths of the other. Machine intelligence will deliver the capacity to monitor vast systems at scale, analyze staggering volumes of data in seconds, and detect subtle patterns invisible to the human eye. Human expertise will supply the context, ethics, empathy, and strategic judgment that machines cannot replicate.[12]

In this environment, the most resilient security organizations will be those that integrate these capabilities seamlessly. Instead of simply bolting on new tools, they will embed machine-driven analytics into their security processes, ensuring that every insight is aligned with organizational priorities and understood within its proper business and operational context. As outlined in Table 8.1, the goal of this new work environment will be to allow each side of the human/machine hybrid program to play to its own strengths. Thus, it allows professionals to make smarter, faster, and more context-aware choices under pressure.

TABLE 8.1 Complementary Strengths in the AI-Enabled ESRM Model

Capability Area	AI Strengths	Human Strengths
Speed & scale	Processes massive volumes of data from multiple sources in milliseconds.	Prioritizes which issues require immediate attention based on organizational priorities and context.
Pattern recognition	Detects subtle correlations and anomalies invisible to the human eye.	Interprets patterns in the context of cultural, operational, and ethical factors.
Consistency	Applies rules and algorithms uniformly, without fatigue or bias drift over time.	Adjusts judgment based on evolving circumstances, incomplete data, and emerging nuances.
Monitoring	Provides continuous, 24/7 surveillance across physical, cyber, and operational systems.	Engages in situational assessment, de-escalation, and dynamic problem-solving during live incidents.
Prediction	Forecasts likely outcomes using historical and real-time data models.	Weighs predicted outcomes against acceptable risk tolerance, organizational values, and stakeholder expectations to ensure alignment.
Automation	Executes repetitive or complex technical tasks at scale (e.g., log correlation, credential checks).	Makes discretionary calls in ambiguous or high-stakes situations where rules may conflict.
Adaptability to data	Rapidly incorporates new datasets and adjusts model outputs accordingly.	Learns from experience, intuition, and informal cues that cannot be codified in algorithms.
Scalability	Expands capabilities quickly across systems and geographies.	Builds trust, fosters relationships, and establishes consensus — elements critical to effective risk ownership across the enterprise.

INSIGHT: TABLE 8.1—COMPLEMENTARY STRENGTHS IN THE AI-ENABLED ESRM MODEL

Table 8.1 highlights a core truth about the AI-enabled ESRM model: technology and people excel in different areas, and the strength of a modern security program lies in combining these capabilities. AI excels at processing vast amounts of information with unmatched speed, consistency, and scalability, making it an ideal partner for tasks like large-scale monitoring, anomaly detection, and predictive modeling. Humans bring context, adaptability, and the ability to weigh complex trade-offs, especially when decisions involve ethics, cultural understanding, or ambiguous circumstances. When both sets of strengths are intentionally integrated, the result is a security function that can operate at a speed and scope unattainable by humans alone, while maintaining the judgment and nuance that only people can provide.

The future lies in *insight-based security*, where the value of technology is measured not by its technical specifications, but by the quality of the decisions it supports. ESRM, by design, is a decision-support model. It forces leaders and teams to ask the right questions:

- What risks will have the most impact on the organization?
- Who owns those risks, and are they prepared to manage them?
- What mitigation options deliver the maximum effect, given the current context and constraints?

When the power of AI is paired with the rigor of ESRM, the process becomes even more powerful. Automated systems can surface high-priority risks in near real time, flagging anomalies before they escalate into incidents. Humans can then evaluate those alerts against business goals, operational realities, and ethical considerations. They are the ones deciding not only *what* action to take, but also *when* and *how* to take it.

Security Leaders: From Technology Operators to AI-Enabled Strategists

This shift will fundamentally redefine the competencies, mindset, and day-to-day responsibilities of security leaders. The leaders of tomorrow will not be measured solely by their ability to operate sophisticated tools, administer systems, or enforce policies. Instead, their value will lie in their capacity to interpret, integrate, and strategically apply machine-generated intelligence in ways that protect the enterprise, enable its objectives, and uphold its values.[13] In the AI-driven security environment, success will depend on the ability to blend technological fluency with human judgment, business acumen, and ethical discernment.

Future security leaders will need to demonstrate a diverse portfolio of skills, including the ability to:

- Interpret AI insights
  Understanding not just what an algorithm reports, but how it arrived at that conclusion, what assumptions it relied on, and where its blind spots may lie. Leaders will need to be able to translate complex models, probability scores, and statistical outputs into concise, actionable narratives that senior executives and operational teams can understand and trust. This includes being transparent about the technology's limitations and the confidence level of its recommendations.
- Balance automation with human oversight
  Resisting the temptation to defer entirely to machine outputs, especially in situations that involve human safety, legal exposure, or reputational risk. This means leaders will be responsible and need to be capable of establishing clear thresholds for when human review is mandatory, as well as designing workflows that allow for human intervention without slowing legitimate automated responses.
- Anticipate unintended consequences
  Recognizing that even well-designed AI systems can generate outcomes that are operationally disruptive, reputationally damaging, or legally problematic. Leaders will need to think several steps ahead, identifying where a decision might produce secondary or tertiary effects. For example, how might an automated lockdown procedure inadvertently trap employees in unsafe areas, or how could a false positive in facial recognition result in discriminatory treatment?
- Collaborate across disciplines
  Working seamlessly with legal, HR, compliance, IT, operations, finance, and even marketing teams to ensure

that security technology supports and never undermines the organization's broader goals. In many cases, security leaders will also need to explain their decisions to external stakeholders such as regulators, insurers, and strategic partners, making cross-functional credibility and diplomacy critical skills.

- Shape governance and policy frameworks

  Contributing to the creation of organizational standards, escalation protocols, and ethical guidelines for the use of AI in security. Leaders will need to operate within these frameworks as well as help design them, ensuring they reflect both security imperatives and the organization's values.

In this new reality, leaders who take a risk-led approach to their security programs will be uniquely positioned to thrive. Their cross-functional mindset, emphasis on aligning security with business priorities, and experience with integrated risk assessment make them natural translators between technical teams and executive decision-makers. They are accustomed to weighing diverse risk factors, reconciling competing priorities, and ensuring that responses serve both immediate operational needs and long-term strategic goals.

In the coming AI era, risk will not be a separate "security problem" that happens somewhere else in the organization. It will be embedded in product design, supply chain decisions, marketing strategies, customer interactions, and day-to-day operations. Leaders who understand this and can navigate it, who can interpret machine-driven insights, apply them ethically, and communicate them effectively, will be indispensable to their organizations and define what effective security leadership looks like in the decades to come.

Security Professionals: Expanding Front-Line Roles in the AI-Enabled ESRM Environment

The transformation driven by AI, automation, and integrated data systems will not be limited to security leaders. Every security professional, from front-line operators to specialized analysts, will see their roles evolve. In the AI-security world, these professionals will operate in a more connected, data-rich environment, where technology handles many of the repetitive, time-intensive monitoring tasks, allowing humans to focus on higher-value work that requires interpretation, communication, and nuanced decision-making. Refer to Table 8.2 for a side-by-side comparison of how security leaders and front-line personnel will need to adapt in the AI era.

TABLE 8.2 Evolving Roles in the AI-Enabled ESRM Environment

Focus Area	Security Leaders	Security Professionals
Core role evolution	From technology operators to AI-enabled strategists who align security programs with business priorities.	From task-based monitoring to proactive, insight-driven risk managers at the operational level.
AI interaction	Interpret complex AI outputs, weigh risks, and make strategic, ethical decisions about their application.	Operate AI tools daily, validate alerts, investigate anomalies, and provide feedback to refine system performance.
Decision-making	Translate machine intelligence into actionable strategies for executives and cross-functional teams.	Apply contextual knowledge to determine the urgency and nature of AI-generated alerts in real time.
Collaboration	Partner with executives, legal, compliance, HR, IT, operations, and external stakeholders to ensure AI supports organizational goals.	Coordinate with peers and supervisors to escalate incidents, share situational insights, and execute response plans.
Risk perspective	Focus on enterprise-wide, long-term risk management and resilience planning.	Focus on immediate, localized risk detection, mitigation, and prevention within their operational scope.
Skill development	Strategic thinking, cross-domain fluency, ethical decision-making, governance, and advanced data interpretation.	Analytical skills, technology stewardship, communication, situational judgment, and adaptive incident response.
Key deliverable	Security strategy that balances innovation, ethics, and risk tolerance.	On-the-ground application of AI insights to maintain safety, security, and operational continuity.
Value to ESRM	Ensures AI adoption is risk-informed, business-aligned, and adaptable to change.	Ensures AI tools are effective in daily operations and that human judgment remains central to security outcomes.

AI will take on much of the "first pass" work, including continuously scanning access control logs for anomalies, flagging irregular badge activity, monitoring social media for emerging threats, and utilizing computer vision to detect unusual behavior in surveillance feeds. But AI must not be left to act in isolation. Security professionals will investigate those alerts, determine whether they indicate a genuine risk, and decide how to escalate the issue. This will require:

- Enhanced analytical skills
  Understanding the outputs generated by AI systems, knowing how to validate them against other data sources, and spotting when results may be incomplete or misleading.
- Operational judgment
  Using real-world context to determine whether a flagged event is actionable or a false positive, and whether immediate intervention is warranted.
- Incident coordination
  Working with cross-functional teams during live events to provide the human context that AI cannot, ensuring that responses are proportionate and aligned with operational needs.
- Technology stewardship
  Learning how to operate, configure, and provide feedback on AI-powered tools so they continue to improve in accuracy and relevance.

The introduction of AI will also broaden the scope of what security professionals can accomplish. With automation handling many routine tasks, security staff will have more time to engage in proactive measures like conducting targeted patrols, building relationships with employees and visitors, and identifying environmental or procedural vulnerabilities before they are exploited.

The shift, however, will also place new expectations on the workforce. Security professionals will need to become comfortable with constant change, as AI tools evolve rapidly and require frequent updates in both technology and procedure. Training will need to go beyond physical protocols and situational awareness to incorporate data literacy, understanding of AI system limitations, and the ability to communicate technical insights in plain language to supervisors and colleagues.

INSIGHT: TABLE 8.2—EVOLVING ROLES IN THE AI-ENABLED ESRM ENVIRONMENT

Table 8.2 shows how AI will reshape the responsibilities of both security leaders and security professionals, not by replacing either role, but by redefining their contributions within an ESRM framework. Leaders will shift from being primarily technology operators to acting as strategic interpreters of AI-generated intelligence, ensuring that decisions are aligned with business priorities, risk appetite, and ethical standards. Professionals on the front lines will see their scope expand from routine, reactive monitoring to proactive engagement, validating alerts, conducting investigations, and applying operational judgment in real time. The interplay between these roles, each informed and enhanced by AI, creates a layered security posture where strategic direction and tactical execution are both strengthened, producing an enterprise-wide capability greater than the sum of its parts.

Within the ESRM framework, as part of continual assessment and improvement of the program, these evolving roles will ensure that the human element remains essential. AI can process patterns; people can understand intent. Machines can detect anomalies; professionals can engage, de-escalate, and adapt in the moment. The most effective future security teams will be those where technology extends the reach and efficiency of the human workforce, and where every professional sees themselves not just as a guard or operator, but as a risk manager contributing to the organization's overall resilience.

As AI capabilities continue to advance, the operational role of security professionals will expand beyond today's imagination. Future front-line teams may routinely interpret AI-generated threat forecasts, coordinate live responses to multi-domain incidents, and act as the human bridge between autonomous systems and the people they protect. In this environment, the professionals who can combine technological fluency with human adaptability will be essential to sustaining trust, ensuring safety, and driving resilience in the decades ahead.

Whether at the strategic level of senior leaders or the operational level of front-line professionals, these evolving roles only deliver their full value when they operate as part of a unified approach to risk.

The ESRM Advantage in a Complex World

In a future that is simultaneously more technological, more unpredictable, and more interconnected than anything security professionals have experienced before, resilience will not be defined solely by the speed at which organizations adopt new technologies. The real differentiator will be how effectively those technologies are woven into a cohesive, values-driven risk framework that ensures tools are applied with purpose, oversight, and strategic alignment. ESRM is that framework.

Its core principles of risk ownership, business alignment, continuous improvement, and cross-functional governance are designed to endure even as the tools and tactics of both security and threat actors evolve. These principles do not rely on a specific technology stack or control library; instead, they focus on ensuring that every security decision starts with a clear understanding of what is being protected, why it matters, and who is responsible for managing that risk. This approach ensures that technology serves the mission, not the other way around.

By adopting ESRM today, organizations are not just addressing current risks; they are building the strategic "muscle memory" needed to adapt to whatever emerges next. The risk landscape of the next decade will almost certainly introduce threats that are difficult to imagine now—quantum computing that can render current encryption obsolete[14] overnight, decentralized autonomous organizations operating outside traditional legal frameworks, AI-enabled insider threats[15] capable of manipulating both digital systems and human decision-making, or global supply chain disruptions triggered by climate events or geopolitical realignments.

In each of these scenarios, ESRM gives enterprises a structured way to:

- Integrate new risks quickly into decision-making—Ensuring that novel threats are not treated as exceptional cases, but incorporated into the same disciplined, organization-wide risk processes that manage existing hazards.
- Respond with agility without compromising ethics or compliance—Enabling rapid action that still respects legal obligations, privacy standards, and organizational values.
- Maintain trust with customers, regulators, and employees in uncertain times—Reinforcing that the organization's

approach to risk is deliberate, transparent, and aligned with its mission, even under pressure.

This is the ESRM advantage: the ability to operate with clarity and transparency when the environment is anything but clear. It transforms the security function from a set of isolated controls into an adaptive, enterprise-wide capability. Security becomes a factor that is designed to absorb, adapt to, and emerge stronger from disruption. In a complex world, that capability is the foundation for long-term viability.

ESRM as a Strategic Framework and Guardrail in the AI Age

One of ESRM's greatest strengths is its resilience to change. It is not anchored to a specific threat vector, technology platform, or prescriptive control set. Instead, it operates around three enduring principles: asset value, risk ownership, and business alignment. These principles are timeless because they focus on why security actions are taken, not just how they are executed. In practice, this means that as new tools are introduced—whether AI-powered detection systems, automated incident response platforms, or immersive training environments—ESRM ensures they are implemented with intention and purpose. The guiding questions remain constant:

- What am I trying to protect?
- What do I need to protect it from?
- How can I most effectively and efficiently protect it?

This discipline helps organizations avoid the "shiny object syndrome" that often accompanies the adoption of new technology. In the AI age, the temptation is strong to deploy the latest tool as a quick fix or a competitive signal. But an uncritical "buy now, figure it out later" approach risks creating a cluttered architecture filled with disconnected point solutions, duplicated controls, and operational friction. Over time, this patchwork can be as dangerous as the threats it is meant to counter.

Pro Tip: Treat every new integration as both an opportunity and a potential risk. Apply the same due diligence to internal projects that you require from external vendors.

ESRM acts as the guardrail against that cycle. It is not about slowing innovation but about channeling it with discipline and purpose. Under ESRM, no technology is implemented in isolation. Each is evaluated for its alignment with enterprise value, its fit with existing processes, and its potential to both mitigate and introduce risk. In a time when innovation often outpaces regulation, this structured approach provides what is frequently lacking in AI adoption: effective governance.[16] ESRM requires that AI-enabled defenses be integrated into transparent workflows, monitored for performance, and periodically reassessed for relevance. This prevents organizations from overcommitting to tools that deliver short-term gains but fail to support long-term objectives,[17] or worse, create liabilities through bias, misconfiguration, or misuse.

Importantly, ESRM now serves as a bridge not only between cyber and physical domains but also between human and machine domains. Just as convergence demands that physical and digital security teams share a common operational picture, the integration of AI requires that human judgment and automated capabilities operate from the same playbook. ESRM provides the connective tissue that binds people, processes, and technology into a governance structure resilient enough to withstand rapid, unpredictable change.

The value of this discipline becomes even clearer in real operating environments. Security is rarely a monolithic function. It is typically a patchwork of teams, systems, and contracts, spread across geographies and vendors. Without a unifying framework like ESRM, AI adoption risks amplifying fragmentation, creating siloed deployments that cannot share data, coordinate responses, or support enterprise-wide situational awareness. ESRM ensures that every new capability strengthens the core rather than pulling resources in divergent directions.

In the AI age, the most resilient organizations will be those that leverage innovation to enhance their existing program foundations. ESRM is not anti-technology. It is pro-strategy. It treats emerging tools as powerful enablers, not as "magic wands." By requiring adoption to proceed with intention, governance, and context, ESRM turns AI into a force multiplier for well-designed security programs rather than a distraction from their core mission. The result is an organization that can move quickly when needed, but never blindly. When decisions must be made in seconds and consequences may unfold on a global scale, that distinction can mean the difference between resilience and collapse.

Taken together, these qualities show why ESRM is both a strategic framework and a practical guardrail. It gives leaders the confidence to integrate new technologies without losing sight of core principles, while preventing hasty decisions that undermine resilience.

ESRM Today Prepares You for Tomorrow

The organizations investing in mature ESRM programs today are building the strategic capacity to thrive in an environment defined by uncertainty. These are the businesses that will:

- Navigate regulatory changes with confidence—Adapting quickly to new compliance requirements, privacy laws, and industry standards without halting operations or losing market position.
- Respond to emerging threats with agility—Mobilizing resources and making risk-informed decisions in hours or even minutes, rather than weeks or months.
- Earn trust from customers, partners, and regulators—Demonstrating that their approach to security is not reactive or superficial, but deliberate, transparent, and tied to organizational values.
- Innovate securely without sacrificing speed or integrity—Launching new products, adopting new technologies, and entering new markets without opening dangerous gaps in their risk posture.

ESRM does not promise stability in an unstable world. Such a promise would be unrealistic. What it offers instead is a disciplined, repeatable method for managing instability in ways that are flexible, ethical, and aligned with the organization's mission. This means that when a change occurs, whether it is a sudden regulatory shift, a disruptive technology, or an unexpected threat, the response is not chaotic. It is coordinated and proportional.

ESRM equips organizations to embed risk management into the fabric of their decision-making processes. It is a way of seeing and managing risk that evolves alongside the business, adapts to technological advancements, and responds to external pressures. Organizations that embrace it now are shaping how they will respond to and even influence the events that define their industries.

The future will test the limits of every organization's resilience. But with ESRM as the foundation, those limits can be expanded. Security can become more than a protective shield; it can be a driver of confidence, enabling bold decisions, a source of agility allowing rapid adaptation, and a catalyst for innovation, ensuring that progress is pursued with both speed and integrity. In the AI age, that combination may be the single most valuable asset an organization will possess.

Key Takeaways for the Future of ESRM

- The threat environment is accelerating and interconnecting. ESRM provides the structure to adapt quickly, prioritize effectively, and sustain decision quality in the face of constant change.
- AI and automation are double-edged forces. ESRM ensures emerging technologies are integrated as strategic enablers, not reactive add-ons, aligning them with long-term business value.
- Security domains are no longer separate. Physical, cyber, and operational risks now overlap and must be managed as one ecosystem. ESRM provides a unified, cross-functional framework to achieve this.
- The role of security professionals is evolving. Leaders must become AI-literate strategists, and front-line teams must become proactive risk managers—each balancing machine capability with human judgment.
- ESRM is inherently future-ready. Its core principles—asset value, risk ownership, and business alignment—are durable across technologies, threat actors, and operational models yet to emerge.

- Trust is an asset built in advance. ESRM programs that establish credibility during calm periods position security as a go-to partner when rapid change or crisis hits.

Security Leader Toolkit for the Future of ESRM

ESRM Implementation Checklist

- Have I identified emerging technologies in use or being considered (AI, IoT, robotics, automation, cloud, etc.)?
- Have I assessed whether each new technology creates additional or new risks?
- Have I identified a clear business owner for each emerging technology (not just security)?
- Have I achieved security input early in the adoption or procurement process?
- Have I evaluated how new technology could impact critical assets (confidentiality, availability, safety, reputation)?
- Have I ensured that new systems are tested before deployment (red-teaming, pen testing, tabletop exercises)?
- Have I planned for ongoing monitoring (patching, updating, auditing, and sunset plans)?
- Have I identified potential regulatory, legal, or ethical obligations associated with new technology?
- Have I ensured that residual risk decisions will be escalated to leadership, rather than being left solely to the project team?

Horizon Scanning Worksheet (Template)

Use this template to capture early signals of change that may impact your security program.

How to Use It

1. Review sources regularly (intel feeds, regulatory bulletins, business media, industry groups).
2. Capture signals of change in each category.
3. Rate potential impact and assign a time horizon.
4. Flag what actions security should take now vs. later.
5. Share a quarterly horizon scan briefing with executives.

Category	Signal of Change	Source (News, Report, Intel, Internal Trend)	Potential Impact on Assets/Operations	Time Horizon (Short: 0–1 yr, Medium: 1–3 yrs, Long: 3–5 yrs)	Next Action
Example: Technology	Rise of generative AI tools used for fraud	Industry reports, law enforcement alerts	Threat to financial transactions & brand trust	Short–Medium	Test employee awareness, monitor fraud cases
Example: Geopolitics	Increased trade restrictions in Asia	Business press, gov't reports	Supply chain disruption for manufacturing sites	Medium	Diversify suppliers, increase stockpiles
Example: Environment	More severe hurricanes in the Gulf region	Climate forecasts	Facility outages, insurance costs	Long	Update BCP, invest in flood resilience
Example: Hybrid Threats	Disinformation campaigns linked to activist groups	Social media monitoring	Reputational harm, regulatory attention	Short	Stand up crisis comms protocol

Notes

1 Adeleke Ayobami, "Leveraging AI for Information and Cybersecurity," *ISACA*, 2024, https://www.isaca.org/resources/news-and-trends/industry-news/2024/leveraging-ai-for-information-and-cybersecurity.

2 FBI, "Senior U.S. Officials Impersonated in Malicious Messaging Campaign," *IC3*, May 15, 2025, https://www.ic3.gov/PSA/2025/PSA250515.

3 Cybersecurity and Infrastructure Security Agency, "Emotet Malware," *CISA*, July 20, 2018, https://www.cisa.gov/news-events/alerts/2018/07/20/emotet-malware.

4 Brian Allen, Brandon Bapst, and Terry Allen Hicks, *Building a Cyber Risk Management Program: Evolving Security for the Digital Age* (O'Reilly Media, 2024).

5 Dustin Volz and Katherine Sayre, "MGM Hackers Exploited IT Help Desk in Casino Cyberattack," *Wall Street Journal*, September 14, 2023, https://www.wsj.com/tech/cybersecurity/mgm-hack-casino-hackers-group-0366c641.

6 According to the 2023 Verizon Data Breach Investigations Report (DBIR), 74% of all breaches involve the human element, so focusing your effort on cybersecurity alone is leaving a gaping hole in your security posture. Verizon, *2023 Data Breach Investigations Report* (Verizon Business, 2023), accessed April 28, 2025, https://www.verizon.com/business/resources/reports/dbir/2023/summary-of-findings.

7 George Tziakouris, "The Rise of AI-Powered Criminals: Identifying Threats and Opportunities," *Cisco Talos Blog*, August 14, 2023.

8 Europol, *EU Serious and Organised Crime Threat Assessment (EU-SOCTA) 2025* (The Hague: Europol, March 2025), https://www.europol.europa.eu/cms/sites/default/files/documents/EU-SOCTA-2025.pdf.

9 World Economic Forum, *Global Risks Report 2025* (Geneva: World Economic Forum, January 2025), https://reports.weforum.org/docs/WEF_Global_Risks_Report_2025.pdf.

10 Filipe Beato, Luna Rohland and Margi Van Gogh, "Why Transport and Supply Chain Ecosystems Need to Be Cyber Secured," *World Economic Forum*, June 20, 2024.

11 Kevin Doyle, "Stronger Together: AI and Human Collaboration in the Battle Against Evolving Threats," *Information Security Buzz*, October 17, 2024.

12 Rachelle Loyear and Jeff Slotnick, "From Guards to Guardians: Reimagining Security Work in the Age of AI and Robotics," *Security Management*, August 1, 2025, https://www.asisonline.org/security-management-magazine/articles/2025/08/guards-to-guardians/.

13 Kevin Megas, "Managing Cybersecurity and Privacy Risks in the Age of Artificial Intelligence," *National Institute of Standards and Technology (NIST)*, September 19, 2024; Wilberforce Murikah, Jeff Kimanga Nthenge and Faith Mueni Musyoka, "Bias and Ethics of AI Systems Applied in Auditing," *Scientific African* 25 (2024): e02281.

14 Mark Hovarth, "Begin Transitioning to Post-Quantum Cryptography Now," *Gartner*, September 30, 2024, https://www.gartner.com/en/articles/post-quantum-cryptography.

15 Nineta Polemi et al., "Challenges and Efforts in Managing AI Trustworthiness Risks: A State of Knowledge," *Frontiers in Big Data* 7 (2024): 1381163.

16 Patrick Rooney, "CIOs Look to Sharpen AI Governance Despite Uncertainties," *CIO*, November 4, 2024.

17 Gartner, "Gartner Hype Cycle," *Gartner*, accessed August 14, 2025, https://www.gartner.com/en/research/methodologies/gartner-hype-cycle.

Glossary

In security risk management, even familiar words can take on different meanings. "Vulnerability," "resilience," and "risk" mean one thing to a hacker, another to an executive, and sometimes something else entirely to your operations team.

This glossary defines the key terms used throughout the book, focusing on real-world usage that bridges business and security. Think of it as a translator—helping security leaders and stakeholders stay aligned, informed, and ready to act.

Assets

Any tangible or intangible item or resource valuable to the organization. Assets can include people, physical property, information, brand reputation, or intellectual property.

Business Continuity

An organization's ability to maintain essential operations during and after a disruptive incident, minimizing downtime and protecting business functions.

Business Impact Analysis (BIA)

A process that evaluates and prioritizes potential impacts of business disruptions on an organization's operations, helping prioritize assets and recovery strategies.

Compliance-Based Security

Security activities are primarily focused on meeting regulatory standards or industry checklists, rather than directly addressing prioritized business risks.

Control Gap

The difference between the security measures currently in place and those needed to fully mitigate a known risk. Identifying control gaps helps prioritize resource allocation for the most impactful security improvements.

Crisis Management

Coordinated organizational responses to major incidents or emergencies, designed to stabilize the situation, communicate effectively, and restore normal operations.

Criticality (Asset Criticality)

A measure of how essential an asset is to an organization's business operations. High-criticality assets, if compromised, would have a severe impact on operations or financial stability.

Data-Driven Decision-Making

Using empirical data, rather than instinct or anecdote, to guide security decisions and risk prioritization.

Effects-Based Security

A strategic approach to security that focuses on achieving specific desired outcomes or "effects," rather than merely deploying standard security tools or procedures.

Enterprise Security Risk Management (ESRM)

A holistic, business-aligned approach to managing all forms of security risk, integrating physical, cyber, information, and operational security into a cohesive strategy that supports organizational objectives.

Executive Buy-in

Achieving commitment and active support from organizational leaders for security initiatives is crucial for the successful implementation of ESRM.

Holistic Security

A comprehensive approach to security that integrates physical, cyber, and operational security measures into a unified strategy, rather than managing them separately.

Incident Response

Organized actions taken immediately following a security event or breach, aimed at limiting damage, restoring operations, and learning from the event to prevent future occurrences.

Insider Threat

A security risk originating from current or former employees, contractors, or business associates who have access to or knowledge of the organization, intentionally or unintentionally causing harm.

Intangible Assets

Non-physical assets, such as intellectual property, brand reputation, customer trust, and proprietary data, that are crucial to an organization's value but challenging to quantify and protect through traditional means.

Key Performance Indicators (KPIs)

Quantitative metrics are used to measure the effectiveness, efficiency, and impact of security programs in achieving strategic objectives.

Mitigation

Strategies and actions designed to reduce or eliminate risks by addressing vulnerabilities or minimizing potential harm.

Proactive Security

An anticipatory approach to security focused on identifying and preventing risks before they occur, rather than reacting after an incident takes place.

Reactive Security

A tactical approach to security focused on responding to security incidents or threats after they have occurred, typically involving immediate corrective actions without broader strategic planning.

Residual Risk

The remaining level of risk after all practical mitigation measures have been implemented, requiring acceptance or further management.

Resilience (Organizational Resilience)

The capability of an organization to withstand and rapidly recover from disruptions, leveraging robust security and continuity planning to ensure ongoing operational effectiveness.

Risk

The potential for loss or damage when a threat exploits a vulnerability against a valued asset. Risk is evaluated based on the likelihood of occurrence and the potential impact.

Risk Assessment

A systematic process for identifying, analyzing, and prioritizing risks based on their likelihood, potential impact, and the effectiveness of existing security controls.

Risk-Based Security

Security activities focused explicitly on managing prioritized risks, informed by business objectives, threat intelligence, and strategic decision-making.

Risk Tolerance/Appetite

The level of risk organizational leaders are willing to accept in pursuit of the company's mission and objectives before implementing mitigations.

Security Controls

Safeguards or countermeasures (administrative, physical, or technical) put in place to mitigate specific security risks.

Security Culture

The collective mindset and behaviors within an organization regarding security practices and policies. A strong security culture promotes proactive risk management behaviors across all levels.

Security Oversight

Formal mechanisms, often involving leadership or governance committees, responsible for ensuring ongoing compliance, strategic alignment, and effectiveness of the organization's security programs.

Stakeholders

Individuals or groups within or outside an organization who have an interest in, influence over, or are impacted by security and risk management decisions.

Strategic Alignment

Ensuring security objectives directly support and complement an organization's broader business strategy and goals.

Tangible Assets

Physical assets such as buildings, equipment, vehicles, inventory, and infrastructure that have clear monetary value and are generally straightforward to inventory and secure.

Threat

Any potential danger or harm to an asset. Threats can be intentional (like cyberattacks), accidental (such as human error), or environmental (natural disasters).

Threat Intelligence

Actionable information about existing or emerging threats gathered from internal sources, industry partners, and external agencies to inform security decision-making.

Vulnerability

A weakness or gap in security measures that could be exploited by a threat, increasing the potential for damage or loss.

Zero Tolerance Policy

A strict organizational stance that certain behaviors or actions, such as fraud or violence, will not be tolerated, with clearly defined and consistently enforced consequences.

Index

Note: **Bold** page numbers refer to tables and *italic* page numbers refer to figures.

For Product Safety Concerns and Information please contact our EU
representative GPSR@taylorandfrancis.com
Taylor & Francis Verlag GmbH, Kaufingerstraße 24, 80331 München, Germany

www.ingramcontent.com/pod-product-compliance
Ingram Content Group UK Ltd.
Pitfield, Milton Keynes, MK11 3LW, UK
UKHW021832260926
475702UK00049B/490

* 9 7 8 1 0 4 1 1 9 3 6 1 6 *